Assessment in the Literacy Classroom

Margaret E. Gredler

University of South Carolina

Robert L. Johnson

University of South Carolina

PEARSON

Boston   New York   San Francisco
Mexico City   Montreal   Toronto   London   Madrid   Munich   Paris
Hong Kong   Singapore   Tokyo   Cape Town   Sydney

Series Editor: *Aurora Martínez Ramos*
Series Editorial Assistant: *Erin Beatty*
Senior Marketing Manager: *Elizabeth Fogarty*
Production Administrator: *Anna Socrates*
Composition and Prepress Buyer: *Linda Cox*
Manufacturing Buyer: *Andrew Turso*
Editorial Production Service: *Susan McNally*
Electronic Composition: *Peggy Cabot*

For related titles and support materials, visit our online catalog at www.ablongman.com

Between the time Website information is gathered and then published, it is not unusual for some sites to have closed. Also, the transcription of URLs can result in unintended typographical errors. The publisher would appreciate notification where these occur so that they may be corrected in subsequent editions.

Library of Congress Cataloging-in-Publication Data

Gredler, Margaret E.
    Assessment in the literacy classroom / Margaret E. Gredler, Robert L. Johnson.
            p.   cm.
Includes bibliographic references.
        ISBN 0-205-34426-7
    1. Language arts—Ability testing.   2. Reading—Ability testing.   3. Literacy—Evaluation.   I. Johnson, Robert L.   II. Title.

    LB1576.G739 2004
    372.6—dc21

                                                    2003050030

Printed in the United States of America

10 9 8 7 6 5 4 3 2 1   08 07 06 05 04 03

Contents

Tables and Figures

Preface

The major purpose of this text is to provide a strong knowledge base on the range and variety of assessment methods for the literacy classroom, their advantages and disadvantages, examples, and guidelines for use. Chapter 1 discusses the importance of assessment and the relationship to literacy instruction. Chapter 2 discusses the characteristics of effective assessment. Included are some ways to ensure that the decisions based on assessments are accurate and reliable, the importance of using situations that are authentic, and the issues in representing the diversity of the classroom.

Chapters 3 through 7 each describe an important component of the three basic approaches to classroom assessment. These approaches are observing, questioning and interviewing, and sampling student work. Described in Chapter 3 are methods for recording teacher observations of the fluid, dynamic, and often unstructured student verbalizations and interactions in the classroom. The focus of Chapter 4 is the forms of teacher questioning in the classroom. Discussed in this chapter are instruction-embedded questions and questioning in student–teacher conferences.

Chapter 5 describes the criteria for performance assessments and the various types that are useful in the classroom. Included are evaluating children's emergent writing in preschool and kindergarten settings, story retelling, and various types of writing assessments.

The focus of Chapter 6 is scoring guides that reflect the purpose of the performance assessment. Discussed are the characteristics and advantages and disadvantages of checklists and analytic and holistic scoring rubrics.

Another type of authentic assessment is the student portfolio. Discussed in Chapter 7 are the major types of portfolios, their role in the classroom, and the resources and conditions essential for effective implementation.

A key characteristic of today's classrooms is diversity. Classrooms include students whose native language is not English, those who speak dialects, and students with learning problems who are mainstreamed into regular classroom instruction. Chapter 8 describes the characteristics of these students and discusses the implications for assessment.

Chapter 9 addresses a different issue in classroom assessment, that of diagnosing the problems of students who are not making adequate progress in literacy. Included are running records, miscue analysis, and informal reading inventories.

In addition to classroom assessment, teachers are responsible for reporting student progress to external audiences. Discussed in Chapter 10 are various reporting methods, including letter grades, pass/fail designations, and narrative reports. Also described are criteria for evaluating the appropriateness of a reporting system and the role of the parent–teacher conference.

Teachers develop many of the classroom assessments they use. However, other assessments, such as text-based assessments, can provide useful information. Chapter 11 discusses the characteristics of these and other published assessments, and offers guidelines for reviewing such assessments. In addition to discussing the issues associated with each type of assessment, each chapter concludes with questions for discussion.

Acknowledgments

We would like to thank the following reviewers of this text: Georgianna Duarte, University of Texas, Brownsville; Ann Rethlefsen, Winona State University; and Ann Russell, Southwestern Oklahoma State University.

1

Introduction

Even the supposedly simple task of reading a newspaper requires critically reviewing the editorial, interpreting the slope of a Dow graph on the financial pages, and understanding a pictogram about U.S. imports or a diagram in a science article about waste conversion.

—Wolfe et al., 1988, p. 123

In one literacy classroom, Josh conducts an inquiry project on diseases of the brain by interviewing experts online and obtaining information from the Internet and books (Owens, Hester, & Teale, 2002). His teacher faces several challenges as Josh and other students begin to develop information with the technology. Included are assisting them to refine key-word searches, to adapt to a nonlinear model of finding information, and to evaluate nontextual features, such as images and graphs (Sutherland-Smith, 2002).

In other words, functioning in an information-driven society requires literacy capabilities unheard of in prior generations. Architects, for example, are expected to be able to explain three-dimensional house plans generated by computer, and auto mechanics must be able to understand diagrams for computer-driven fuel systems.

The centrality of literacy in society is reflected in the 2001 federal legislation "No Child Left Behind." Briefly, the goal is to ensure that all students achieve high standards in literacy that allow them to function at their maximum potential. This goal requires sensitivity to individual differences, knowledge and expertise in appraising student progress, diagnosing student difficulties, and implementing and determining the effectiveness of different instructional strategies. An essential element in meeting this goal is the information provided by classroom assessments. For example, a teacher's anecdotal notes may indicate that children are expressing their thoughts clearly in their personal reflections, but that some children are having difficulty in using simple punctuation. She makes a note to conduct a brief lesson on the use of commas and periods. One role of classroom assessments, in other words, is to inform teachers about students' strengths and weaknesses and their developing skills and understandings. This information serves as the basis for identifying instructional needs in the classroom.

Literacy assessments also inform students about the capabilities that are important in the classroom (Taylor & Nolen, 1996). For example, oral assessments that focus on word pronunciation send the message that pronouncing words correctly is the goal of reading. If oral assessments do not include story retelling, the message that reading involves the construction of meaning is not conveyed.

In addition, assessments inform students about themselves. They learn how well they are progressing in developing important capabilities. Teacher feedback on a student's draft of a story, for example, may state, "Good control of the setting description. I felt I was really there." Students also use the information from assessments to make decisions about their need to study and their potential in a subject area (Stiggins, 1992).

Outside the classroom, summary information developed from assessments informs parents, administrators, and others. Assessments are the basis for information about both individual student learning and the extent to which identified curriculum priorities are being met. For parents, narratives, checklists, or portfolio summaries are particularly useful for reflecting students' strengths and weaknesses.

The varied communicative roles of assessment are important reasons for literacy teachers to become knowledgeable about the characteristics, uses, and strengths and weaknesses of different kinds of classroom assessments. Another reason is the range and variety of available classroom assessments that can provide information about student literacy. Among them are anecdotal records, checklists, teacher questioning and interviewing, student portfolios, diagnostic assessments, and a variety of performance assessments. Some assessments are appropriate for providing feedback to the teacher on student understanding and difficulties; others can reflect the richness and depth of learning to students and parents. However, other assessments may more clearly reflect student progress to other external audiences, such as district administrators and legislators. Moreover, some assessments are time consuming and should be used sparingly, and all have advantages and disadvantages.

In addition to learning about the specific details of different kinds of assessment methods, developing a framework for assessment in the classroom also is important. Briefly, an assessment framework is a mechanism for linking the selection of assessments to classroom goals and curriculum goals or standards. In the absence of such a framework, the teacher risks collecting pages of anecdotal notes, recordings of students' reactions to literature, or other data that are difficult to interpret in a meaningful way (Teale, 1990).

The purpose of this text is to describe and discuss the various types of classroom assessment methods; their characteristics, appropriate uses, advantages and disadvantages; and guidelines for development or implementation. Discussed in this chapter are the current views of literacy, the relationships of assessment models to literacy learning, and the role of curriculum frameworks in literacy assessment. The chapter concludes with an overview of the text.

Literacy and Assessment

Two factors are influential in determining the role of assessment in the literacy classroom. First, basic beliefs about the nature of literacy and the role of literacy in individuals' lives establish the foundation for the types of assessment activities considered appropriate for classroom use. Second, the type of teaching-assessment model adopted in the classroom specifies the relationship of assessment to instruction.

Views of Literacy

The concepts of literacy and literacy assessment have changed in major ways since the early days of American education. At that time, participating in society required only basic reading skills and simple addition and subtraction. Spelling tests, recitation, and essay questions on factual knowledge were appropriate assessment methods for this level of literacy.

   In subsequent years, the emphasis shifted to the teaching of discrete literacy skills followed by student practice of each skill. The curriculum emphasized (1) decoding written messages, (2) encoding spoken messages into writing, and (3) coping with the demands of everyday life that involve written language. Included are completing a questionnaire or writing a routine report (Wells, 1990).

   In this context, literacy assessment consisted of measuring student performance on isolated specific skills. The belief was that these skills would lead to the ability to obtain information from textbooks and other references. Wells (1990) describes this focus as the information level of literacy. That is, an individual is able to consult a reference book on a topic of interest, such as identifying an unknown flower or bird (p. 373). However, as indicated in Table 1.1, today the informational level of literacy would be assessed in a more meaningful way. For example, informational note cards preparatory to writing an essay is a more authentic assessment than a test of discrete skills.

A Multidimensional Concept of Literacy.   Since the 1980s, consensus has formed for the perspective that literacy involves more than proficiency on isolated skills (Hiebert, 1991). The current view of language development differs in two major ways from the discrete skills perspective. One difference is the current emphasis on broad interrelated capabilities. That is, language development consists of four related strands of reading, writing, speaking, and listening (Bembridge, 1994). In the workplace, for example, individuals should be able to read and write reports and also to present information orally to others and listen to their views (Secretary's Commission on Achieving Necessary Skills [SCANS], 1991).

   In addition to these four strands, Cooper (2000) includes (1) communicating through technology and (2) "viewing." Technology includes computers, CD-ROMS, and the World Wide Web. In contrast, viewing involves critically examining visual information, such as a television program or movie (Cooper, 2000, p. 6). Further, Myers and Spalding (1997) add "representing," which refers to preparing graphics for a speech or filmed drama (p. 7).

The second key difference between the current perspective of literacy and the discrete skills approach is the focus on the learner's construction of meaning. This involvement with text can occur at either of two levels of literacy that go beyond the informational level. As indicated in Table 1.1, one level involves engaging with the text "for the pleasure of constructing and exploring a world through words" (Wells, 1990, p. 373). Referred to as *re-creational,* this level of constructing meaning may involve the individual's own words or those of another author. Included are reading imaginative literature and writing expressively, such as letters to friends and entries in a personal journal (p. 373). For example, Mandy writes "I know a special place where a brook runs down a hill, through some daisies, and just as the brook turns to cross the hill, there is a big reddish rock" (Graves, 1983, p. 123). Assessment activities related to exploring through words include children's retellings of their favorite stories, tape recordings of their reactions to stories, and students writing and reworking their own stories.

The informational and re-creational forms of text engagement are important aspects of constructing meaning. However, they do not extend the individual's thinking and understanding about ideas, issues, beliefs, and values. A third level of constructing meaning is identified as an essential component in being fully literate (Wells, 1990). This level involves seeking to achieve "insights of feeling and understanding" that go beyond one's own knowledge (p. 373). This third level of constructing meaning, referred to as *epistemic,* from the Greek word for knowledge, involves several steps. First, the individual asks questions such as "What is the writer's meaning? Is the text internally consistent?" and "Does this text make sense with my experience?" (Wells, 1990, p. 373). In addition, the reader may make notes about the text that capture her insights and connections for later review and critical examination. Subsequent review of these notes can lead to further development of her understanding. Classroom assessments that reflect epistemic

TABLE 1.1   *Levels of Literacy and Related Assessments[1]*

Literacy Levels	*Definitions*	*Related Assessments*
Informational	Consulting a reference book and obtaining information about a topic of interest, such as identifying an unknown flower	Student submits note cards on facts about the Battle of Bull Run, preparatory to writing an essay
Re-creational	Engaging with text "for the pleasure of constructing and exploring a world through words" (Wells, 1990, p. 373)	Student retells a story from imaginative literature; student writes an expressive piece on knowing his grandfather
Epistemic	Achieving "insights of feeling and understanding" that go beyond one's own knowledge (Wells, 1990, p. 373)	Student develops her own concept of tragedy in English literature based on her analysis of several plays

[1]Summarized from Wells (1990)

engagement with text include students' critiques of political or philosophical essays, developing richly detailed understandings of broad ideas.

Engaging with text to develop new understandings and insights is important for at least two reasons. First, it leads to advances in understanding that would be difficult to achieve by other means (Wells, 1990). Second, such understandings are essential to developing the analytical skills involved in applying information to the solution of important problems.

In summary, literacy in today's society involves far more than the encoding and decoding of simple messages, the informational level of engagement with text. Instead, literacy involves proficiency in the interrelated strands of listening, speaking, reading, writing, communicating through technology, and critically examining visual information. Further, the construction of meaning from text also includes exploring a world through words and achieving insights that go beyond one's own knowledge.

Classroom Activities. The current broad orientation toward literacy has led to discussions about the kinds of classroom activities appropriate for instruction. One perspective that has grown over the last twenty years is the approach referred to as whole language. A basic belief of this perspective is that all forms of language, including written language, are most easily learned in the context of use. Therefore, literacy development requires immersion in authentic literacy events. To be authentic, activities should depend on the functional use of language and have personal meaning for the student (Goodman, 1986). An example in the early childhood classroom is setting up a grocery store where children read labels and purchase items. Middle school students, in contrast, may be writing letters to the editor of the local newspaper on an issue of interest to them.

Proponents of the whole language perspective do not support the teaching of arbitrary rules, such as standard spelling. The view is that this practice deprives learners of opportunities to move through their personalized discovery process from "invention to convention" (Goodman & Goodman, 1992). Some research studies, however, indicate that combinations of whole language approaches with explicit instruction in key skills, such as phonemic awareness, have produced achievement gains (e.g., Englehart et al., 1994; Snow, Burns, & Griffin, 1998). Further, Au (1994) and Cooper (2000) suggest a balanced approach to developing literacy. Important are including real opportunities for students to read, write, speak, listen, and think (p. 71). Such activities are referred to as authentic literacy experiences (Cambourne, 1988). Also important is teaching prerequisite skills, such as letter–sound associations, at the beginning of reading (Cooper, 2000, p. 6). This instruction, however, should be combined with meaningful text experiences. A balanced literacy approach, in other words, incorporates the best elements of direct instruction (explicit teaching) and indirect instruction. In indirect instruction, the teacher establishes situations in which children can learn by themselves or from each other. Examples include peer review of drafts of students' stories and independent reading time.

Discussions continue about the role of word identification, various teaching materials, and instructional texts in the development of literacy (Bembridge, 1994). However, one basic tenet is supported by the different approaches. It is that instruction must focus on the students' construction of meaning either from texts written by others or through generating text for others (Bembridge, 1994; Hiebert, 1991).

This text does not endorse a particular approach to the classroom development of literacy. Instead, the purpose is to discuss the various types of assessments that are useful for different purposes and emphases in the classroom.

Teaching Assessment Models

Basic beliefs about the nature of literacy establish the broad capabilities to be addressed in the classroom and suggest the kinds of assessment activities that can provide information about these capabilities. When simple decoding was the focus in early American schools, recitation and spelling tests were sufficient. The current broad view of literacy, in contrast, permits a variety of assessment activities.

Also important in clarifying the role of assessment in relation to instruction is the type of teaching assessment model implemented in the classroom. Three models that reflect different relationships between teaching and assessment may be identified. They are (1) the summative assessment model (Bloom, Hastings, & Madaus, 1971), (2) the formative assessment model (Bloom et al., 1971), and (3) the integrated teaching/assessment model (Gredler, 1999).

The Summative and Formative Assessment Models.   In the summative model, assessment is outside of or after instruction. The goal is not to provide feedback to teachers or students that can inform the selection of either teaching or study activities. Instead, assessment occurs at the end of identified units of instruction. The function of assessment is to document students' levels of achievement in order to assign grades. Assessments typically are limited to classroom tests and formal student products such as research papers. That is, they consist of standardized procedures that are administered under prescribed conditions (Harris & Hodges, 1995).

Although the summative model is prevalent in higher education, variations may be found in some public school classrooms, particularly at the high school level. One variation, formerly found in reading, was the focus on measuring student performance on specific skill elements (Hiebert, 1991). Teachers typically administered tests at the end of instruction to determine whether students had mastered particular skills.

Like the summative model, the formative assessment model is also related to the mastery of specific skills and content. It represented an improvement, compared to the summative model, because it added a feedback role for assessment. However, this model did not expand the types of assessment methods implemented in the classroom. The teacher administered a test at the designated point in instruction, typically at the end of an identified unit (Block, 1975; Bloom et al., 1971). Students who did not meet the mastery standard on that administration received feedback on their weaknesses. Targeted instruction followed, with a subsequent opportunity to take another test on the skills and/or content.

The problems with these two models are the limited information provided for instruction and the limited assessment formats. Further, the complex processes involved in developing literacy cannot be understood adequately through infrequent assessment.

The Integrated Teaching/Assessment Model. The curriculum reform of the 1980s introduced a new model of teaching and assessment, referred to as the integrated teaching/ assessment perspective (Gredler, 1999). A key role for assessment in this model is to inform instruction. Therefore, assessment is closely intertwined with instruction and is an ongoing process. Examples include teacher questioning to determine students' knowledge of the topic prior to reading a new selection, teacher notations while students read aloud, and analyses of drafts of students' writing. These and other assessment activities inform instruction when the teacher revises her instruction on the basis of results, analyzes which students need more practice, and confers with students about their strengths and areas that need improvement (Chappuis & Stiggins, 2002, pp. 40–41).

Several characteristics differentiate this model from the prior teaching assessment models. First, because assessments are closely linked to instruction, they address dimensions of literacy that previously were not considered. Among them are the reading and writing strategies used by learners, the level of students' explicit understanding of the processes they use when reading and writing, learners' attitudes toward reading and writing, and the extent of control that students exercise over the forms of language (Cambourne & Turbill, 1990, p. 343). In other words, the model supports a multifaceted role for assessment. As illustrated in Figure 1.1, assessments provide information for different types of decisions in various areas of student development across the different forms of literacy.

Second, a variety of formats and activities can inform teachers of students' strengths and weaknesses as instruction progresses. In contrast to prior assessment models, the integrated teaching/assessment model includes both formal and informal assessments. Formal assessments are planned, structured assessments conducted under prescribed conditions. Story retelling, for example, can provide information about children's oral language development and their understanding of story structure. Further, students' expository paragraphs about particular topics can provide information about their capabilities to organize facts coherently. Informal assessments, in contrast, are unstructured, usually spontaneous methods that document student behavior. For example, a fifth-grade teacher notes that

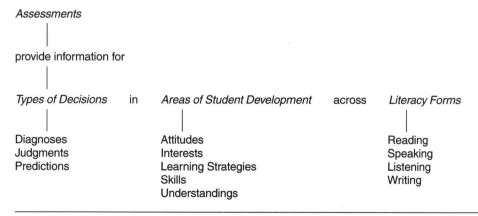

FIGURE 1.1 *The Expanded Role of Assessment in the Integrated Assessment Model*

Bart and Jack, who previously were unengaged in writing, are beginning to work together on writing stories (Gomez, Graue, & Block, 1991, p. 620).

Third, assessments should focus on students' capabilities related to real-world tasks. Such assessments are referred to as authentic to illustrate this relationship. Examples include students sharing stories they have read, writing persuasive letters on topics of importance to them, and writing radio plays for Halloween.

Finally, the integrated teaching/assessment model supports the altered roles of teachers and students that are essential in developing complex literacy capabilities. Specifically, the teacher's role is not that of a transmitter of information. Instead, he or she often functions as coach, guide, and facilitator. Moreover, the teacher also assesses and evaluates the processes students engage in during their literacy activities rather than administering tests or similar assessments at certain points in the school year. In the literacy classroom, for example, the teacher observes children's strategies during independent reading and writing, peer editing, and other activities (Hiebert, 1991).

Further, an expectation for students is that they learn to communicate in various ways and to construct meaning from different types of text. Emphasis on the construction of meaning as a priority requires that students develop intentional strategic activities in their reading and writing. For example, they must learn ways to determine the meanings of words that are new for them and strategies for summarizing the information they have read.

In summary, two factors are influential in determining the role of assessment in the literacy classroom. One is the basic beliefs about the nature of literacy and the role of literacy in individuals' lives. In today's society, individuals are expected to be proficient in several broad interrelated capabilities. They are expected to be able to construct meaning from text beyond the informational level. That is, students should be able to explore new worlds by reading imaginative literature and writing expressively. They also should be able to achieve new insights and understandings through interacting with text. Appropriate assessments for these levels of constructing meaning include children's retelling of their favorite stories, writing and reworking their own stories, and critiquing serious compositions such as political or philosophical essays.

The second factor that influences the type and variety of classroom assessments is the classroom assessment model. The summative and formative models are limited to assessments that can provide information about the skill and content mastery of students. In contrast, a key role for the integrated teaching/assessment model is to inform instruction. Assessments are closely linked to instructional activities, provide information about the various dimensions of literacy, and include both formal and informal assessments that focus on students' capabilities related to real-world tasks. Finally, the integrated teaching/assessment model supports the altered roles of teachers and students.

Frameworks for Classroom Assessment

The current view of literacy emphasizes the importance of acquiring broad interrelated capabilities accompanied by a classroom model that integrates instruction and assessment. This perspective has greatly expanded the opportunities for assessment in the literacy classroom. However, a framework is needed that can guide the focus of classroom instruction and assessment.

General priorities typically are stated in the form of broad expectations for student achievement. For example, the Reading Excellence Act passed by Congress states that reading refers to the ability to read fluently and involves the development of appropriate active strategies to construct meaning from print (Roller, 2000). To facilitate planning, curriculum priorities in the form of national and state standards serve as focal points for developing instruction and assessments.

National and State Standards

To develop standards for the English language arts field, the International Reading Association (IRA) and National Council of Teachers of English (NCTE) brought together teachers, administrators, professors, parents, and others to define the body of knowledge and skills that can ". . . ensure that all students are knowledgeable and proficient users of language" (p. vii, 1996). The resulting twelve standards, illustrated in Table 1.2, reflect six essential areas of literacy: reading, writing, listening, speaking, viewing, and visually representing.

Standards, Stiggins (2002) noted, "frame accepted, valued definitions of academic success" (p. 759). These standards are the broad expectations for students in literacy. They are not prescriptions for instruction. For example, standard six refers to the use of language structures and conventions, media techniques, figurative language, and genre in the creation, critique, and discussion of print and nonprint texts. However, the standard does not state explicitly the language conventions or genres to be taught. In other words, the national standards are broad statements of expectations that serve as guidelines for further planning.

State and school district standards provide further clarification of national standards. For example, the state standards shown in Table 1.3 clarify expectations about students' capabilities to write in various genres, a focus of standard six in the national standards. As indicated, a seventh-grade teacher should plan instruction to prepare students to write reports, poems, stories, songs, essays, and plays. Assessments should consist of student examples of these various types of compositions. Further, student work, such as stories, reports and essays, should include drafts as well as final products to illustrate student growth.

In addition to clarifying national literacy standards, school and district standards fulfill three other functions. As illustrated in Table 1.3, a second function is to define expectations by grade or developmental (age) levels. As indicated, students are expected to develop the ability to write in a variety of forms; however, the nature of their understanding will differ. For example, the second-grader may learn the conventions associated with particular genres such as the treatment of dialogue in plays. In contrast, the seventh-grader should understand that authors may, for a particular purpose, violate the convention of a genre. An example in concrete poetry is arranging the lines to form the shape of the object that is the subject of the poem. The lines in a poem about a cat, for example, would be arranged to form the head, body, and tail. Another example is the lack of capitalization in the poetry of e. e. cummings.

TABLE 1.2   *National English Language Arts Standards*

1. Students read a wide range of print and nonprint texts to build an understanding of texts, of themselves, and of the cultures of the United States and the world; to acquire new information; to respond to the needs and demands of society and the workplace; and for personal fulfillment. Among these texts are fiction and nonfiction, classic and contemporary works.
2. Students read a wide range of literature from many periods in many genres to build an understanding of the many dimensions (e.g., philosophical, ethical, aesthetic) of human experience.
3. Students apply a wide range of strategies to comprehend, interpret, evaluate, and appreciate texts. They draw on their prior experience, their interactions with other readers and writers, their knowledge of word meaning and of other texts, their word identification strategies, and their understanding of textual features (e.g., sound-letter correspondence, sentence structure, context, graphics).
4. Students adjust their use of spoken, written, and visual language (e.g., conventions, style, vocabulary) to communicate effectively with a variety of audiences and for different purposes.
5. Students employ a wide range of strategies as they write and use different writing process elements appropriately to communicate with different audiences for a variety of purposes.
6. Students apply knowledge of language structure, language conventions (e.g., spelling and punctuation), media techniques, figurative language, and genre to create, critique, and discuss print and nonprint texts.
7. Students conduct research on issues and interests by generating ideas and questions, and by posing problems. They gather, evaluate, and synthesize data from a variety of sources (e.g., print and nonprint texts, artifacts, people) to communicate their discoveries in ways that suit their purpose and audience.
8. Students use a variety of technological and informational resources (e.g., libraries, databases, computer networks, video) to gather and synthesize information and to create and communicate knowledge.
9. Students develop an understanding of and respect for diversity in language use, patterns, and dialects across cultures, ethnic groups, geographic regions, and social roles.
10. Students whose first language is not English make use of their first language to develop competency in the English language arts and to develop understanding of content across the curriculum.
11. Students participate as knowledgeable, reflective, creative, and critical members of a variety of literacy communities.
12. Students use spoken, written, and visual language to accomplish their own purposes (e.g., for learning, enjoyment, persuasion, and the exchange of information).

Another role of state and local standards is to guide the development and review of curriculum materials. School districts form committees of teachers and administrators to review textbooks for possible adoption according to alignment with the standards. Additionally, at the district level, subject-area specialists and teachers develop curriculum documents with examples of instructional units and assessments to guide other teachers in developing their own units.

TABLE 1.3 *Examples of Grade-Level Writing Standards*

Second Grade

The student will publish a variety of texts, such as stories, poems, plays, directories, newspapers, charts, and diagrams.

Seventh Grade

The student will select and use a variety of forms in writing.

Vary writing to fit given purpose and audiences.

Compose personal writing (thank you notes, letter of request, etc.) in conventional forms.

Compose in other genres, such as research, poetry, stories, songs, essays, articles, and drama scripts.

Practice written forms in which conventions may be waived, such as poetry, advertisements, certain examples of fiction, and dialogue.

Tenth Grade

The student will compose in a variety of forms, such as personal writing, stories, poems, skits, expository texts, business letters, memos, persuasive pieces, electronic mail, formal writing (appropriate for audience), readers' theater (dramatic), recitation, speechmaking (expressive), debate (clear statements of issues with proper support and logic), plays, exposition (precise, accurate, clear, and organized), reports (informative), applications, resumes, and hypertext.

Source: Reading/English Language Arts: South Carolina Curriculum Standards (1998)

Finally, standards structure the development of assessments used in state testing programs. As indicated in Table 1.3, seventh-grade students are expected to compose letters, poetry, stories, songs, essays, articles, and drama scripts. In developing state assessments, test writers, who are often teachers in the subject area, review the standards and write items that will measure student learning. Thus, students may be asked to demonstrate their understanding of any of the forms of writing specified in the grade-level standards. Student performance on the assessment is then reviewed to document student progress in attaining the standards.

Developing Lesson Goals

The level of generality in national and state standards, in some cases, requires translation into more targeted learning goals for the classroom. Table 1.4 illustrates examples of student learning goals from a set of state curriculum standards for the six literacy strands and illustrates associated examples of assessments. One example is developing a plan for writing and an appropriate assessment is the completion of a concept map or web.

The illustrated goals provide a framework for planning instruction and assessment. However, not all states include goals that indicate specificity. In such situations, teachers develop lesson goals by asking "What should students be able to do after completing this

TABLE 1.4   *Examples of Learning Goals and Assessment Tasks*

Grade Level	Literacy Strand	Learning Goal* (Students will . . .)	Examples of Assessment Tasks
Kindergarten	Listening	identify rhyming words	contribute rhyming words during shared writing to complete a poem
1	Speaking	tell stories in a logical sequence	share stories about events that occurred in the classroom or at home
2	Reading	identify characters, settings, and major events in a story	complete a story map with elements of the narrative
3	Writing	develop a plan for writing	construct a concept map or web to develop ideas and structure for the narrative
4	Viewing	plan and conduct research by accessing information from video and online resources	summarize information from a video and website for use in a report
5	Representing	integrate simple computer graphics into reports	import clipart, diagrams, graphs, or tables into appropriate sections of a report
6	Reading	compare and contrast plot and character development in narrative poems, short stories, and longer fiction stories	construct a Venn diagram to illustrate the similarities and differences in the genres
7	Reading	vary strategies, such as skimming, scanning, using subheadings, and reading rate, to read a variety of texts effectively	complete a survey of metacognitive awareness (Jacobs & Paris, 1987)
8	Writing	revise writing for word choice, relevant details, appropriate organization, sequence of events, consistent point of view, and transition among paragraphs	review revisions in an interview with the teacher
9	Reading	read and follow instructions to perform tasks, such as use computer software	demonstrate the use of a word-processing program to create and format a table
10	Listening	listen, question, and respond appropriately during conferences and interviews	participate in peer conferences during the editing phase of writing
11	Speaking	illustrate ideas in an oral presentation through anecdotes and examples	debate a social or political issue and build the arguments on anecdotes and examples
12	Writing	establish criteria for self and peer evaluation of written text	develop checklists or rubrics for evaluating their drafts

*From the Reading/English Language Arts: South Carolina Curriculum Standards (1998) unit of study?" For example, a seventh-grade teacher may translate the national and state standards that focus on genre into the following lesson goals:

- Identify the literary elements that are common across genres and those elements that are unique to each genre
- Analyze texts to identify the form of the narrative (e.g., historical and realistic fiction)
- Compose in various genres by incorporating the literary elements associated with realistic fiction, fantasy, and historical fiction into their stories

The specificity of these lesson goals guides instructional planning and assessment.

In summary, national literacy standards represent broad expectations for student achievement. These curriculum priorities typically are further clarified by state and school district standards. Other functions of state and local standards are to define developmental or grade-level expectations, and to serve as guides for the development and review of curriculum materials and state assessments. National and state standards are then translated into learning goals for the classroom. In situations in which states or districts do not include specific goals, the teacher develops lesson goals to guide instruction and the development of assessments.

Discussion Questions

1. Why is positive feedback to a student on an assessment task important?

2. Leu (2000, p. 747) stated that, in today's society, "power and influence accrue to those who are most effective at using information for solving problems." What does this mean?

3. What are some of the deficiencies of the summative and formative assessment models for literacy instruction?

4. What are some real-world tasks that can serve as a basis for literacy assessment in the classroom?

5. Standard 8 in the National English Language Arts Standards addresses using a variety of technological and informational resources to gather and synthesize information. What are some ways to assess this standard?

References

Adams, M. J. (1990). *Beginning to read: Thinking and learning about print.* Cambridge, MA: MIT Press.

Au, K. (1994). Portfolio Assessment: Experiences at the Kamehameha Elementary Education Program. In S. W. Valencia, E. H. Hiebert, & P. Afflerbach (Eds.), *Authentic reading assessment* (pp. 103–126). Newark, DE: International Reading Association.

Bembridge, T. (1994). A multilayered assessment package. In S. W. Valencia, E. H. Hiebert, & P. Afflerbach (Eds.), *Authentic reading assessment* (pp. 167–184). Newark, DE: International Reading Association.

Block, J. H. (1975). *Mastery learning in classroom instruction.* New York: Macmillan.

Bloom, B. S., Hastings, J. T., & Madaus, G. F. (1971). *Handbook on formative and summative evaluation of student learning.* New York: McGraw-Hill.

Cambourne, B. (1988). *The whole story: Natural learning and the acquisition of literacy in the classroom.* New York: Ashton-Scholastic.

Cambourne, B., & Turbill, J. (1990). Assessment in whole-language classrooms. *Elementary School Journal, 90*(5), 337–349.

Chappuis, S., & Stiggins, R. (2002). Classroom assessment for learning. *Educational Leadership, 60*(1), 40–43.

Cooper, J. D. (2000). *Literacy: Helping children construct meaning.* Boston: Houghton Mifflin.

Englehart, C., Raphael, T., & Marriage, T. (1994). Developing a school-based discourse for literacy learning: A principled search for understanding. *Learning Disability Quarterly, 17,* 12–32.

Gomez, M. L., Graue, M. E., & Block, M. N. (1991). Reassessing portfolio assessment: Rhetoric and reality. *Language Arts, 68*(8), 620–628.

Goodman, K. S. (1986). *What's whole in whole language.* Portsmouth, NH: Heineman.

Goodman, Y., & Goodman, K. (1992). Vygotsky in a whole-language perspective. In L. Moll (Ed.), *Vygotsky and education* (pp. 223–250). New York: Cambridge University Press.

Graves, D. H. (1983). *Writing: Students and teachers at work.* Portsmouth, NH: Heinemann.

Gredler, M. (1999). *Classroom assessment and learning.* New York: Longman.

Harris, T. L. & Hodges, R. E. (Eds.). (1995). *The literacy dictionary.* Newark, DE: International Reading Association.

Hiebert, E. (1991). Teacher-based assessment of literacy learning. In J. Flood, J. M. Jensen, D. Lapp, & J. R. Squire (Eds.), *Handbook of research on teaching the language arts* (pp. 510–520). New York: Macmillan.

International Reading Association and National Council of Teachers of English (1996). *Standards for the English language arts.*

Leu, D. J. (2000). Literacy and technology: Deictic consequence for literacy education in an information age. In M. L. Kamil, P. B. Mosenthal, P. D. Pearson, & R. Barr (Eds.), *Handbook of reading research, Vol. III* (pp. 743–800). Mahwah, NJ: Lawrence Erlbaum Associates.

Myers, M., & Spalding, E. (1997). *Standards exemplar series: Assessing student performance grades K–5.* Urbana, IL: National Council of Teachers of English.

Owens, R. F., Hester, J. L., & Teale, W. H. (2002). Where do you want to go today? Inquiry based learning and technology integration. *Reading Teacher, 55*(7), 616–625.

Reading/English language arts: South Carolina Curriculum Standards. (1998). Columbia: South Carolina Department of Education.

Rhodes, L. K., & Nathenson-Mejia, S. N. (1999). Anecdotal records—A powerful tool for ongoing literacy assessment. In S. J. Barrentine (Ed.), *Reading assessment: Principles and practices for the beginning teacher.* (pp. 83–90). Newark, DE: International Reading Association.

Roller, C. (2000). The International Reading Association responds to a highly charged political environment. *Reading Teacher, 53*(8), 626–636.

Secretary's Commission on Achieving Necessary Skills (SCANS). (1991). *What work requires of schools.* Washington, DC: U.S. Department of Labor.

Snow, C., Burns, M. S., & Griffin, P. (Eds.). (1998). *Preventing reading difficulties in young children.* Washington, DC: National Academic Press.

Stiggins, R. (2002). Assessment crisis: The absence of assessment FOR learning. *Phi Delta Kappan, 83*(10), 758–765.

Stiggins, R. (1992). High quality classroom assessment: What does it really mean? *Educational Measurement: Issues and practices, 11*(2), 35–39.

Sutherland-Smith, W. (2002). Weaving the literacy web: Changes in reading from page to screen. *Reading Teacher, 55*(7), 662–669.

Taylor, O., & Nolen, S. B. (1996). A contextualized approach to teaching teachers about classroom assessment. *Educational Psychologist, 31*(1), 77–88.

Teale, W. H. (1988). Developmentally appropriate assessment of reading and writing in the early childhood classroom. *The Elementary School Classroom, 89*(2), 173–183.

Teale, W. H. (1990). The promise and challenge of informal assessment in early literacy. In L. M. Morrow & J. K. Smith (Eds.), *Assessment for instruction in early literacy* (pp. 45-61). Englewood Cliffs, NJ: Prentice Hall.

Wells, G. (1987). Apprenticeship in literacy. *Interchange, 18*(1 & 2), 109–123.

Wells, G. (1990). Talk about text: Where literacy is learned and taught. *Curriculum Inquiry, 20*(4), 369–405.

Wolf, D., Davidson, L., Davis, M., Walters, J., Hodges, M., & Scripp, L. (1988). Beyond A, B, and C: A broader and deeper view of literacy. In A. D. Pellegrino (Ed.), *Psychological bases for early education* (pp. 123–152). New York: John Wiley & Sons Ltd.

2

Effective Assessment in the Classroom

Assessments for teachers are successful only to the extent that they improve instruction for individual students.

—Winograd, Paris, & Bridge, 1991, p. 113

Jeremy's fifth-grade teacher is reviewing the anecdotal notes she has taken during students' independent writing time. The class is using resource books checked out of the library and sources they have found on the Internet. Her notes indicate that three of the student research pairs are having difficulty in relocating sources of interest identified in their initial searches. She adjusts her lesson plan for the next day to include a demonstration of online bookmarking.

Assessments that are successful for teachers in improving instruction are those that are effective in assisting their decision making. That is, the assessments provide accurate and dependable information about students' needs. Assessments in the classroom also are implemented for other purposes. Among them are documenting student growth, identifying students' strengths and weaknesses, and reporting student progress to parents, administrators, and other audiences.

Several characteristics are important in ensuring that all such assessments are effective. One of two essential criteria discussed in this chapter is that assessments provide accurate information for decision making, referred to as the validity of an assessment. The other critical criterion is that assessments lead to dependable decisions about student performance, referred to as reliability. Also important for effective assessments is that the tasks should be meaningful. Factors contributing to this goal, discussed in this chapter, are authenticity, the representation of diversity, and student involvement in assessment.

Ensuring Appropriate Decisions about Student Learning

Assessments that provide information about instructional needs, student strengths and weaknesses, and student progress are conducted in busy, often fast-paced classrooms. Several practices are important in ensuring that the assessments lead to valid (accurate) and reliable decisions.

Documenting Patterns in Performance (Reliability)

Teachers are aware that students' responses to classroom tasks vary from day to day. One reason is the physical or emotional state of the learner. For example, Brigitte is anxious about being in a new school and Mike is preoccupied with being the starting pitcher in his team's game that afternoon, and their full attention is not on school tasks.

Other factors that can influence student performance are time of day of the assessment, the specific questions, and the literature selections. That is, a student's performance on essay questions will vary for different essay prompts, and he will react differently from one literary selection to the next. Also, factors that influence children's oral retellings of stories are text length and predictability of the text. Of particular importance is that, in young children, some performances do not stabilize for an extended period of time. For example, when young children have progressed to using invented spellings in their emergent writing, they also may continue to use drawings as a writing form, and may do so until age 6 or 7 (Sulzby, 1990a, 1990b). For these reasons, a conclusion about performance based on limited observations is considered unreliable.

Reliability in assessment is defined as a decision about a student's attitudes, capabilities, or strategies that is based on consistent patterns of student performance. Patterns may be evident in students' scores, when, for example, some students with emergent literacy skills have consistently low scores in letter identification. Patterns also may be noted in more qualitative terms. In a writing class, for example, one student may consistently develop strong characters but weak setting descriptions. Another student, however, typically develops strong plots but does not observe the mechanics of punctuation and grammar.

Detecting patterns, however, requires assessment across many contexts to obtain information that is consistent with a student's typical performance. Thus, student performances should be observed across many occasions, questions, test items, types of reading selections, and writing topics (IRA/NCTE Joint Task Force on Assessment, 1994). In practice, this means assessing students frequently and documenting student progress over time (Hiebert, Valencia, & Afflerbach, 1994). An example is noting the patterns in children's oral reading of several literature selections on different occasions in class and tape recordings completed during independent reading. In this way, assessments can provide "a representative picture of the student's true performance—not a fluke, not a matter of chance or luck" (Brookhart, 1993).

Tapping into different contexts and types of assessments over time reflects the view that assessment and evaluation are ongoing and cyclic processes intricately interwoven with teaching and learning (Hancock, Turbill, & Cambourne, 1994, p. 46). However, a tension exists in that assessment of students should not be overdone (Kohn, 1994). Kohn warns that excessive concern with performance may deter curiosity, reduce quality of performance, and result in students avoiding difficult tasks to avoid negative evaluations (p. 40). The challenge is for teachers to assess often enough to note patterns in student capabilities and characteristics, but not to "overuse" assessments. Anecdotal records of students' classroom activities and review of work developed in scheduled writing activities, for example, can reduce the emphasis on "on-demand" assessments.

Table 2.1 illustrates key questions that reflect the conditions essential for reliable decisions about students' capabilities, interests, and strategies of learning. Question 1 addresses the opportunities for the student to demonstrate actions that reflect this learning. For example, observations of student engagement in writing should focus on one student at a time for several days and in several activities. Question 2 provides a reminder that decisions are more reliable when based on more, rather than fewer, questions. One essay question at the end of a unit, for example, does not adequately reflect the extent of student understanding developed during the unit. Question 3 indicates that assessments should use a wide variety of reading selections.

In summary, reliance on any one student performance may result in information that does not reflect a student's ability to read and write. To be effective, assessments must provide information that leads to consistent decisions about student performance. Consistency is achieved when a teacher observes patterns in students' learning, reading strategies, and attitudes. Required, however, are assessments on multiple occasions, several rather than one essay question, and a variety of topics for students' reading experiences.

TABLE 2.1   *Reliability Questions to Frame the Review of Classroom Assessments*

Review Questions	*Assessment Contexts*	*Conclusions*
1. Do students have multiple opportunities to demonstrate their understanding, skills, or interests?	1. On several occasions during a grading period, students write summaries about the literary selections that they read.	The teacher has sufficient information to indicate a consistent pattern in the level of student understanding.
2. In a test, are there a sufficient number of questions that are related to the instructional goals?	2. After reading a novel, students complete a ten-item computer-based test to assess their understanding.	With so few items to assess student understanding of an entire book, student scores would likely be different on another quiz with ten different questions.
3. Do the texts used in the assessment represent a variety of topics?	3. During a study of realistic fiction, a teacher varies the story plots that students encounter in small-group reading because student reactions to text vary from topic to topic.	The teacher's estimate of student engagement in reading will be more consistent with a student's actual level of engagement.

Patterns in performances indicate, for example, a consistent demonstration of learning achievements or difficulties, and provide information for decisions about both student learning and instructional needs.

Supporting Accurate Decisions (Validity)

In addition to reliability, the effectiveness of an assessment also depends on its ability to generate valid decisions about student capabilities (Messick, 1993). For example, if a school is implementing a process-writing curriculum, the decisions to be made involve students' growth in gaining control of their writing through peer review, self-editing, and revising their work. Therefore, ongoing assessments of students' work at various stages in the writing process are needed to provide accurate information. Similarly, in a literature-based language arts curriculum, teachers assess reading growth by documenting the ways that students read, understand, and respond to trade books (Winograd, Paris, & Bridge, 1991, p. 110).

   The importance of the accuracy of decisions about students' capabilities is illustrated in the inappropriate use of a particular rating scale by one school system. The purpose was to determine which students were ready to learn to read and could benefit from instruction in the first grade (Gredler, 1992). Many of the items on the scale, however, assessed motor skills, such as the ability of a child to ties his shoes. In terms of validity, one should ask, "Are decisions about a child's reading readiness likely to be accurate when based on an instrument weighted heavily with items on motor skills?" The answer is no, because shoe tying is not related to reading readiness.

   Four classroom practices are important in developing assessments that provide information for making accurate inferences about students' capabilities, strategies, and attitudes. They are (1) establish a focus for assessments, (2) align assessments with the identified focus, (3) ensure that instruction provides students the opportunity to learn the identified capabilities and strategies, and (4) ensure that the selected assessments provide an opportunity for students to demonstrate their learning.

Identify a Focus for Assessments.   Hiebert et al. (1994) noted that "without clear definition of goals . . . assessment will be ambiguous in both nature and purpose. . . ." As discussed in Chapter 1, national and state committees of teachers, administrators, professors, and parents convened to define the knowledge and skills essential for students to develop in the English language arts. These standards are further clarified by curriculum guides and other materials and developed into learning goals for the classroom, which serve as focal points for assessments. An example is telling stories in a logical sequence (see Table 1.4). Valid assessments of this capability include documentation of the child's shared stories about events at home and the completed scoring guides for scheduled retellings in the classroom (see Chapter 5).

Align Assessments with the Identified Learning Focus.   This requirement includes two components. One is that assessments must draw out the learning identified as the focus. For example, a multiple-choice test cannot address students' capabilities to select and organize key information to develop a report on a particular subject. Second, the assessment must capture the key dimensions of complex capabilities. For example, the dimensions in developing a case for a particular course of action may include (1) a clear statement of the student writer's position, (2) an explication of supporting arguments, and (3) a refutation of opposing arguments. Two assessment types that may address this focus and the key dimensions are writing a persuasive letter, and engaging in a formal oral debate. (Chapters 5 and 6 address the identification of dimensions for assessment for assessment tasks.)

Ensure Student Opportunity to Learn. For assessments to be valid, instruction must address the capabilities and strategies that are the focus of learning. For example, students should not be assessed on analyzing challenging texts, taking risks, or exploring diverse interpretations unless teachers spend time teaching students to be critical thinkers (Winograd et al., 1991, p. 111).

Similarly, instruction should include any novel or unusual formats that may be incorporated into an assessment. An example is an assessment that asks students to construct story maps to reflect their understanding of narrative structure (i.e., the characters, setting, problem, plot, climax, and resolution) (Cunningham & Allington, 1999; Fountas & Pinnell, 2001). Prior to use as an assessment, the teacher should first demonstrate the use of story maps. That is, she talks through the process of selecting important events from the story and linking them in a visual portrayal (Fountas & Pinnell, 2001). Then, during small group and class discussions, students practice constructing story maps to illustrate stories they have read.

Some authors suggest that assessments should engage students in higher-level thinking (Hiebert et al., 1994). This criterion implies that instruction engaged students in learning such capabilities through, for example, analyzing propaganda techniques used in advertisements, critiquing the arguments in a speech, or developing a poem based on the stylistic elements of ballads. In these situations, assessments that require analysis, evaluation, and synthesis, respectively, would be appropriate.

Ensure That Assessments Provide Students an Opportunity to Demonstrate Their Learning. Four major characteristics of assessments affect students' opportunities to demonstrate their learning. They are response format, situational circumstances, time requirements, and task directions. First, studies indicate that students perform differently for different formats of an assessment (e.g., Shavelson, Baxter, & Gao, 1993). For example, open-ended formats that require written responses should not be the only method used with children to assess their ability to interpret and respond to text (Garcia & Pearson, 1991; Hiebert, 1991) (see Chapters 5 and 8). The reason is that children's understanding is often greater than they can demonstrate in writing. Therefore, oral retellings and oral interviews also should be used to assess students' comprehension (Shepard, 1993).

Situational circumstances also may prevent students from demonstrating their learning. For example, a shy student may not speak out in small group discussions, but may communicate one-on-one with the teacher in an interview. In addition, providing adequate time to complete an assessment is important. Students with special needs may need more time than their peers to complete a task (see Chapter 8).

Finally, clear directions are essential for all students so they understand the nature of the task. For example, in story retellings, the teacher must state that the child is to retell the story as though the listener had never heard it before (Morrow, 1990). Otherwise, the child is likely to omit important elements (see Chapter 5).

The questions posed in Table 2.2 provide a framework to review the accuracy of decisions based on classroom assessments. Question 1 focuses on whether the tasks to assess student learning reflect key concepts, skills, and strategies in the language arts that were the focus of student learning. Question 2 reminds teachers that the assessment must align with the learning goals. The congruence of instructional methods and the method of assessment are the focus of question 3. Question 4 directs attention to the issue of whether an assessment provides all students an opportunity to demonstrate their knowledge.

Summary

Effective assessments support the accuracy of decisions and inferences about student development such as students' understanding of literary selections, their reading and writing strategies, and their attitudes toward the language arts. Decisions about student development in the language arts are supported when instruction and assessment focus on those skills identified in the standards as important capabilities. Also, teachers' decisions about student learning are supported when an assessment aligns with the identified learning focus. This requires that the assessment draw out the learning identified as the focus and capture the key dimensions of complex capabilities. In addition, inferences about student learning are supported when instruction includes learning opportunities in which students

TABLE 2.2   *Validity Questions to Frame the Review of Classroom Assessments*

Review Questions	*Assessment Scenarios*
1. Does the assessment reflect key concepts, skills, and/or processes identified as the focus of learning?	1. A language arts teacher focused instructional activities on the learning goal of "develop a plan for writing." His assessment of student learning used their information webs developed as part of an inquiry project.
2. Does it align with the particular learning goal(s) it is intended to assess?	2. A learning goal states that students will use sentence structure, line length, and punctuation to convey mood of a poem. An assessment based on student analysis of a poem in a literature discussion circle would not be valid because students are required to analyze a poem, not use the elements to write a poem.
3. Does the assessment reflect the instructional methods in the classroom?	3. To prepare students to make presentations about their inquiry projects, as part of instruction, a teacher modeled the process of identifying major points, organizing those points, creating visuals, and delivering the speech.
4. Does it provide students with an opportunity to demonstrate their learning?	4. Students who comprehend a story may experience difficulty in providing a written summary; however, in a conference they may provide detailed retellings of the narrative.

express their understanding in the same format to be used in the assessment. Finally, the accuracy of decisions about student development depends on whether the assessment provides students an opportunity to demonstrate their learning. Important are attention to response format, situational circumstances, adequate time to complete the assessment, and clear task directions.

Developing Meaningful Contexts

Validity and reliability are the two criteria essential for effective assessment. Also contributing to the effectiveness of assessment is the development of meaningful contexts. The three qualities that contribute to the development of meaningful assessments are the authenticity of the tasks, the representation of diversity, and self-assessment and collaboration.

Authenticity in Instruction and Assessment

Authenticity requires that, whenever possible, assessment situations closely resemble the actual context in which students will use the particular capabilities to be learned (Hiebert et al., 1994; Wiggins, 1993). For example, as Scott crafts dialogue, scenes, and comic sketches for a play-writing project, he displays an understanding of the elements of plays that goes beyond a simple recall of facts about the genre (Zessoules & Gardner, 1991). Wiggins (1993) suggests that authentic assessments (1) engage students in worthy problems that reflect the challenges faced by professionals and adult citizens, (2) are faithful to the contexts encountered by adults, (3) are multistage problems that require students to use their understanding of the subject area to make judgments, and (4) require the student to develop a quality product or performance (pp. 206–207). He also states that authentic tasks require students ". . . to be critical in an ill-structured situation" (Wiggins, 1993, p. 204).

However, the extent to which an assessment is authentic varies along a continuum. In writing, for example, multiple-choice tests on mechanics lack authenticity. Actual samples of writing for a directed performance assessment, such as the directive to write a letter to a pen pal in England on an identified topic, are next on the continuum (Thomas & Oldfather, 1997). Samples of writing collected from projects in which students write for real purposes and audiences are at the top of the continuum. An example is letters to the editor about an issue of concern to the students (p. 109).

In the language arts, authentic assessment includes those "activities that represent the literacy behavior of the community and workplace, and that reflect the actual learning and instructional activities of the classroom and out-of-school worlds" (Hiebert et al., 1994). To illustrate, consider the teacher who wants to assess his students' ability to read and understand a wide range of print and nonprint texts. Adults, for example, may rely on newspapers, broadcast news, or news magazines in forming their opinions about current events. To design an assessment of student understanding of a variety of news sources, the teacher may establish a context in which students identify a current event of interest and compare the information provided in print and nonprint sources. Students may identify details that appear in both types, details that appear to present contradictory information, and additional information found in some sources but not others.

Zessoules and Gardner (1991) note that "such rich modes of assessment cannot be activated in a vacuum. . . . Educators interested in reform must recognize and examine the need for a classroom culture that will sustain the values, merits and practices of more authentic forms of assessment" (p. 49). Piluski (1994) offers an additional caution: "The most authentic, valid, responsive, naturalistic assessment procedures are worthless unless classroom teachers find them doable" (p. 63). Of importance here is that the teacher consider authenticity in planning multiple forms of student assessment that can reasonably be integrated into the classroom.

In summary, authenticity in an assessment requires that students apply their language arts skills in contexts similar to those in the community and the workplace. These contextualized assessments require students to apply their understanding and make judgments as they solve complex problems. For such assessments to support accurate inferences about student development, the language arts teacher must provide learning experiences aligned with authentic assessment practices.

Representing the Diversity of the Classroom

Instruction and assessment activities that involve students in real-world problems are anchored in a context that includes people. That is, through photographs and scenarios, people are portrayed as to their physical appearance, dress, environment, and activities (Macmillan-McGraw Hill, 1993). These portrayals should reflect diversity in culture and be free of biases based on ethnic group, gender, nationality, religion, socioeconomic condition, sexual orientation, and physical disability (IRA/NCTE Joint Task Force on Assessment, 1994, p. 22). To gauge the attainment of this goal in assessment, one asks, "Do the assessment procedures used with students reflect their ethnic and community cultures?" (Banks, 2001, p. 343).

Assistance in addressing Banks' question is offered in *Reflecting diversity: Multicultural guidelines for educational publishing professionals* (Macmillan-McGraw Hill, 1993), a resource for the development of curriculur and instructional materials. Attention to these guidelines can assist a teacher to reduce bias in assessment by avoiding stereotypical representation, contextual invisibility, and historical distortions. The result is a balanced portrayal of people by gender, ethnicity, disability, age, sexual orientation, and socioeconomic status.

Stereotypical Representation. Individuals are presented in stereotypical ways when the narrative and art in curriculum materials project inaccurate generalizations on the basis of characteristics unrelated to behavior. That is, physical appearance, dress, or activities are depicted to convey a particular impression of a group (Macmillan-McGraw Hill, 1993). For instance, always portraying older characters in a narrative or illustration as sitting in rocking chairs, recliners, or porch swings is a stereotype. The inference is that older individuals are inactive and not in the mainstream of society. Similarly, the depiction of disabled students as always being the recipients of help from able-bodied students, and never the providers of assistance, perpetuates inaccurate generalizations of the disabled as being helpless.

Also, correspondence, literature, and other text materials from earlier periods may portray individuals in particular ways that are unacceptable by today's standards. For example, an excerpt from the Jamestown governor's diary in a history chapter indicates that he used the word *savages* to describe Native Americans (Afflerbach & VanSledright, 2001).

Sexist stereotypes occur when the narrative or art explicitly or implicitly narrows and defines a person's life according to gender (Macmillan-McGraw Hill, 1993). Such was the case when a fourth-grade teacher read a popular legend in which a father offered his daughter in marriage to any man who could perform a specified feat (Cruz-Janzen, 1998). The father's offer of marriage is made without the consent of the daughter. One fourth-grader responded, "That's a stupid way to find a husband. Just because some guy can ride a horse and throw a ball on your lap doesn't mean that you are going to like him. You just don't marry anyone off the street" (p. 5). On reflection, the teacher realized that the legend perpetuated a bias of women as passive and for whom men make all the decisions. Similarly, stereotypes are perpetuated when lawyers are all males and nurses are all female.

Sexist words and phrases send subtle messages of exclusion to female readers. Texts and assessments that rely on gender-based words such as *mankind* and *spokesman* instead of gender-neutral terms such as *humanity* and *spokesperson* subtly exclude female students from the narrative. Sexist language also narrows the behaviors acceptable for students based on gender. An example is the connotation that some behaviors are inappropriate for males by labeling a male who has displayed sensitivity to and understanding of others as a "sissy."

Racial stereotypes are perpetuated in materials that convey the assumption that racial characteristics determine a person's behavior and capacities (Macmillan-McGraw Hill, 1993). Examples include portraying African American, Native American, or Hispanic American persons in service jobs, but not in executive positions. In selecting or developing an assessment, a teacher should review the narrative and art to assure that ethnic groups are portrayed in a variety of professions, activities, and environments (see question 1, Table 2.3).

Contextual Invisibility.   The underrepresentation of groups, lifestyles, or customs in curricular materials is referred to as contextual invisibility (Macmillan-McGraw Hill, 1993). Underrepresentation indicates to students that some groups, lifestyles, and customs are of less value and significance than others. Applebee (1991) provided an example in the language arts. He reported that diversity in the selections of short stories, poems, and nonfiction in anthologies had increased; however, he also noted that book-length works by women or minorities were less often part of required reading.

In contrast, multicultural education describes "the histories and experiences of people who have been left out of the curriculum" (Lee, 1995, p. 9). For example, students may read only about the issues addressed by upper-class white women at the 1848 Seneca Falls, New York, women's rights conference. That is, they may not be exposed to the issues faced by enslaved African American women, Native American women relocated in

TABLE 2.3 *Questions to Frame the Review of Classroom Assessments for Diversity*

Review Questions	Assessment Scenarios
1. Are people presented without stereotype in descriptions of their physical appearance, dress, environment, and activities?	1. Texts to assess student reading level contain illustrations that portray characters with disabilities in physically active situations.
2. Does the assessment represent diverse groups, lifestyles, or customs and avoid contextual invisibility?	2. An English literature class completed a poetry unit that focused on the authors' experiences in American culture. To determine which poems her students would use in their critical analysis, the teacher selected poems that addressed issues of gender, ethnicity, and sexual orientation.
3. Does the assessment accurately portray the complexity of history and avoid the historical distortions that occur when (a) materials present only one interpretation of an issue or (b) controversial or sensitive topics are avoided?	3. A reading list of historical fiction contained novels that portrayed the settlement of America only through the viewpoints of European settlers. A teacher supplemented the list with a novel about the forced relocation of the Cherokee tribe. In her final exam, one essay question required students to reinterpret a scene from a European-based historical fiction novel through the viewpoint of Native Americans.

the Trail of Tears, and Mexican women in the new territory of New Mexico (Bigelow, 1999). In the selection of literary works and development of assessments, a teacher should ask whether the materials omit or underrepresent groups, life-styles, or customs (question 2, Table 2.3).

Historical Distortions. Presentation of only one interpretation of an issue or the avoidance of controversial or sensitive topics is referred to as historical distortion (Macmillan-McGraw Hill, 1993). In the literacy classroom, historical texts provide a context for students to develop critical reading skills (Afflerbach & VanSledright, 2001). For example, students begin to develop intertextual reading strategies as they examine historical materials that include primary sources, as well as excerpts from other sources. Through the comparison of the information from different sources, students begin to understand that authors attend to some information and may fail to address other details. That is, through comparison, students develop the understanding that history is, in part, a portrayal by different authors. When using historical texts, teachers should sensitize students to this phenomenon.

An example of a sensitive topic that Takaki identifies as "a hidden reality of American history" is class structure (in Halford, 1999, p. 10). "We overlook class, but class is central to the ethnic experience, including the experience of European immigrant groups"

(p. 10). He outlined the history of the need for a labor class and the use of indentured Irish and English servants by Virginia planters in the 1600s. After indentured servants burned down Jamestown in Bacon's Rebellion in 1676, the Virginia planters shifted from indentured white laborers to enslaved African laborers. Later, the labor of Jews supported the garment industry. Irish laborers built railroads and worked in textile mills, and Japanese laborers worked on the sugar plantations of Hawaii.

In one tenth-grade classroom the teachers provided guiding questions, from which students chose their focus for their research projects. One question, for example, selected by a student who researched the life of blues singer Billie Holliday, was "How do people face and fight destructive beliefs, powers, and prejudice?" (Kordalewski, 2000, p. 48). In other words, students were able to pursue sensitive topics in their research activities.

When asked to define multiculturalism, Takaki stated that "multiculturalism . . . is a serious scholarship that includes all American peoples and challenges the traditional master narrative of American history. The traditional master narrative we've learned in our schools says that this country was founded by Americans of European ancestry and that our ideas are rooted in Western civilization" (in Halford, 1999, p. 9). However, he challenged this portrayal by describing a diverse culture composed of peoples from Africa, Latin America, and Asia. He argued it is "more accurate to recognize this diversity. The intellectual purpose of multiculturalism is a more accurate understanding of who we are as Americans" (p. 9). Therefore, classroom assessments must also acknowledge this diversity.

In summary, curriculum materials use narrative and art to portray people in their physical appearance, dress, environment, and activities. These portrayals may bring a multicultural perspective to instruction and assessment or they may promote biases. In the selection and development of instructional and assessment materials, teachers want to eliminate biases based on ethnicity, gender, nationality, religion, socioeconomic condition, sexual orientation, and physical disability. To bring a multicultural perspective to instruction and assessment, teachers should review materials for stereotypical representations, contextual invisibility, and historical distortions. By attending to the portrayals of people in literature, instructional materials, and assessments, teachers can reduce bias in the representation of people who are citizens of this society and who include the students in the classroom.

Self-Assessment and Collaboration

As stated in Chapter 1, assessments can support the decision making of students. That is, they learn how well they are progressing in developing important literacy capabilities. In addition, assessments should (1) involve students in learning to evaluate their strengths and areas that need improvement (Chappuis & Stiggins, 2002; International Reading Association [IRA] Commission on Adolescent Literacy, 1999; Kohn, 1994; Stiggins, 2002), and (2) include instances that involve collaboration (IRA Commission on Adolescent Literacy, 1999). Involvement of students in their own assessment requires that they participate in the selection or discussion of the dimensions that are the focus of the performance (Chappuis & Stiggins, 2002; Kohn, 1994). However, learning to self-assess is not second nature for students (see Chapter 7). With instruction and class discussion, children can learn to set goals for their learning and to reflect on their progress (Courtney & Abodeeb, 2001). Also, students can learn to use scoring guides to evaluate their own work and identify their strengths and areas of challenge (Chappuis & Stiggins, 2002). They also can participate in the development of practice tests based on their understanding of the class material.

An example of collaboration and self-assessment is provided by Michael, a third-grade student with learning disabilities. A struggling reader, Michael's primary focus in reading has been the accurate reproduction of words, not the construction of meaning. Michael and a literacy researcher, Prisca Martens, listen to an audiotape of the third-grader's earlier reading session (Martens, 1998). As they follow the original text and listen to Michael read *Owl at Home* (Lobel, 1975), the two discuss miscues in his reading. They attempt to determine why a word substitution occurred, if the substitution made sense, how much it resembled the actual text, if it was corrected, and if it should be corrected. At one point in the reading, Michael read "said Owl" instead of the author's text "he said." In his discussion with Martens, the third-grader questions why the author had not written the phrase as he had read it. Michael's contribution to the analysis indicated that he "was understanding that just as authors make decisions on how to create meaning in their stories, readers also make those decisions for themselves. He was seeing that as a reader, he had the responsibility of constructing a meaningful text that made sense to him" (Martens, 1999, pp. 156–157). In this collaborative assessment of Michael's reading, he revealed to Martens that he was beginning to consider the construction of meaning in stories, an insight available only through the student's contribution.

In conclusion, this chapter has described the characteristics of effective assessments. But not all forms of assessment meet the demands of a particular instructional purpose. Therefore, the classroom teacher selects the assessment strategy that is most appropriate for a particular purpose. The following chapters describe different assessment approaches for use in the classroom. To assist teachers in selecting assessments for various classroom contexts, the strengths and weaknesses of each approach are discussed.

In considering the approach to use in a particular context, a teacher will want to consider the audience for the information, the age and number of students who will be assessed, and the literacy goals that are the focus of instruction and assessment (Hiebert et al., 1994, p. 14). Also, some assessment approaches are most useful to review the progress of a few students, whereas other approaches may be used to collect information about all students in the classroom. These issues are addressed in this text in the discussion of each approach so that teachers can make informed decisions about which assessment should be used in a given context.

*Discussion Questions*_____

1. Name two assessment practices that a teacher can implement in her classroom in order to be more effective in making decisions about student performance.

2. What are the elements of an authentic assessment? Describe an authentic assessment of students' ability to distinguish between facts and opinions.

3. The following item overlooks which multicultural issue?

In *A Wrinkle in Time*, the character of Charles Wallace is to rational as the character of Meg is to _____.

  a. emotional*

  b. intellectual

  c. logical

  d. practical

4. Portfolios are purposeful collections of students' work in an area of learning. The contents of the portfolio represent student performance across time and types of assessments. For example, a reading portfolio may contain several examples of both taped retellings and written summaries that a student has completed during a report period. The student and teacher work together to select work samples that show the student's understanding. Which of the criteria for effective assessment may be addressed in the use of a portfolio assessment?

References

Afflerbach, P., & VanSledright, B. (2001). Hath! Doth! What? Middle graders reading innovative history text. *Journal of Adolescent and Adult Literacy, 44*(8), 696–707.

Applebee, A. (1991). Literature: Whose heritage? In E. Hiebert (Ed.), *Literacy for a diverse society: Perspectives, practices, and policies* (pp. 228–236). New York: Teachers College Press.

Banks, J. (2001). *Cultural diversity and education: Foundations, curriculum, and teaching* (4th ed.). Boston: Allyn and Bacon.

Bigelow, B. (1999). Why standardized tests threaten multiculturalism. *Educational Leadership, 56*(7), 8–13.

Brookhart, S. (1993). Assessing student achievement with term papers and written reports. *Educational Measurement: Issues and Practices, 12*(1), 40–47.

Chappuis, S., & Stiggins, R. (2002). Classroom assessment for learning. *Educational Leadership, 60*(1), 40–43.

Cruz-Janzen, M. (1998). Culturally authentic bias. *Rethinking schools, 13*(1), 5.

Courtney, A. M., & Abodeeb, T. L. (2001). *Journey of discovery*. Newark, DE: International Reading Association.

Cunningham, P., & Allington, R. (1999). *Classrooms that work: They can all read and write* (2nd ed.). New York: Longman.

Fountas, I., & Pinnell, G. (2001). *Guiding readers and writers (Grades 3–6)*. Portsmouth, NH: Heinemann.

Garcia, G., & Pearson, P. D. (1991). The role of assessment in a diverse society. In E. H. Hiebert (Ed.), *Literacy for a diverse society: Perspectives, practices, and policies* (pp. 253–278). New York: Teachers College Press.

Gredler, G. (1992). *School readiness: Assessment and educational issues*. Brandon, VT: Clinical Psychology Publishing.

Halford, J. (1999). A different mirror: A conversation with Ronald Takaki. *Educational Leadership, 56*(7), 8–13.

Hancock, J., Turbill, J., & Cambourne, B. (1994). Assessment and evaluation of literacy learning. In S. Valencia, E. Hiebert, & P. Afflerbach (Eds.), *Authentic reading assessment: Practices and possibilities* (pp. 46–70). Newark, DE: International Reading Association.

Hickman, J. (1987). Looking at response to literature. In A. Jagger & M. Smith-Burke (Eds.), *Observing the language learner*. Newark, DE: International Reading Association.

Hiebert, E. (1991). Teacher-based assessment of literacy learning. In J. Flood, J. M. Jensen, D. Lapp, & J. R. Squire (Eds.), *Handbook of research on teaching the language arts* (pp. 510–520). New York: Macmillan.

Hiebert, E., Valencia, S. & Afflerbach, P. (1994). Definitions and perspectives. In S. Valencia, E. Hiebert, & P. Afflerbach (Eds.), *Authentic reading assessment: Practices and possibilities* (pp. 6–21). Newark, DE: International Reading Association.

International Reading Association Commission on Adolescent Literacy (1999). Adolescent literacy: A position statement. *Journal of Adolescent and Adult Literacy, 43*(1), 97–112.

IRA/NCTE Joint Task Force on Assessment (1994). *Standards for the assessment of reading and writing*. Newark, DE: International Reading Association.

Kohn, A. (1994). Grading: The issue is not how but why. *Educational Leadership, 52*(2), 38–41.

Kordalewski, J. (2000). *Standards in the classroom: How teachers and students negotiate learning*. New York: Teachers College Press.

Lee, E. (1995). Taking multicultural, anti-racist education seriously: An interview with Enid Lee. In D. Levine, R. Lowe, Peterson, & R. Tenorio (Eds.), *Rethinking schools: An agenda for change* (pp. 9–16). New York: The New Press.

Lobel, A. (1975). *Owl at home*. New York: Harper & Row.

Macmillan-McGraw Hill (1993). *Reflecting diversity: Multicultural guidelines for educational publishing professionals*. New York: Author.

Martens, P. (1998). Using retrospective miscue analysis to inquire: Learning from Michael. In S. Barrentine (Ed.), *Reading assessment: Principles and practices for elementary teachers* (pp. 152–159). Newark, DE: International Reading Association.

Messick, S. (1993). Validity. In R. Linn (Ed.), *Educational measurement,* (3rd ed., pp. 13–103). Washington: American Council on Education.

Morrow, L. M. (1990). Assessing children's understanding of story through their construction and reconstruction of narrative. In L. M. Morrow & J. K. Smith (Eds.), *Assessment for instruction in early literacy* (pp. 110–134). Englewood Cliffs, NJ: Prentice Hall.

Pikulski, J. (1994). [Commentary on the chapter Assessment and evaluation of literacy learning]. In S. Valencia, E. Hiebert, & P. Afflerbach (Eds.), *Authentic reading assessment: Practices and possibilities* (pp. 63–70). Newark, Delaware: International Reading Association.

Shavelson, R., Baxter, G., & Gao, X. (1993). Sampling variability of performance assessments. *Journal of Educational Measurement, 30*(3), 215–232.

Shepard, L. (1993). Evaluating test validity. In L. Darling-Hammond (Ed.), *Review of Research in Education, 19* (pp. 405–450). Washington, DC: American Educational Research Association.

Stiggins, R. (2002). Assessment crisis: The absence of assessment FOR learning. *Phi Delta Kappan, 83*(10), 758–765.

Sulzby, E. (1990a). Children's emergent reading of favorite story books: A developmental study. *Reading Research Quarterly, 20*(4), 458–481.

Sulzby, E. (1990b). Assessment of emergent writing and children's language while writing. In L. M. Morrow & J. K. Smith (Eds.), *Assessment for instruction early literacy* (pp. 83–109). Englewood Cliffs, NJ: Prentice Hall.

Thomas, S., & Oldfather, P. (1997). Intrinsic motivation, literacy, and assessment practices: "That's my grade. That's me." *Educational Psychology, 32*(2), 107–123.

Wiggins, G. (1993). Assessment: Authenticity, context, and validity. *Phi Delta Kappan, 75*(3), 200–208, 210–214.

Winograd, P., Paris, S., & Bridge, C. (1991). Improving the assessment of literacy. *The Reading Teacher, 45*(2), 108–116.

Zessoules, R., & Gardner, H. (1991). Authentic assessment: Beyond the buzzword and into the classroom. In V. Perrone (Ed.), *Expanding student assessment* (pp. 47–71). Alexandria, VA: Association for Supervision and Curriculum Development.

3

Observations

Classroom observation is a key method of inquiry about children; specifically, the processes they participate in and the social situations in which teaching and learning occur.

—Genishi, 1985, p. 247

Structured assessment tasks, such as story retelling and writing paragraphs, provide important information about students' progress in literacy. However, they are "snapshots" at particular points in time. These assessments do not reveal students' difficulties during learning, their strategies, their "breakthroughs" in understanding, or their interactions with a peer. For these goals, observing the fluid, dynamic, and often unstructured stream of student verbalizations and interactions is essential.

Referred to as "kidwatching" by Goodman (1978, 1985), observation includes targeting such activities as children's approaches to new learning tasks, and children's conversations as they discuss their favorite book. For example, a teacher may learn that Juanita looks through available picture books and other sources for topics prior to writing a story. She also systematically rules out different possibilities (e.g., "I like elephants better than snakes"). Lois, in contrast, immediately starts writing on a topic, then, after a few paragraphs, discards it for another. The next day she replaces it with another topic. The teacher records this information and makes a note to probe further into possible reasons for Lois' approach.

In other words, students' ongoing behavior in the classroom is a rich source of information for the teacher. Also important is that, unlike tests, classroom observations impose few restrictions on student performance. Observations may be obtained, for example, during independent reading and writing, peer interactions in literacy activities, and literature circles. Further, observations are unobtrusive (Teale, 1988, p. 175). That is, the teacher first identifies a purpose for the observation, such as the relationships between a child's emergent writing and his emergent reading. Then she documents the child's words and interactions with his work or with a peer in a way that does not disturb the flow of the child's activity. Observational methods discussed in this chapter that are appropriate for documenting aspects of students' literacy activities are anecdotal records, checklists, tape recordings, and teacher logs or journals.

Introduction

Discussed in this section are the role of planned observations in the literacy classroom, general requirements, and the role and limitations of informal observations.

Role in the Literacy Classroom

In the literacy classroom, observations of ongoing behavior can provide several important kinds of information. They are

1. students' involvement in language use for different purposes and in a variety of contexts
2. the reading, writing, and problem-solving strategies in student responses to literacy tasks (Rhodes & Nathenson-Mejia, 1999)
3. student attitudes toward different literacy activities and situations
4. instructional needs in the classroom

First, students' language use for different purposes depends on both linguistic competence and communicative competence (Genishi, 1985). Linguistic competence includes the learner's knowledge about sounds, meanings, and syntax. For example, planned observations conducted in the writing center can provide information about young children's letter–sound knowledge in relationship to their writing. In one kindergarten classroom, Kayla read her sentence "LAEYMLABCDLPK" as "I like rainbows because they have so many colors" (Teale, 1988, p. 180). The sentence appears to indicate little understanding of sound–letter relationships. However, the teacher's observation of Kayla as she wrote the sentence indicated that she systematically used one letter for each syllable, and also repeated the sentence and counted the letters (p. 181).

Communicative competence refers to the child's capability to speak and interact appropriately in different situations. A child may speak quite differently in a testing situation with the resource person, at lunchtime, and in conversation with the teacher (Genishi, 1985, p. 132). Observations of the child's interactions with others can provide information about his or her knowledge of rules for different situations.

Second, observations can indicate the extent to which students are using effective strategies to manage their learning and to solve problems when they arise. These strategies, and the knowledge of when and where to use them, are referred to as *metacognition*. For example, in the case of Lois, mentioned previously, her switching from topic to topic after a few paragraphs may be the result of her lack of knowledge of how to narrow a particular topic.

Third, observations can indicate a student's approach or avoidance actions toward particular literacy tasks (an indicator of the student's preferences or attitudes). For example, during silent reading, the teacher may note a student who is off task by his actions of flipping through the book instead of actually reading (Keefe, 1993, p. 223).

Finally, in addition to students' developing capabilities and their difficulties, observations can inform the teacher about classroom instructional needs. For example, observations may indicate that students are not progressing beyond colloquial expressions such as "funny," "dumb," or "neat" in their discussions of selected readings. This information should signal to the teacher that discussion and guidance are needed to provide students with the tools to evaluate their readings and clearly communicate their critiques.

In other words, classroom observation can identify processes and situations that cannot be addressed by more formal assessments. Included are the ways that children approach (or avoid) different language tasks, the methods they use to address difficulties they experience in reading and writing, leadership roles they may take in interactive situations, and insights they develop about literacy. The social situations that may be addressed, for example, include literature circles, paired reading, independent reading, independent writing, and shared writing activities. By implementing focused observations of ongoing situations in conjunction with performance assessments, teachers can obtain a representative picture of the child's strengths and weaknesses and also identify instructional needs (Teale, 1988).

General Requirements

Recall from Chapter 2 that two important characteristics of effective assessments are validity and reliability. Specifically, assessments should lead to accurate inferences about students' capabilities and they also should be reliable. Establishing the validity of classroom observations requires attention to both the planning and implementation of observations.

Planning.   The first step is to identify a purpose for the observation. To observe without knowing at least fairly well the purpose and focus of the observation is usually to blunder (Dollaghan & Miller, 1986, p. 108). Without a framework, too much information for unclear reasons is likely to be collected. In other words, to be effective, observational methods should be used selectively.

One way to identify focal points for observation is to develop a list entitled "Things I Want to Know" (Keefe, 1993). Cambourne and Turbill (1990) suggest developing "markers" to be observed. They are the overt forms of behavior that provide evidence of the presence of linguistic knowledge, skill, or aptitude (p. 343). Examples include developing a sense of audience when communicating and developing control of the conventions appropriate to language contexts, such as attentiveness to pronunciation or spelling.

Second, identify the settings, situations, and/or activities that can provide information about the identified purpose. For example, information about a student developing a sense of audience when communicating can be obtained from observing peer conferences on the student's draft of a story and the student's review and editing of her work. Third, ensure that the selected contexts and situations provide adequate opportunities for the student to demonstrate her developing capabilities. In a literature circle or other group discussion, for example, the student may not have an adequate opportunity to express her thoughts and conclusions. In other words, to be effective as assessments, observations focus on an identified purpose and appropriate settings and activities. This requirement does not mean that the teacher cannot take note of unexpected events. However, the notation will be in reference to a particular purpose.

Important in addressing the reliability of observations is to collect information on several occasions. For example, Larry may agree with Sophie's peer review comments that the opening of his draft story is not clear. However, unless subsequent observations of Larry indicate that he is making adjustments in his story, inferences based on the student conversation are unreliable. In planning observations to obtain adequate information, the teacher identifies one child as the focus for several occasions, and then systematically focuses on other children in turn.

Implementation. In conducting observations, the task for the teacher is to record student actions in ongoing classroom situations. On occasion, the teacher may be inclined to record observations about student capabilities during activities in which the teacher also is a participant. However, observations to document a student's emerging capabilities must be as accurate as possible. When the teacher is involved in exchanges with students, important information may be missed. To be fair, observations about student abilities should be reserved for situations in which the teacher is not a participant. Also, part of the rationale for nonparticipant observation is that the observer who is removed from the action may be cooler and more objective than an observer involved in the activity (Genishi, 1985, p. 134).

Implementing observations requires that the teacher select the format (anecdotal record, checklist, or tape recorder); document the day, time, and setting; and then conduct the observation. In the case of Lois noted earlier, an anecdotal record is appropriate. The teacher records "Lois writes her topic and a few paragraphs, scratching through her work 15 minutes later, and begins with new topic." (The next day, the teacher records Lois' rejection of her second topic.)

One issue associated with the use of observational methods is classroom management. That is, if the teacher intends to observe one activity for 10 to 15 minutes, the concern is that disruptions may occur among the other students. The key is to establish classroom routines whereby students develop responsibility for working on their own. Required are providing specific guidance to the groups and making clear that they are accountable for having completed the announced tasks or activities when the teacher returns.

A second issue is that classroom observations generate considerable data for review. Arranging for time to review the information is essential, such as the beginning of the planning period. Of importance is that, when combined with analyses of student products and performance tasks, observational methods contribute to a comprehensive view of students' strengths, weaknesses, strategies, and attitudes toward reading and writing.

The Role and Limitations of Informal Observations

As stated, to meet the criteria of validity and reliability, observations of ongoing events in the classroom should be planned, conducted systematically, and recorded. They differ from the teacher's informal observations, which are spontaneous, unstructured, and usually covert. That is, informal observations are not verbalized in oral or written form. A typical example is relying on students' facial expressions, posture, eye contact, and questions to know whether or not to redirect a lesson. Another is recognizing potential behavior problems before they occur (Airasian, 1991). In such situations, the teacher must make an instantaneous decision about a course of action. For example, the teacher may decide to call on Larry, because he is beginning to look out the window, or ask Mike to describe his understanding of "audience" because some children have puzzled looks on their faces.

In situations that require immediate instructional or management decisions, informal observations are an asset to the teacher. However, their widespread use is not recommended because they have serious limitations. For example, in the first few days of school a teacher may consider relying on informal observations to determine the kinds of students who are in his or her classroom. One problem is that students' characteristics, such as intelligence, motivation, self-concept, and anxiety, cannot be directly observed and informal observations are very likely to be inaccurate. Inferences about these characteristics are based on a small sample of behavior, are influenced by the observer's beliefs and attitudes, and are uncorroborated by other types of evidence. That is, the observations are limited to students' actions when the teacher happens to be looking their way. Therefore, they do not meet the criteria of validity and reliability—criteria essential for making decisions about students' capabilities.

A second problem is that brief, informal observation can lead to teacher actions that negatively influence students. For example, Good (1980) lists eleven ways that students perceived as low achievers are treated differently in the classroom. Among them are seating low achievers farther from the teacher, asking them fewer questions, requiring less work of them, and providing less detailed feedback (p. 88).

Third, perceptions based on initial informal observation may create a self-fulfilling prophecy (Good & Brophy, 1997). In the preceding example, students will soon perceive they are not capable of being successful. Further, teacher perceptions of low ability can lead to teacher reactions of sympathy or pity for the student. Such reactions, however, typically convey to the student that he or she cannot succeed (Graham, 1984; Graham & Weiner, 1983; Weiner, Graham, Stern, & Lawson, 1982).

Finally, another problem with early inferences about students based on limited observations is that subsequent disconfirming information may not be noticed (Sadler, 1981). That is, research indicates that people tend not to process information that conflicts with a prior hypothesis. The issue is not that individuals deliberately ignore disconfirming instances. Instead, these instances simply are not perceived (p. 28). In other words, prejudgment interferes with the teacher's ability to make a valid and fair assessment of a student.

Summary

Classroom observation is a key method of inquiry about children. It is important because it can provide information about students' reading, writing, and problem-solving strategies; their involvement in language use for different purposes; their attitudes toward different literacy situations; and their metacognitive strategies. In conjunction with performance assessments, observations can provide a comprehensive picture of students' strengths and weaknesses.

Establishing the validity of classroom observations requires the identification of a purpose for the observation, such as the interaction between a child's emergent writing and reading. Second, the settings, situations, or activities that can provide the needed information are identified. Third, the teacher should ensure that the selected situations provide the student with adequate opportunities to demonstrate emerging capabilities. Important in establishing reliability is to collect information on several occasions.

In conducting observations, the teacher selects the format; documents day, time, and setting; and then conducts the observation. When the teacher is recording the information, she should exclude situations in which she is a participant. The reason is to be as fair as possible when documenting students' emerging capabilities.

Two issues associated with the use of observational methods are classroom management and the amount of data to be reviewed. By establishing classroom routines and clear expectations for small-group work, the teacher can focus on a particular activity. Further, planning for time to review observational information in advance is essential.

A third issue is the role of informal observations, which are spontaneous, unstructured, and usually covert. Appropriate uses are in situations that require immediate instructional or management decisions.

Widespread use of informal observation is not recommended. An example is relying on informal observations during the first days of school to determine the kinds of students in the classroom. Four problems are associated with this use. First, student characteristics, such as intelligence and motivation, cannot be directly observed and inferences are likely to be inaccurate. Second, inferences can lead to teacher actions that negatively influence students. Third, a teacher's negative perceptions based on initial informal observations often contribute to similar student perceptions. Fourth, subsequent disconfirming information is unlikely to be perceived by the teacher.

Anecdotal Records

One mechanism for addressing the weaknesses of informal observations is the use of anecdotal records. They are a systemic method of collecting information about students' language processes, aspects of metacognition, and interactions. They also assist in identifying instructional needs.

Definition and Criteria

Anecdotal records consist of brief, written descriptions of concrete actions or events observed by the teacher (or other observer). That is, they are factual, not inferential, and several examples are obtained before conclusions are reached about the student.

Anecdotal records also are open-ended; the teacher determines the general types of information to record, depending on the student who is observed, the context, previous assessment data, and instructional goals (Rhodes & Nathenson-Mejia, 1999, p. 83). An anecdotal record, for example, may document a student's engagement in reading and writing, interactions with others about reading and writing, the planning and problem-solving strategies of students, and their insightful comments and misconceptions. In these roles, anecdotal records are particularly useful in capturing a potential problem or a change of direction by a student. For example, one fifth-grade teacher observed that Jack and Bart, who had previously been unengaged in writing, had begun to work together on writing stories. She notes on the card for Jack, "Nuclear War, using story to collaborate, tests ideas" (Gomez, Graue, & Black, 1991, p. 620).

In another classroom, the teacher observed that, in at least two reading pairs, one child typically immediately supplied the word when the weaker reader had a problem. These observations led to interviewing the second-grade class about their strategies in word identification. After learning that most of the children relied on simply telling the other child the word, the teacher discussed other strategies with the class (Rhodes & Nathenson-Mejia, 1999).

As indicated by these examples, an important role for anecdotal records is to inform instruction. Others are to help parents and others see the child in the same way as the teacher, and to generate new questions for the teacher (Rhodes & Nathenson-Mejia, 1999). This topic is discussed in more depth in the section on the hypothesis-test method in this chapter.

Important criteria for anecdotal records from Thorndike and Hagen (1977), reported in Rhodes and Nathenson-Mejia (1999), are as follows. Each record should

1. describe a specific event
2. report factual information rather than evaluations or interpretations
3. relate the material to other facts known about the child

An example of a specific event that may be captured by anecdotal records is noting the first time a child sounded out words as she wrote "PADENDSNO" (I played in the snow) (Rhodes & Nathenson-Mejia, 1999, p. 84). Another is recording a child's attending to phonemes (SID for side), after formerly writing only consonants (SD). This incident may be related to a shift to a firmer concept of words by the child (Teale, Hiebert, & Chittenden, 1987, p. 776), or it may be an isolated action. It is a signal to the teacher to be attentive to further similar actions.

Also, notes should be concrete and factual and not interpretations or evaluations. For example, a teacher should record that a student leaves his desk frequently (not that he is nervous, uninterested, or unmotivated). Interpretations of a student's actions are important, but they should be made after several observations and/or in conjunction with other information. Genishi (1985) suggests that any interpretations, plans, or guesses from several observations should be separated from the observations with parentheses (p. 136). In addition, related information about the child's capabilities may be noted briefly in parentheses.

Of particular importance is that the statements in an anecdotal record should not be judgments of behavior as good or bad. Examples of this error are "Jimmy showed a bad attitude when told to stop talking," and "Marie looks out the window a lot when she's not busy, she's such a daydreamer." First, such observations do not inform instruction or indicate the students' strengths and weaknesses; instead, they are character statements.

Second, such broad judgments may well be inaccurate. For example, perhaps Marie does not have enough to do and she looks out the window, or she may be thinking about a story she has read or one she has written.

Guidelines for Implementation

Because anecdotal records are time consuming to record and analyze, they should be reserved for processes that are not easily documented through other mechanisms (such as checklists). For example, teachers can listen for and record evidence of language growth during times when individual children are sharing the details of books they have read or pieces they have written. Other examples include student actions during independent reading and writing activities and paired reading and writing.

Table 3.1 illustrates the steps to be followed in using anecdotal records. Steps 1 through 3 are important to avoid acquiring unrelated notes that are not informative. In one fifth-grade class, for example, the teacher had recently implemented a writing period. Her observations first focused on students' approaches to writing stories (purpose of the observation—step 1). Observations of Simon over several days indicated that he used the option of working in the adjacent library to go in and out of the classroom seven to ten times an hour. Although he carried paper and pencil, he only occasionally stopped in a location long enough to write more than a few words. He alternated between going in and out of the library, strolling among his classmates, and pausing for a minute or two at a desk or table to jot down a few words. These observations suggested that Simon's actions were an effort to avoid dealing with his poor writing skills (Gomez, Graue, & Block, 1991, p. 604). This information suggests a situation that requires the hypothesis-test method for addressing problems (discussed in the following section).

TABLE 3.1 *Guidelines for the Implementation of Anecdotal Records*

Steps	Examples
1. Identify a purpose for the observation in advance	1. Student engagement in reading, oral language, control, approach to writing
2. Select the activity or situation, focusing on one area at a time	2. Silent reading, paired reading, peer editing
3. Develop observational notes that can inform instruction and/or assess progress	3. An example is the observation that Marie asks for help when she does not know a word, does not try other strategies
4. Develop a systematic method to keep track of observations	4. Observation notebook, sticky notes transferred to a notebook
5. Obtain adequate samples of a student's actions prior to making an interpretation	5. As already noted, the fifth grade teacher observed Simon in independent writing for 4 to 5 successive days
6. Plan time for analysis	6. Beginning of each planning period

The use of a focused approach to developing anecdotal records does not rule out taking note of unexpected events. An example is a student's sudden insight that consonant letter strings should include vowel sounds.

Because teachers often must observe "on the run" (Genishi, 1985, p. 134), a systematic mechanism of keeping track of observations is essential (step 4). Moreover, it helps the teacher to remember more details. There is no single correct method; the teacher should select an approach that he or she feels comfortable with and is efficient (Keefe, 1993). Some teachers use an observation notebook with three to five blank pages per child (p. 219). One teacher uses a 25-picture photo album filled with cards, one for each child. Others divide the pages in a three-ring binder with index tables for quick flipping and recording (Hemme & Goyins, 1992).

Whatever the method, the recording of observations should be unobtrusive. One teacher noted that children were more focused when she carried her clipboard and began writing (Rhodes & Nathenson-Mejia, 1999, p. 89). An alternative is to use sticky notes that are later transferred to a notebook. Although unobtrusive, this format can present a problem because notes may be lost before they are transferred.

The Hypothesis-Test (HT) Process

Most children, with some hesitations and difficulties, make adequate progress in developing literacy. However, a few children may be experiencing more serious difficulties. The hypothesis-test (HT) process is a means of recording and analyzing observations about students whom the teacher is worried about as readers or learners (Stephens & Story, 2000, p. 8). A major purpose of this method is to better understand students who have problems and to avoid moving quickly to "fix-it" strategies that may be inappropriate and/ or miss subtle aspects of the problem.

The HT process is unique in that interpretations of the observations lead to hypotheses to be tested instead of conclusions about the child's problem. The four recursive components of the HT process are observations, interpretations, hypotheses, and curricular decisions. They are illustrated in the partial record about Karen, a second-grader, in Figure 3.1. Like anecdotal records, observations (step 1) are detailed, concrete, and factual. In this way, each observation serves as the basis for interpretations (step 2). Stephens and Story (2000) suggest brainstorming at least five likely interpretations for each observation to avoid premature conclusions.

Next, the teacher reviews the interpretations and identifies possible patterns, which are recorded as hypotheses to explore. In the case of Karen, interpretations from the shared reading lead to the hypotheses of lack of experience with print, lack of personal confidence in reading, and lack of understanding about ways to self-monitor reading. Of importance is that hypotheses are possible reasons for the particular behaviors that are to be explored. That is, hypotheses are not conclusions (such as "works best in one-on-one situations") (Tsuchiyama, 2000, p. 48). The process does this by helping teachers to slow down the thinking process. This process is difficult because it runs counter to the tendency to "fix" children as soon as possible. It is, instead, a way to study a child who is struggling, one for whom previous well-intended quick fixes were unsuccessful (Stephens & Story, 2000, p. 14).

FIGURE 3.1 *Example of the HT Process Described by Stephens & Story (2000)*

Name   Karen

Teacher

Observations	Interpretations (by Observation Number)	Hypotheses	Curricular Decisions
1. During shared reading with me, Karen began at the beginning of the story, "Tom and Me Go Fishing." She did not go beyond the first two pages, saying she was tired. She had difficulty with syntax and pronunciation. During pauses in her reading, she looked intently at the pictures in the story.	1a. Karen seems to understand basic concepts about text; she began on the first page.	1. Karen may have had little experience with print text (given her sustained attention to the pictures and her problems with syntax).	1. Talk to Karen's mother to learn about Karen's background in reading.
	1b. Saying she is tired may be a way for Karen to escape a task that is unpleasant and/or unfulfilling.	2. Karen lacks confidence in her reading.	2. Confer with Karen on the ways she perceives reading.
	1c. Karen may have had little experience with books.	3. Karen may not understand ways to self-monitor her reading.	3. Observe Karen in other situations that involve reading, including examples of easier texts.
	1d. The text may be too difficult for her reading level, she seems to get the meaning from the pictures.		
	1e. Karen may not understand basic sound/symbol correspondences.		
	1f. Karen may not be interested in a story about the friendship of two boys.		

39

Other Implementation Issues

Other important issues, when anecdotal records are used to document learner capabilities, are advantages, limitations, and validity and reliability. The advantages of anecdotal records are that they can (1) capture behaviors that may otherwise go unnoticed, (2) document actions as they occur in ongoing situations, and (3) contribute to a rich, contextualized description of students' strengths and weaknesses.

One limitation of anecdotal records is the time required to write them and to analyze the data. A related limitation is that isolated and infrequent observations, completed in the absence of a systematic plan for collecting information, will likely yield a distorted or uninformative view of a student's progress. That is, the inferences from the observations are unreliable.

Anecdotal records, when used appropriately, can serve as valid and dependable indicators of student progress. However, validity is affected by contextual circumstances that may limit or influence a particular student's behavior. For example, some educators have suggested developing anecdotal notes on the behaviors of individual children in group classroom activities, such as playing grocery store and exchanging views in literature circles. However, individual children's reactions to the print labels used in the grocery store activity and their contributions to a literature discussion depend, in part, on opportunity and on the actions of others. Further, a shy student may rarely contribute to a literature circle, but interact one-on-one in a peer-editing situation. Thus, decisions about a child's accomplishments may be faulty in such cases. The remedy is to record concrete observations over many occasions and in a variety of instructional settings.

Summary

Anecdotal records, which are brief, concrete, written descriptions of behavior, are a mechanism for addressing the weaknesses of informal observations. Uses include documenting students' emerging capabilities, including aspects of metacognition, informing instruction about student weaknesses to be addressed, helping parents and others see the student in the same way as the teacher, and generating new questions for the teacher.

Criteria for anecdotal records are that they should describe a specific event, report factual information, and relate the material to other facts known about the child. Statements should not be judgments of behavior as good or bad because such inferences are character statements that do not inform instruction.

Because anecdotal records are time consuming, they should be reserved for processes that are not easily documented by other methods. In addition to focusing on one area at a time, notes should inform instruction or assess progress. Also, adequate samples should be obtained, and a systematic method for keeping track of the observations should be used. Examples include photo albums and three-ring binders.

The hypothesis-test (HT) process is a means of recording and analyzing observations of students who are having problems. The four recursive components are observations, interpretations, hypotheses, and curricular decisions. The purpose is to generate several interpretations and hypotheses to explore for each observation. Curricular decisions are the plans for testing the hypotheses. A purpose of the HT approach is to slow down the teacher's thinking processes and avoid premature "fix-it" strategies.

Advantages of anecdotal records include capturing behaviors that may go unnoticed and documenting actions in ongoing situations. Disadvantages include the time requirements and the possibility of obtaining uninformative observations. Of importance also is that infrequent observations and contextual circumstances may jeopardize validity and reliability.

Other Observational Methods

Discussed in this section are checklists, tape recordings, and teacher logs or journals.

Checklists

Anecdotal records are open-ended observations. That is, the teacher, within a general focus, documents relevant student verbalizations and actions. In contrast, a checklist is a predetermined set of key behaviors that typically represent an activity of interest or a phase of literacy development. For example, a checklist may state behaviors related to independent reading (such as attending to the task), or it may document observed progress in literacy over time. Like anecdotal records, checklists record behaviors or characteristics that are concrete and observable; the teacher places a check beside each observed behavior. (Chapter 6 provides a detailed discussion of checklists.) When applied to ongoing events in the classroom, checklists should be used when (1) information is identified that is to be gathered on every child in the classroom, and (2) important behaviors associated with particular activities can be identified in advance.

One application of a checklist is to assess young children's developing awareness of letters, sounds, and their relationships, referred to as emergent writing (Sulzby, 1990). Researchers have identified particular forms of emergent writing, as illustrated in the checklist in Table 3.2. However, the transitions in emergent writing do not occur through invariant, hierarchically ordered stages. For example, a child who has begun to use invented spelling may, for a time, continue to scribble (Sulzby, 1990). Teale (1988) suggests observing children in the writing center over several months. Combining observational data with writing samplers in the children's writing folders can provide a longitudinal picture of children's emerging capabilities (p. 181).

Checklists also may be used to document student responsibilities in interactive situations with others, such as peer review. First, the teacher, through modeling and explanation, instructs students on the responsibilities of the roles of both the writer and the reviewer (Spandel, 2001). For example, a responsibility of the writer is to read aloud the particular passage he or she has selected for review with intonation and expression for the reviewer. Responsibilities of the reviewer include describing the scene or context this reading creates and, if appropriate, the feelings created by the passage (Spandel, 2001). Both the writer and reviewer should use the language of writing, such as "consider using synonyms" and "organize the paragraph." As illustrated in Table 3.3, these responsibilities may be organized into a checklist that addresses both roles. In this way, the teacher obtains systematic information about students.

An advantage of a checklist, related to the fact that it specifies particular dimensions for observation, is that it can assist the teacher to focus on key characteristics of literacy

TABLE 3.2   *Checklist of Writing Development*[1]

Name: _____

Time period: From _____ to _____

| *Dates* | _____ | _____ | _____ | _____ | _____ | _____ |

Writing Forms

Drawing

Scribble

Letter-like words

Random letters

Patterned letters

Letter-named elements

Copies environmental print

Invented spelling:

   Syll./early phon.

   Full letter-name

   Transitional

Conventional spelling

[1]Adapted from Teale (1988)

across different situations. A limitation is that, unless carefully constructed, the checklist may record trivial events.

Tape Recordings

Tape recordings are well suited to small-group discussions and activities in which the teacher is a participant and unable to take notes. The two purposes for which tape recordings of small-group activities are appropriate are (1) identifying student interest in a particular literature selection during literature circles, and (2) student difficulties or issues that instruction should address.

Tape recordings also may be used to supplement anecdotal notes or checklists of peer review sessions to provide the speech of the students. Because cassette recordings capture actual speech, they can contribute to a more comprehensive assessment of the ways that children are using language for different functions (Genishi, 1985, p. 138). Among them are instrumental (to get what we want), interactional (to establish and define social relationships), personal (to express individuality), regulatory (to control the behavior of others), imaginative (to express fantasy), heuristic (to explore and investigate), and informative functions (Pinnell, 1985). For example, young children's verbalizations in different activities include "Why don't you paint your ashtray?" (regulatory), "You can be

TABLE 3.3 *Checklist of Writer and Reader Responsibilities in Peer Review*

Students	As a Writer		As a Reviewer			As a Writer and as a Reviewer
	Initiates contact with peer reviewer	Reads the passage with expression for the reviewer	Describes the scene or context that the passage creates	States the feelings created by the passage	Raises questions based on the passage	Uses language of a writer
Steven B.						
Astrid C.						
John C.						
Denzel F.						
Janette J.						

my sister, only I'm older" (imaginative), and "You make a 1 and you make a 0" [to make a 10] (informative). If observations over a period of time indicate that some language functions appear rarely, then the teacher can organize activities in which they are important. Situations that require sharing materials, for example, can facilitate interactional language and real problems for children to solve can facilitate heuristic language (Pinnell, 1985).

In small-group activities, tape recordings can capture the direction of the discussion as well as the perspectives of students. For example, one reading teacher recorded fourth-graders' discussion of the book *Ultra-violet Catastrophe or The Unexpected Walk with Great Uncle Magnus Pringle* by Mahy (1975). She found that children's perceptions of the story seemed to go beyond their limited vocabulary (e.g., "dumb," "funny," "neat"), but were not expressed appropriately. One boy commented that the book was "funny and dumb at the same time," and one girl noted "The old Pringle guy was havin' fun. Old guys don't have much fun. That is why it's a neat book" (Hickman, 1985, p. 217). Of importance is that the activity, unstructured by an adult, suggests that follow-up discussions with the teacher and the other children may help them develop more formal ways to express their evaluations of readings.

Prior to taping selected activities, the teacher should conduct a trial recording. This serves to check the equipment and determine if the speech is intelligible (Genishi, 1985). If the tape recorder is a novelty for the children, the teacher should set it up a few times prior to collecting the data so they become accustomed to its presence.

A disadvantage of using a tape recorder is the time required to review the data. Repeating the tape is essential to note the information. A major advantage, however, is that it permits the identification of children's language patterns and their use of language for different purposes. Another advantage is that preserved tapes facilitate comparison of children's speech at the beginning of the semester or year with their verbalizations at the end of the year. Such comparisons are useful in parent conferences.

Teacher Logs or Journals

Anecdotal records and checklists provide information about the emerging capabilities of individual students. That is, the unit of analysis is the student. However, teachers also need information about group and class situations that have implications for instruction. Examples are (1) the effectiveness of different planned activities, (2) the sequences of events and shifts of focus in a group's discussion (Hickman, 1985, p. 216), (3) a group's attitude toward a particular genre or activity, and (4) students' difficulties that should be addressed through instruction. For example, students may be skilled at making predictions from the introductory paragraphs of a story, but may have difficulty in summarizing information.

Teacher logs or journals are useful for these purposes. The teacher may record student actions and reflections on a particular activity, or the entries may relate to various bits of information such as anecdotal records. In the early childhood classroom, for example, the teacher may set up a grocery store activity accompanied by print props such as signs and labels. Journal notes are useful for documenting the extent to which children attend to the print information.

Another group activity for which journal notes are useful is the literature circle or literature discussion. In this activity, children who have read the same book discuss and react to it. The purpose is to permit students to construct their meanings of the text. Each discussion typically lasts from 10 to 20 minutes, depending on the age of the students. Information that may be recorded in the log or journal includes student involvement in the story in the form of identifying important parts of the story, favorite parts or characters, the extent to which students relate the story to their own experiences or compare it to other stories, and their reaction to the genre.

The major advantage of such a record is that it helps the teacher reflect on the various events in the classroom. A limitation is that it is time consuming.

Summary

Unlike anecdotal records, which are open-ended, checklists are sets of behaviors or capabilities identified as important for language growth. They should be used for important information that is to be collected on every child in the classroom.

Tape recordings are useful in situations in which the teacher is a participant and cannot take notes, and for recording small-group discussions. Because cassette recordings document actual speech, they can contribute to a more comprehensive assessment of the ways children use language for different functions, and capture the direction of the discussion as well as the perspectives of the students. Important in using this method is to first conduct a trial recording and use it a few times prior to collecting data.

Notes recorded in teacher logs or journals, in contrast, provide information about the effectiveness of different planned activities and the sequence of events and shifts of focus in a group discussion. Other purposes are to identify students' difficulties that should be addressed through instruction, and to summarize teacher reflections.

Discussion Questions_____

1. What are the reasons for identifying a purpose for a classroom observation?

2. Why should anecdotal records be reserved for events and situations that cannot be documented in other ways?

3. A teacher notices that Julian is withdrawn the first few days of school. He does not make eye contact with her, and he does not engage in verbal conversation with the other children. She concludes that he will have difficulties in learning. What are the problems with this situation?

4. A teacher wants to record students' use of the language of writing (e.g., plot, word choice) when they are discussing the elements of a story in a literature circle. Which would be most appropriate—anecdotal notes, checklists, or tape recording? Why?

References_____

Airasian, P. W. (1991). Perspectives on measurement instruction. *Educational Measurement: Issues and Practice, 10*(1), 13–16.

Cambourne, B., & Turbill, J. (1990). Assessment of emergent writing and children's language while writing. In L. M. Morrow & J. K. Smith (Eds.), *Assessment for instruction in early literacy* (pp. 83–109). Englewood Cliffs, NJ: Prentice Hall.

Davila, L. (1998). Using anecdotal records in writing conferences. In T. Thomason. *Writer to writer: How to conference young authors* (pp. 67–70). Norwood, MA: Christopher-Gordon.

Dollaghan, C., & Miller, J. (1986). Observational methods in the study of communicative competence. In F. L. Schiefelbusch (Ed.), *Language competence: Assessment and intervention* (pp. 99–129). San Diego, CA: College-Hill Press.

Genishi, C. (1985). Observing communicative performance in young children. In A. Jaggar & M. T. Smith-Burke (Eds.), *Observing the language learner* (pp. 131–142). Newark, DE & Urbana, IL: International Reading Association and National Council of Teachers of English.

Gomez, M. L., Graue, M. E., & Block, M. N. (1991). Reassessing portfolio assessment: Rhetoric and reality. *Language Arts, 68*(8), 620–628.

Good, T. (1980). Classroom expectations: Teacher-pupil interactions. In J. H. McMillan (Ed.), *The social psychology of school learning* (pp. 70–122). New York: Academic.

Good, T., & Brophy, J. (1997). *Looking in classrooms*. New York: Longman.

Goodman, Y. (1978). Kidwatching: An alternative to testing. *National Elementary Principal, 57*(4), 41–45.

Goodman, Y. (1985). Kidwatching: Observing children in the classroom. In A. Jaggar & M. Trika Smith-Burke (Eds.), *Observing the language learner* (pp. 9–18). Newark, DE: International Reading Association.

Graham, S. (1984). Communicating sympathy and anger to black and white children: The cognitive attributional consequences of affective cues. *Journal of Personality and Social Psychology, 47*(1), 40–54.

Graham, S., & Weiner, B. (1983). Some educational implications of sympathy and anger from an attributional perspective. In R. Snow and M. Farr (Eds.), *Aptitude learning and instruction: Vol. 3. Conative and affective policy analysis* (pp. 199–221). Hillsdale, NJ: Erlbaum.

Hemme, E., & Goyins, T. (1992). Portfolio, please! *Instructor, 101*(8), 49.

Hickman, J. (1985). Looking at responses to literature. In A. Jagger & M. T. Smith-Burke (Eds.), *Observing the language learner* (pp. 212–219). Newark, DE & Urbana, IL: International Reading Association and National Council of Teachers of English.

Keefe, C. H. (1993). Response assessment for special learners. *Reading and Writing Quarterly: Overcoming learning difficulties, 9*, 215–226.

Mahy, M. (1975). *Ultra-violet catastrophe or the unexpected walk with great uncle Magnus Pringle*. Illustrated by Brian Freud. New York: Pergamon.

Pinnell, G. S. (1985). Ways to look at the functions of children's language. In A. Jaggar & M. T. Smith-Burke (Eds.), *Observing the language learner* (pp. 57–72). Newark, DE & Urbana, IL: International Reading Association and National Council of Teachers of English.

Rhodes, L. K., & Nathenson-Mejia, S. (1999). Anecdotal records: A powerful tool for ongoing literacy assessment. In S. J. Barrentine (Ed.), *Reading Assessment* (pp. 83–90). Newark, DE: International Reading Association.

Sadler, R. (1981). Intuitive data processing as a potential source of bias in naturalistic evaluations. *Educational Evaluation and Policy Analysis, 3*(4), 25–31.

Schnickedanz, J. A. (1986). *More than the ABC's: The early stages of reading and writing*. Washington, DC: National Association for the Education of Young Children.

Spandel, V. (2001). *Creating writers* (3rd ed.). New York: Addison Wesley Longman.

Stephens, D., & Story, J. (Eds.). (2000). *Assessment of inquiry: Learning the hypothesis-test process*. Urbana, IL: National Council of Teachers of English.

Sulzby, E. (1990). Assessment of emergent writing and children's language while writing. In L. M. Morrow & J. K. Smith (Eds.), *Assessment for instruction in early literacy* (pp. 83–109). Englewood Cliffs, NJ: Prentice Hall.

Sulzby, E., & Teale, W. H. (1985). Writing development in early childhood. *Educational Horizons, 64*, 8–12.

Teale, W. H. (1988). Developmentally appropriate assessment of reading and writing in the early childhood classroom. *Elementary School Journal*, *89*(2), 173–183.

Teale, W. H., Hiebert, E. H., & Chittenden, E. A. (1987). Assessing young children's literacy development. *Reading Teacher, 40*, 772–777.

Tsuchiyama, E. (2000). Devin. In D. Stephens & J. Story (Eds.), *Assessment of inquiry: Learning the hypothesis-test process* (pp. 46–57). Urbana, IL: National Council of Teachers of English.

Weiner, B., Graham, S., Stern, P., & Lawton, M. (1982). Using affective cues to infer causal thoughts. *Developmental Psychology, 18*, 278–286.

Wilkinson, L. C., & Silliman, E. R. (1994). Assessing students' progress in language and literacy: A classroom approach. In L. M. Morrow & J. K. Smith (Eds.), *Integrated language arts: Controversy to consensus* (pp. 241–260). Boston: Allyn & Bacon.

4

Teacher Questioning

> We sometimes forget that a good conference is a conversation about writing in progress—not an interrogation. . . . We are poised, ready to engineer a breakthrough in revision with the right question. . . . But faith in the power of the right question is misplaced. There are no magic questions.
>
> —Sowers, 1988, p. 130

Although there are no "magic" questions, the ebb and flow of many group and individual activities is at least partially structured by the nature and form of the teacher's questions. Examples include "What can you tell me about tropical rain forests?," "What do you think will happen next in the story?," and "What did you learn from the story about Stephanie's first day at school?"

The first question asks the students to recall information they know about the topic of an upcoming thematic unit. The students' answers inform the teacher of any gaps in their knowledge that may be essential to understanding the reading, as well as any misconceptions. The second question, posed after the teacher reads the title of a story and a few lines to the class, provides the children with practice in making predictions. It also helps them develop a framework as they read. The third question asks the children to think about the story they have read and assesses their learning.

As indicated by these examples, teacher questioning is an informal assessment tool that can fulfill any of several roles in the literacy classroom. Teacher questions also are a key component of the classroom communication between the teacher and the students. As suggested in the above statement by Sowers (1988), teacher questions during an individual writing conference are part of a conversation with the student. The goal is to help the student develop new insights about his writing.

Particularly important is that the nature of the teacher's questions and the ways they are used send messages to students about the classroom. That is, students learn whether thinking and problem solving or rote learning are important (Lucking, 1985). For example, questions about historical figures in a reading selection may ask what they wanted badly, what opposing tensions they faced because of what they wanted, and what they learned from the events they were involved in (Graves, 1999, p. 39). Such questions provide students with opportunities to think deeply about literature selections or other texts they have read.

Questions also assist or hinder students in taking responsibility for their own learning, and they indicate whether risk taking is valued in the classroom. The use of questions for which the teacher has predetermined right answers discourages these important aspects of learning.

In the classroom, teacher questioning occurs primarily in two contexts. One is during the flow of class or small-group instruction (instruction-embedded questions). The other setting is one-on-one interactions with students, specifically, conferences and interviews. Important in both types of activities is that the questions should not form an interrogation, but should emerge from the particular context and instructional activity.

Instruction-Embedded Questions

Questioning is a cued-recall measure of the child's knowledge or understanding (Leslie, 1993, p. 21). In the context of ongoing classroom activities, teachers use questions for various purposes. In the introduction of a new topic or reading selection, questions assist in getting students' attention and focusing their thinking. As an informal assessment tool, instruction-embedded questions provide the teacher with two general types of information about students' capabilities. One is students' prior knowledge about a new topic. The other, after completion of a unit or a reading selection, is their understanding of key ideas and the meanings they have developed. Because reading processes are not directly observable, they must be inferred from student actions (Davey, 1989; Farr & Carey, 1986), particularly their responses to questions. This section discusses the role of prior knowledge in learning, types of questioning strategies for addressing students' background knowledge, and questions to determine student understanding and facilitate the development of meaning.

Developing a classroom environment that supports students' responses and reactions to literature, however, depends on more than the ways that the teacher asks questions. It also involves the ways that the teacher reacts to student responses (Cooper, 2000; Graves, 1999). Teacher reactions and appropriate follow-up actions also are discussed in this section.

The Role of Prior Knowledge

A major influence in learning is the extent and variety of prior knowledge the student brings to the learning situation. Prior knowledge serves as the framework for identifying new ideas and details, influences the inferences learners make about new information, and minimizes the potential confusion among similar types of information. For example, in reading about John Dean in *All the President's Men,* one does not confuse him with King John, Pope John, or a former classmate John (Adams, 1989).

Research indicates that the learner's background knowledge is a key factor in the process of making meaning through interacting with text (whether listening, speaking, reading, or writing) (e.g., Alexander, 2000, 1996; Bernhardt, 2000; Holmes, 1983; Tierney & Cunningham, 1984). Specifically, the learner's prior knowledge predicts both the rate of learning and retention scores for factual learning, general topics, and word meanings (Leslie & Caldwell, 1990). In other words, lack of sufficient background knowledge about text structure, topics, and ideas impairs students' comprehension and their writing skills (Heller, 1999).

Assessing students' background knowledge fulfills three functions (see Table 4.1). One is to detect gaps in their knowledge that will influence their understanding of a thematic unit or a reading selection. For example, if a child has never been to a museum, as is the case with many young children, then a story called "Going to the Museum" will be difficult to understand without first discussing the related concepts (Heller, 1999, p. 73). Similarly, prior to the class reading a selection about birds in winter, the teacher should address the concept *blizzard* (Cooper, 2000).

A second function is to detect students' misconceptions that are highly unlikely to be corrected by the reading. Across all ages and ability levels, readers use their knowledge base as a filter to interpret and construct meaning from text passages (Dole et al., 1991). When the material is in conflict with or contradicts the learner's knowledge base, learner knowledge typically prevails (Dochy, Segers, & Buhl, 1999). Discussion can correct minor misconceptions; however, too heavy an emphasis can hamper children's interest in reading (Maria, 1990).

Third is to ensure that the students' cognitive resources are brought to bear on the classroom task. Information that is not in the learner's conscious or working memory is referred to as inert. That is, it is inactive and cannot assist the learner in processing new information. The role of questions is to activate inert knowledge.

TABLE 4.1   *Functions of Assessing Students' Prior Knowledge*

Function	Rationale
To detect gaps in students' knowledge	Omissions or gaps in knowledge relevant to the task increase students' processing difficulties and lead to misconceptions.
To detect students' misconceptions	Students' misconceptions are unlikely to change from reading new information, particularly for poor readers (Holmes & Roser, 1987).
To activate students' relevant knowledge	Students' prior knowledge cannot be applied to an imminent task unless the information is in the learner's conscious memory.

Strategies for Assessing Prior Knowledge

Different areas of prior knowledge are important in instruction. In the early childhood classroom, an area essential to reading is young children's concepts about print. Interactive story-reading/questioning activities are appropriate for assessing this aspect of the child's prior knowledge. Another important area, at all levels of education, is the student's background knowledge and knowledge about topics and concepts in upcoming reading selections. One approach to assessing students' background knowledge is through introductory questions. Another approach integrates assessing prior knowledge with the identification of a purpose for the reading.

Assessing Young Children's Concepts about Print.   An example that develops information about a child's concepts of print is the exercise developed by Marie Clay (1989) that uses specially designed booklets. The texts, *Sand* (Clay, 1972) and *Stones* (Clay, 1979), are approximately twenty pages in length with a picture on one page and text (one to three sentences) on the facing page. Some of the words have reversed letters, for example, "Would it tsop by the gaet?" (Clay, 1979, p. 13), an upside-down picture on one page, and upside-down print on another. The exercise requires 5 to 10 minutes and is useful in the first year of schooling. The purpose of the exercise is to determine where the child's visual and mental attention are directed. If the child focuses on the wrong page, the wrong part of the page, or on a letter instead of a word, for example, the child will have difficulty benefitting from reading (Clay, 1989, p. 269).

In this exercise, teacher questions are interspersed with the activity of the teacher reading the story. The teacher begins by telling the child she is going to read him or her a story, but wants the child to help. She first hands the booklet to the child, holding it vertically by the spine, and asks the child to show her the front of the book (Clay, 1985, p. 29). She then asks the child to show her where to begin reading and which way to go.

The teacher then reads the story, periodically pausing to ask the other predetermined questions in the exercise. Among them are "Show me the bottom of the picture" (on the page with the inverted drawing), "Where do I begin?" (page with inverted print), and other questions about reordered letters in a word, and word concepts. Each of the twenty-four questions is scored one point for a correct answer. However, the importance of the items is that they indicate concepts about print yet to be learned or confusions to be untangled (Clay, 1985, p. 31). The exercise also is a way to record progress in the early months of instruction (Clay, 1979).

Assessing Background Knowledge through Introductory Questions.   Two components of students' knowledge are essential prior to their reading new text material. They are (1) overall prior knowledge, and (2) text-specific or topic-specific knowledge (Cooper, 2000). As indicated in Table 4.2, several questioning strategies are available for assessing students' background knowledge. The unstructured discussion relies on students recounting their experiences with the particular topic. For example, for the topic "snake," children may mention seeing snakes in a zoo, the yard, or in picture books. A few may have actually touched a snake.

One purpose of the unstructured approach is motivational; linking the topic to children's personal experiences is a way of developing interest. Further, such a discussion

TABLE 4.2 *Possible Strategies to Assess Students' Prior Knowledge*[1]

Strategy	Description	Advantages	Disadvantages
Unstructured discussion	Teacher asks students about their experiences with the topic	Sometimes used as a motivational device	Appears to be the least helpful method for assessing knowledge about the topic
Free recall	Teacher asks students to think of everything they can about the topic	Requires only a few minutes and one teacher probe	Yields an incomplete picture of students' information and misinformation
Word association	Teacher states a subtopic related to the main topic and asks students to tell everything they can about the word as it relates to the topic	Relatively easy to prepare and administer	Yields an incomplete picture of students' information and misinformation, although slightly better than free recall
Recognition	Questions (one for each subtopic) with more than one correct response in a written format; teacher reads each phrase and the students circle all the true sentence endings	Excellent for assessing students' knowledge; useful for students who may have difficulty in producing information	Requires preparation time; resembles a test
Structured questions	Questions developed on subtopics related to the topic; teacher asks the questions orally	Elicits the greatest amount of information; efficient; students can learn from each other	Requires preparation time; can resemble an oral test

[1]Summarized from Holmes & Roser (1987)

does not resemble an interrogation. The problem, however, is that basic information important for understanding the topic may not be addressed. If the children are reading a story about relationships or families, for example, then an informal discussion of children's experiences can activate their knowledge relevant to the story. However, if the reading selection is an exposition in a thematic unit, then a more precise method of assessing student's background knowledge is needed.

Free recall and word association yield somewhat more information than the unstructured discussion. They also can be organized as game-like exercises. In free recall, for example, the teacher asks students to think of everything they can about the topic. Word association, however, requires that the teacher read the selection in advance and identify concepts central to understanding the text (Leslie, 1993). Then, in the classroom, the teacher says, "I'm going to say a word or words, and I want you to tell me what you think of when I say them" (p. 13). For example, the teacher may say "paws" for the topic *cat*. Likely responses are "a cat has four," "claws," and "pads" (Holmes & Roser, 1987).

One advantage of free recall and word association is that the teacher easily can build on children's responses to fill in gaps in their relevant knowledge. This factor is particularly important for students whose native language is not English or other students whose background knowledge is limited.

The other two approaches, recognition and structured questions, are more formal assessments that can generate accurate information about students' background knowledge. The problem with the recognition format is that it resembles a test. The teacher writes one question in the form of an open-ended phrase for each subtopic. Each phrase is followed by several possible endings and each question may have more than one correct answer. The children select all the endings they believe are correct. For example, the term "cold-blooded" may be followed with "(a) having cold blood, (b) having a constant body temperature, and (c) changing temperature with one's surroundings, and never being too hot" (Holmes & Roser, 1987, p. 648). Administered in a written format, the teacher reads each phrase aloud, with the students circling each correct sentence ending. The class can then discuss their responses. This follow-up provides an opportunity to address misconceptions and gaps in student knowledge.

In the structured questions approach, the teacher develops questions for each subtopic. For example, for the subtopic "snakes shedding their skin," the questions may include "Does a snake live in the same skin all of its life?" "What happens to it?" and "How often does the skin come off?" (Holmes & Roser, 1987, p. 648). The importance of structured questions is that they can elicit the most information about students' thinking—both correct and incorrect (p. 648). However, unless incorporated into a discussion, the questions can resemble an oral test.

Integrating Questioning with Text Reading.   The questioning strategies summarized in Table 4.2 serve, in part, as an introduction to a reading selection or a thematic unit, but they do not interact with it. In contrast, the two strategies discussed in this section incorporate queries about students' prior knowledge as a component of the subsequent reading or research of the students. Further, both strategies assist learners in establishing a purpose for reading. One strategy is KWL, which represents what I *know* (K), what I *want* to learn (W), and what I *learned* and still need to learn (L). This strategy combines activating students' prior knowledge with helping them focus on a purpose for reading expository text (Cooper, 2000; Ogle, 1986). Each student has a worksheet with three columns headed by the three phrases and the teacher has a larger version on the chalkboard or overhead transparency (see Figure 4.1).

Teachers and students first brainstorm their information about the topic of the text. For example, if the topic is sea turtles, the teacher should ask, "What do you know about sea turtles?" (Ogle, 1986, p. 565). Students write the ideas in column one on their worksheet and the teacher also records the information on the group chart (Cooper, 2000, p. 110). Disagreements or areas of uncertainty are turned into information categories that are listed in column two. An example is "foods sea turtles eat" (p. 110).

The teacher then asks the students to consider the kinds of things they would like to find out during the reading and writes them on the group worksheet. The topic of black widow spiders, for example, may include such questions as "Do they hurt people?" and "How many baby spiders are born?" (Ogle, 1986). After a few minutes, the teacher asks the students to write the questions they are most interested in on their worksheets. After reading, students write their answers to the questions. Class discussion helps determine the questions that were unanswered in the material and any additional questions the students have.

The second strategy organizes two categories of knowledge in a different format. It was developed to assist teachers and students to work together in using reading and

FIGURE 4.1 *Example of Student KWL Sheet*

Topic: _____

K	*W*	*L*
What I know	*What I want to learn*	*What I learned or still need to learn*

Questions I am most interested in:

writing to learn (Harste, Short, & Burke, 1988, p. 366). The teacher and students first identify a topic they wish to study. Next, they make a web with two sections (What We Know and What We Want to Know) on a large sheet of butcher paper. As indicated in Figure 4.2, the teacher writes the topic in the center in a circle. As he queries the students, he writes the items of information they mention in a web around the topic.

Questions of interest to the students for investigation are listed in a separate section. They are used to form a list of likely research questions or problems (p. 367). Students and teachers then make a list of information sources (books and people) on the topic and bring resources to the classroom. Working as individuals or groups, the students explore the

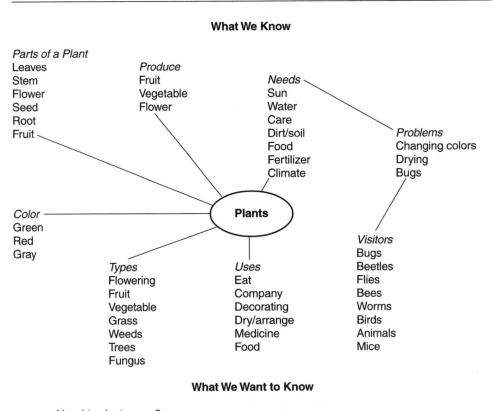

What We Know

Parts of a Plant
Leaves
Stem
Flower
Seed
Root
Fruit

Produce
Fruit
Vegetable
Flower

Needs
Sun
Water
Care
Dirt/soil
Food
Fertilizer
Climate

Problems
Changing colors
Drying
Bugs

Color
Green
Red
Gray

Plants

Visitors
Bugs
Beetles
Flies
Bees
Worms
Birds
Animals
Mice

Types
Flowering
Fruit
Vegetable
Grass
Weeds
Trees
Fungus

Uses
Eat
Company
Decorating
Dry/arrange
Medicine
Food

What We Want to Know

—How big plants grow?
—How many different kinds of plants there are in the world?
—What colors do plants come in?
—How do they make their seeds?
—How do seeds look? How do you know which seed will grow to be a certain plant?
—What is the biggest plant?

FIGURE 4.2 *Theme Cycle of a Plant Web by a Third-Grade Class*

From Harste, Short, & Burke (1988), p. 369

questions that most interest them about the topic. New information and new questions are added to the web as they are developed. At the end of the study, students share their learning with one another in formal or informal presentations.

Summary.   A major influence in learning is the extent and variety of prior knowledge the student brings to the learning situation. Assessing students' background knowledge fulfills three functions. They are to detect gaps in students' knowledge, identify misconceptions that are unlikely to be corrected by reading, and activate relevant student knowledge.

First, in the early childhood classroom, assessing children's concepts about print is important. Interactive story-reading/questioning activities can determine where the child focuses her visual and mental attention as the story is read.

Second, at all grade levels, five questioning strategies for assessing students' knowledge prior to reading new text are available. They are unstructured discussions, free recall, word association, recognition, and structured questions. They vary in effectiveness and in their similarity to real-world discussions.

Another approach is to integrate questioning with text reading. Two strategies are the KWL method and the use of knowledge webs.

Assessing Student Understanding and Facilitating the Development of Meaning

Teachers face a dual responsibility in the classroom in relation to students' reading of expository text and literature selections. One is to assess student understanding of story events and characters in literature selections and the explanatory information in expository text. The second is to assist students to deepen their reading experiences in terms of relating to the characters, whether fiction or nonfiction, and sharing, with the writer, the unfolding of events (Graves, 1999, p. 171). Essential to these goals is to develop a classroom environment in which students' responses and reactions to literature are supported and accepted. In this way, students can develop independence in constructing meaning from text.

Research conducted in the 1980s indicated that the dialogue in classrooms often was unnatural and contrived (Lucking, 1985). In some situations, the majority of questions were the "tell me" type, such as "Tell me which syllable is accented" and "Who can tell me what the noun is in this sentence?" (p. 173). In other classrooms, factual questions predominated even when the teacher's goal was to encourage the children to think (Watson & Young, 1986, p. 126). On occasion, when the question was intended to be open, the form of the question and the teacher's intonation signaled the expected response:

> ***Teacher:***   Some people might say that the theme of the play is exploitation. Have we much evidence for that?
>
> ***Students:***   *(in chorus)* No. (Watson & Young, 1986, p. 127)

In addition, discussions with "yes/no" questions are stilted. Also, students from some cultural backgrounds, such as Native Americans, may not be comfortable in being singled out to respond in this way (Au, Mason, & Scheu, 1995, p. 296).

Instead, as indicated in Table 4.3, when the goal is to assess comprehension, include open-ended questions that promote thoughtful responses. For example, when asking "Where and when does the story take place?," follow-up questions may include "How do you know?" and "If the story took place somewhere else, how would it be different?" (Cooper, 2000, p. 303). Of importance is that these questions elicit basic information about the story, yet they require student thinking. Further, the question on the effects of a change in locale promotes varied responses from the students. Such questions are important to establish an environment in which different perspectives are valued. Other examples of open-ended questions related to story events are "Did the story end the way you expected it to?" and "What clues did the author offer to prepare you to expect this ending?" (Cooper, 2000, p. 303).

Open-ended questions that promote deeper thinking about the selection may be interspersed with comprehension questions. For example, students may be asked about their ideas or feelings generated by the story, and questions they would like to ask the author if she visited the classroom.

For expository text, the teacher may ask, "What did you learn that you didn't know before?" and "What did you learn that surprised you?" Graves (1999) suggests opening up children's thinking about science by developing an understanding of the thinking of scientists as individuals. This understanding can be fostered through reading about individual scientists and their search for understanding events in the universe. Questions that can assist the reader include "What does the scientist want?," "How does he or she go about getting it?," and "What ambiguities does the scientist face and how does he or she deal with them?" (Graves, 1991, p. 93).

Class discussions involve text material that all the students have read. Another classroom activity designed to develop student responses to literature is the literature discussion group or circle. Students, in groups of three to six, meet for 10 to 20 minutes to respond to either a book the class has read or one the group has chosen to read. Literature circles may last from two days to a week or two, depending on the book length and the depth of the discussion (Harste et al., 1988, p. 294). The purpose is for students to explore

TABLE 4.3   *Guidelines for Comprehension Questions*

Class Discussions

1. Avoid questions that can be answered yes/no.
2. Phrase comprehension questions in a way that promotes thinking.
3. Use questions that seek varied responses.
4. Include questions that promote deeper thinking.

Literature Circles

5. Do not control the questioning; the activity is learner directed.
6. Occasionally, use "why" questions so that students support their views.
7. If needed, model appropriate questions.

the meaning of a book with one another, to support and explain their interpretations, and to collaboratively build new understandings of the selections (p. 297).

The goal is for the literature circle to be student directed. The teacher may open the discussion the first day with a broad question such as "What was this story about?" (p. 109). This opener provides the teacher an idea of the most interesting parts of the story for the students. The group members then discuss their reactions and raise questions about aspects that surprise them or that they did not understand. They also make a list of questions to pursue the next few days (p. 295).

A second role for the teacher when meeting with the different groups is to challenge students to support their statements by raising "why" questions. In other words, discussions do not simply accept children's statements. In this way, students are encouraged to probe the relationships among plot, setting, characterizations, and events in literature selections. Finally, a third role for the teacher is to model the types of appropriate questions, if needed. The goal is for the literature circle to be student directed.

In summary, teacher questions should both assess student understanding and assist them to deepen their reading experiences through the meanings they develop. Instead of "tell me" and "yes/no" questions, teachers should use open-ended questions that promote thoughtful responses. Follow-up questions can ask students about their ideas and feelings, such as "What did you learn that surprised you?" In literature circles the teacher may ask a broad opening question, but should confine subsequent involvement to those questions that require the readers to substantiate their statements.

Responding to Students' Answers

Teacher reactions to student answers also send messages to students about the classroom environment. Teachers should avoid right/wrong evaluative reactions to student questions. For example, responding "That's right" to an answer sends the message that the teacher has decided no other answers should be considered. Instead, the follow-up question "How do we know . . ." asks both the responding student and others in the class to seek supporting information from the reading selection. Also, to avoid signaling that a student's answer is wrong, respond with statements such as "That's a possibility; let's hear some other thoughts" (Cooper, 2000, p. 302).

In other words, as indicated in Table 4.4, teachers should avoid the rapid-fire sequence of question/brief answer/evaluative reaction. In such a situation, students quickly learn that their role is insignificant. That is, the apparent goal is to respond with isolated facts that provide the teacher (not the students) an opportunity to elaborate a concept or an idea.

Interspersing follow-up questions that require students to think about the reading with essential comprehension questions sends the message that thoughtful responses are valued. Particularly important is that follow-up questions should not begin with phrases such as "Isn't it true that . . ." and "Don't you think that . . ." (Pearson, 1980, p. 41). These phrases are verbal signals that contribute to student dependence on the teacher to make decisions about meaning.

Another important factor in establishing a meaningful discussion is the extent of wait time for student responses following teacher questions. Research by Rowe (1974,

TABLE 4.4   *Guidelines for Responding to Student Answers*

1. Avoid right/wrong evaluative reactions to content questions. Instead, solicit input from students.
2. Avoid the rapid-fire sequence of teacher question/brief response/evaluation reaction.
3. Allow sufficient wait time for student responses.
4. Encourage student elaboration of responses.

1980, 1986) indicated that, in some classrooms, teachers typically waited 1 second or less for students to initiate a reply. Further, following the student's response, they reacted or posed the next question in less than 1 second (Rowe, 1986, p. 43). This situation reflects the rapid-fire questioning that is not recommended. In such situations, six or seven students provided most of the responses and captured more than half the question-and-answer time. Training teachers on increasing wait time to 5 seconds contributed to lengthier student responses, responses from students who previously had not participated in discussions, and more varied questions from teachers (Gambrell, 1980; Rowe, 1986). Further, disabled readers began to verbalize more in discussions about stories (Gambrell, 1980), and teachers could listen to student answers, enabling them to build on those answers in subsequent questions.

Summary

Teachers use questions in the context of classroom activities in several ways. They are to get students' attention, to determine their prior knowledge about a new topic, to assess their understanding of ideas after completing a unit or a reading, and to facilitate students' development of meaning. Assessing students' prior knowledge is essential because background knowledge serves as a framework for learning, influences the inferences that learners make about new information, and minimizes potential confusion with similar topics. For example, lack of knowledge of basic concepts about print increases a child's difficulty in learning to read. Further, lack of sufficient knowledge of text structure, topics, or ideas impairs both the student's understanding as a reader and her composition as a writer.

Assessing students' background knowledge reveals gaps in essential information, detects misconception about key topics, and can ensure that students' relevant knowledge is activated for the upcoming task. Detecting misconceptions is important because, when new information conflicts with the learner's knowledge base, learner knowledge typically prevails.

Assessing young children's concepts about print is best accomplished in an interactive story-reading/questioning task that determines where the child's visual and mental attention are directed. To assess relevant background knowledge for particular topics, several introductory questioning strategies are available. However, the structured questions approach, in which the teacher poses oral questions on subtopics, yields the most information and is efficient. Two methods that integrate questioning with text reading are KWL and the development of a concept web that includes what the students know and what they want to know.

Following student completion of literature selections or expository text, the teacher's responsibility is to assess student understanding and to help students develop their own meanings. Therefore, comprehension questions should be open-ended and interspersed with follow-up questions that elicit students' ideas or feelings. In literature circles, which are student-directed, the teacher may ask a general question to begin the discussion. The teacher also may ask "why" questions that encourage or prompt students to support their views.

Teacher reactions are also important in implementing effective questioning strategies. When the teacher evaluates student answers as right or wrong, the message is that only the teacher can determine the correct answers. That is, the student's role is only to respond with isolated bits of information. Also important is to avoid rapid-fire questioning and to allow sufficient time for students to respond.

Conferences and Interviews

Class and small-group discussions provide opportunities for students to develop new understandings by building on each other's thoughts and ideas. In contrast, conferences and interviews, although differing from each other in purpose, provide one-on-one interactions between teachers and students. Conferences provide students with opportunities to share their current reading or writing with the teacher and assist the teacher to understand the student as a writer (or reader). Interviews, which are teacher-directed, can inform the teacher about students' strategies in reading and their misinformation about content.

Conferences

A conference is an informal talk or chat between a teacher and a student (Thomason, 1998). The term "conference" typically is used to refer to writing (e.g., Calkins, 1994; Graves, 1999; Spandel, 2001; Thomason, 1998). Two myths about conferences are that the teacher must ask the questions (control events) and use the meeting to "fix" the student's writing (Graves, 1999; Spandel, 2001, p. 365). Instead, conferences are opportunities for teachers to listen to and honor the writer's words (Graves, 1983) and provide personal support to individual students (Spandel, 2001).

Conferences may be brief, on-the-spot exchanges that are spontaneous or they may be scheduled interactions of 5 to 10 minutes. On-the-spot conferences are those times when a teacher stops to chat with a student and listens carefully to the student's statements (Cooper, 2000, p. 477). A brief question such as "What are you reading?" or "What writing piece are you working on?" can yield information about a reader's engagement or lack of it with a selection or a writer's progress or dilemma with a particular passage.

Scheduled conferences should be short (5 to 10 minutes), focused, and student oriented. Equally important, they should be positive, relaxed experiences. For the student who is shy about asking a question in class, the conference can provide a quiet and safe moment to receive help on a specific problem (Spandel, 2001, p. 366).

The teacher's role in the first phase of conferences is to understand the writer (Calkins, 1994, p. 225). Instead of initially looking at the draft, the teacher may begin with questions such as "Can you tell me how you wrote this?," "What problems did you have while writing this?," and "When you read over your text, how do you feel about it?" Follow-up questions then emerge from the teacher's active listening as a reader instead of as a teacher. That is, the focus is on meaning and helping students think through their problems. Examples include "You said this piece needed more description of the spooky old house. Where do you think that description would be most effective?" and "Which would make the most interesting lead?" (Thomason, 1998, p. 34).

The important contribution of the writing conference is that it can make the student writer feel special, and this is its unique contribution to writing instruction (Spandel, 2001, p. 366). Therefore, the teacher's focus is not to improve the student's text. That is, a teacher should not rush in to offer evaluations and solutions (Calkins, 1994; Thomason, 1998). The main reason is that problems with syntax and punctuation often are the result of the child's belief that he has information in his selection that is not there (Graves, 1983, p. 103). When the child develops the information further, language and conventions are more easily adjusted (p. 103).

In addition, the effect of teacher evaluation in the writing conference is to ensure students' dependence on the teacher's judgments, problem approaches, and strategies (p. 194). Instead, the goal should be to interact with children so that they learn to interact with their emerging text (Calkins, 1985, p. 194). To accomplish this goal, the conference must "help writers talk out problems they are having or verbalize their plans for the piece" (Thomason, 1998, p. 32). In this context, teacher questions return authorship or ownership of the piece to the student.

Although writers' conferences focus on empowering the writer, they play an important role in assessment by indicating where the student is in terms of gaining control of his or her writing. Davila (1998) suggests maintaining a weekly class list of students that is headed "Writing Workshop—Conferring Records." Column headings are days of the week, with the far right column labeled "Comments." A checkmark by the student's name under the appropriate day records the conference. Comments may include statements such as "developing a voice" and "strong story beginning."

Second, writing conferences can inform instruction. The teacher does not function as an editor during the conference. Instead, he makes notes about use of conventions and other issues to address later with the class. Davila (1998) suggests reserving several lines at the bottom of the weekly record form to note needed class topics. Examples include "concept of a sentence—using capital letters and punctuation" and notations of the need to address the spellings of high-frequency words.

Content Conferences.   In some writing conferences, referred to as content conferences by Calkins (1985, 1994), the focus is the student's emerging text. One focus for the content conference is to listen to a child's emerging subject and then repeat the story. This active listening, sometimes accompanied by questions to clear up snags that prevent the teacher from hearing the child's emphasis, helps the writer clarify her thinking (Calkins, 1985, p. 195). Of importance is that the questions should not be concocted simply to pull out more information from the writer (p. 195). Instead, the teacher takes in the writer's thoughts and takes his cue from them (Thomason, 1998). A particular benefit of the emphasis on teacher listening is that, for the writer, it reinforces the value of her message. This contributes to both the child's further development of the text and her confidence.

A second focal point for a content conference, in addition to listening to the child's subject, is to help the child focus the topic (Calkins, 1985). A key question, "What are you trying to say?," may be rephrased as "What's the important thing about your topic?," "What do you want to leave the reader with?," or "What's the heart of the piece?" (p. 195).

A third focal point is to assist the writer to add details to a skeleton piece or a brief description. Children typically summarize their content; for example, Eric said "I almost made a home run—made it to third." The teacher may ask, "What exactly happened?," "How did you feel?," or "It's hard for me to picture it when you tell me in one sentence. What was it like for you?" (Calkins, 1994, p. 235). Like the prior questions, the importance of this approach is that it leaves control in the writer's hands. In other words, specific questions intended to pull out more detail are not asked, because the effect of such questions is to pull the writer in different directions (Calkins, 1985, p. 196). Also important is that writers can learn to anticipate the reader's need for information and to anticipate where the reader may be confused (Calkins, 1994, p. 235). In other words, teacher responses that are real questions further this goal.

Process Conferences.   Another type of conference, referred to as a process conference by Calkins (1985, 1994), focuses on children's writing strategies. Of importance is to avoid questions such as "Where will you go next with this writing?" (Spandel, 2001, p. 367). Although such a question is provocative for skilled writers, it is too broad to assist writers who do not know where they are going (p. 367).

Appropriate questions that leave control in the child's hands include "How'd you go about writing this draft?," "What new problems did you run into?," and "How can you put your thinking in words?" (Calkins, 1985, p. 196). Through these questions, children become aware of their intentions and strategies. This awareness is an essential prerequisite to the child's gaining control of his or her own thinking (Donaldson, 1978; Vygotsky, 1934/1987). Also, these questions are guided by the rule of what might help the writer and not what might help the specific piece of writing (Calkins, 1994, p. 228).

Interviews

The primary focus of the writing conference is on understanding and empowering the writer. In contrast, the purpose of the interview is for the teacher to discover new information about the student. Like the conference, the interview consists of open-ended questions. However, one purpose is to develop information about the processes students engage in during their writing and reading. One use is in conjunction with a multifaceted task or on its completion. For example, the teacher may briefly interview students who are working on the final drafts of a research paper. The purpose is to determine (a) the ways that they obtained information from the library and other sources, (b) the preparation of their note cards, and (c) the ways they made decisions about the information to include or omit. Questions should be open-ended, focused, and address concrete steps in the process of developing the research paper.

Another use of interviews is to discover the thinking of readers who are having difficulties. Typically, such interviews occur in the third or fourth grade or later. By this time, children are expected to obtain information from expository text and to use reading as a process for learning (Leslie, 1990, p. 24). This added function requires, first, that children understand the purpose of reading. Young children, for example, sometimes believe that the purpose of reading is to pronounce all the words without mistakes and some believe that good reading involves verbatim recall of the text (Gredler, 2001).

Second, obtaining information from text requires that children develop awareness of and monitor their comprehension. That is, they should check their progress as they read and select appropriate repair strategies when needed. For example, the student should note when he or she has read a sentence without understanding it and read it and the surrounding context again. If this strategy is not successful, then the student may seek assistance from others.

Less-proficient readers, however, may use a "search and destroy" technique (Nicholson, 1984, p. 23). That is, they skip sentences they do not understand, and rely on the words they know and their own experience to create a likely scenario. For example, one less-proficient reader identified learning about cattle to become a stock agent as a reason for migration from South Island to North Island in New Zealand. An interview with the student revealed that he based this view on the word "stockbroker" in the passage, pairing it with his own information about dairy farming (Nicholson, 1984).

Essential to conducting interviews with students who are having difficulty is to schedule them as the student is working through or has just completed a task. In this way, the concrete strategies used by the student may be immediately identified. The interview should begin with a friendly, open question, such as "You look deep in thought—what are you thinking?" (Nicholson, 1984, p. 28). Subsequent questions should be focused, yet open, such as "That's interesting—how did you work that out?" or "Tell me more about . . ." (p. 28).

Also important is to get beyond surface answers by (1) turning the student's comment into a question ("What do you mean it was too hard?"), (2) waiting (saying "mmm," indicating you would like to hear more), and (3) probing further (p. 28). For example, a passage about the reasons for locations of factories included the phrases "transport links" and "available markets." A student, when asked the meaning of markets, responded that they sold things in little stalls (Nicholson, 1984, p. 19). An appropriate probing question, such as "Can you tell me a little more about why you think it means little stalls?" yielded the information that the student, relying on personal experience, was thinking of flea markets.

Also important in interviews is to avoid interpreting the student's words and rushing the student. The effect, in the first case, is to change the student's thinking. In the latter, the student likely will "escape" or close down the interview with phrases such as "I forgot" (Nicholson, 1984). The teacher also should not overpraise the student. Instead, she should remain neutral yet interested.

Some educators suggest using interviews to ascertain students' perceptions of the reading process and their reading strategies. However, several difficulties are associated with students reporting such general abstract information about themselves. Among them are that students may not articulate their strategies clearly. That is, they may be unaware of some of the strategies they use. Younger students, in particular, have difficulty in responding to general questions about unobservable processes. Others unconsciously provide the information the teacher is seeking (a well-known phenomenon in educational research referred to as providing socially desirable answers). Other methods for identifying inadequate strategies are miscue inventories, discussed in Chapter 8.

Summary

Conferences and interviews provide different types of one-on-one interactions between teachers and students. A conference is an informal conversation that is a sharing experience for the student and assists the teacher in understanding the student as a reader or writer. Most conferences, however, address writing. The goal is to empower the writer, not to "fix" a specific piece of writing. That is, the goal is to interact with children so that they develop strategies for interacting with their emerging text.

In the content conference, the focus is on the student's emerging text. Teacher questions should not focus on pulling out more information from the writer. Instead, the content conference reinforces the value of the child's message through the active listening of the teacher. Also, it can help the child focus her topic and, moreover, because most children summarize information, it can help the child see the need for detail. The teacher, however, does not suggest the details to be added. In contrast, the process conference focuses on children's writing strategies. The goal is for the child to develop self-awareness of his thinking. Writing conferences also inform instruction by providing information about conventions and other issues that should be addressed with the class. They also play an important role in assessment by indicating where the student is gaining control of her writing.

The purpose of the interview, in contrast, is to determine specific information about the student. One focus is to develop information about the processes students engage in during reading and writing. Another use is to discover the thinking of readers who are having difficulties. Essential to this focus is to conduct the interview when the student is working through or has just completed a task. Also important is to get beyond the student's surface answers and to avoid interpreting the student's answers to the open-ended questions.

Discussion Questions

1. A first-grade class is preparing to read a selection on festivals of Mexico. What are some topics that should be discussed prior to the reading?

2. Describe the problems in a teacher initiating post-reading questions with "Isn't it true that snakes shed their skins more than once?"

3. During a writing conference the teacher says, "I'm wondering if you see a different way to start your narrative?" (Calkins, 1994, p. 229).

   a. What is the problem with this question?

   b. Suggest alternative questions.

4. In what ways can an interview help the teacher discover the thinking of readers who are having problems?

*References*_____

Adams, M. J. (1989). Thinking skills curricula. *Educational Psychologist, 24*(1), 25–77.

Alexander, P. A. (1992). Domain knowledge: Evolving themes and emerging concerns. *Educational Psychologist, 27*(1), 33–51.

Alexander, P. A. (1996). The past, present, and future of knowledge research: A re-examination of the role of knowledge in learning instruction. *Educational Psychologist, 31*, pp. 89–92.

Alexander, P. A. (2000). Learning from text: A multidimensional and developmental perspective. In M. L. Kamil, P. B. Mosenthal, P. D. Pearson, & R. Barr (Eds.), *Handbook of reading research. Volume III*. Mahwah, NJ: Lawrence Erlbaum Associates.

Alexander, P. A., Schallert, D. A., & Hare, V. C. (1991). Coming to terms: How researchers in learning and literacy talk about knowledge. *Review of Educational Research, 61*(3), 315–343.

Au, K. H., Mason, J. M., & Scheu, J. A. (1995). *Literacy instruction for today*. New York: Harper Collins.

Anderson, R. C., Spiro, R. J., & Anderson, M. C. (1978). Schemata as scaffolding for the representation of information in connected discourse. *American Educational Research Journal, 15*, 433–440.

Bernhardt, E. B. (2000). Second-language reading as a case study of reading scholarship in the twentieth century. In M. L. Kamil, P. B. Mosenthal, P. D. Pearson, & R. Barr (Eds.), *Handbook of reading research, Vol. III* (pp. 791–812). Mahwah, NJ: Lawrence Erlbaum Associates.

Calkins, L. M. (1985). Learning to think through writing. In A. Jaegger & M. T. Smith-Burke (Eds.), *Observing the language learner* (pp. 173–198). Newark, DE: International Reading Association.

Calkins, L. M. (1994). *The art of teaching writing* (2nd ed.). Portsmouth, NH: Heinemann.

Clay, M. (1972). *Sand*. Auckland, New Zealand: Heinemann.

Clay, M. (1979). *Stones*. Auckland, New Zealand: Heinemann.

Clay, M. (1985). *The early detection of reading difficulties* (3rd ed.). Auckland, New Zealand: Heinemann.

Clay, M. (1989). Concepts about print in English and other languages. *Reading Teacher, 42*(4), 268–276.

Cooper, J. D. (2000). *Literacy: Helping children construct meaning*. Boston: Houghton Mifflin.

Davey, B. (1989). Assessing comprehension: Selected interactions of task and reader. *Reading Teacher, 42*(9), 694–697.

Davila, L. (1998). Using anecdotal records in writing conferences. In T. Thomason *Writer to writer: How to conference young authors* (pp. 67–70). Norwood, MA: Christopher-Gordon Publishers.

Dochy, F., Segers, M., & Buhl, M. (1999). The relation between assessment practices and outcomes of studies: The case of research on prior knowledge. *Review of Educational Research, 69*(2), 145–186.

Dole, J. A., Duffy, G., Roehler, L. R., & Pearson, P. D. (1991). Moving from the old to the new: Research on reading comprehension instruction. *Review of Educational Comprehension, 61*(2), 239–264.

Donaldson, M. (1978). *Children's minds*. New York: Norton.

Farr, R., & Carey, R. E. (1986). *Reading: What can be measured?* Newark, DE: International Reading Association.

Gambrell, L. B. (1980). Think-time: Implications of reading instruction. *Reading Teacher, 34*(2), 143–146.

Garner, R. (1990). Children's use of strategies in reading. In K. Bjorklund (Ed.), *Children's strategies: Contemporary views of cognitive development* (pp. 245–268). Hillsdale, NJ: Erlbaum.

Graves, D. H. (1983). *Writing: Students and teachers at work*. Portsmouth, NH: Heinemann.

Graves, D. H. (1999). *Bring life into learning: Create a lasting literacy*. Portsmouth, NH: Heinemann.

Gredler, M. (2001). *Learning and instruction: Theory into practice* (4th ed.). Upper Saddle River, NJ: Prentice-Hall.

Harste, J. C., Short, K. G., & Burke, C. (1988). *Creating classrooms for authors: The reading-writing connection*. Portsmouth, NH: Heinemann.

Heller, M. F. (1999). *Reading-writing connections: Theory into practice*. Mahwah, NJ: Lawrence Erlbaum.

Holmes, B. C. (1983). The effect of prior knowledge on the question answering of good and poor readers. *Journal of Reading Behavior, 15*(1), 1–18.

Holmes, B. C., & Roser, N. L. (1987). Five ways to assess readers' prior knowledge. *Reading Teacher, 40*(7), 646–649.

Leslie, L. (1993). A developmental interaction approach to reading assessment. *Reading and Writing Quarterly: Overcoming Learning Difficulties, 9,* 5–10.

Leslie, L., & Caldwell, J. (1990). *Qualitative reading inventory.* Glenview, IL: Scott Foresman.

Lucking, R. (1985). Just two words. *Language Arts, 63,* 173–174.

Maria, K. (1990). *Reading comprehension interactions: Strategies and issues.* Parkton, MD: York.

Nicholson, T. (1984). You get lost when you gotta blimmin' watch the damn words: The low progress reader in the junior high school. *Topics in Learning and Learning Disabilities, 3*(4), 16–30.

Ogle, D. M. (1986). K-W-L: A teaching model that develops active reading of expository text. *Reading Teacher, 39*(6), 564–570.

Paris, S. G., Wasik, B. A., & Turner, J. C. (1991). The development of strategic readings. In R. Barr, M. L. Kamil, P. Mosenthal, & P. D. Pearson (Eds.), *Handbook of reading research Vol. 2* (pp. 609–640). New York: Longman.

Pearson, C. (1980). Can you keep quiet for three seconds? *Learning,* Feb., 40–43.

Rowe, M. B. (1974). Pausing phenomena: Influence on the quality of instruction. *Journal of Psycholinguistic Research, 3*(3), 203–223.

Rowe, M. B. (1980). Pausing principles and their effects on reasoning in science. *New Directions for Community College, 31,* 27–34.

Rowe, M. B. (1986). Wait time: Slowing down may be a way of speeding up. *Journal of Teacher Education, 37,* 43–50.

Sowers, S. (1988). Reflect, expand, select: Three responses in the writing conference. In Newkirk & Atwell (Eds.), *Understanding writing* (2nd ed., pp. 130–141).

Spandel, V. (2001). *Creating writers* (3rd ed.). New York: Addison Wesley Longman.

Thomason, T. (1998). *Writer to writer: How to conference young authors.* Norwood, MA: Christopher-Gordon Publishers.

Tierney, R. J., & Cunningham, J. W. (1984). Research on teaching reading comprehension. In B. D. Pearson (Ed.), *Handbook of reading research* (pp. 609–655). New York: Longman.

Vygotsky, L. S. (1987). Thinking and speech. In R. W. Rieber & A. S. Carton (Eds.), *Problems of general psychology, Vol. 1. The collected works of L. S. Vygotsky* (pp. 39–285). New York: Plenum Press.

Watson, K., & Young, B. (1986). Discourse for learning in the classroom. *Language Arts, 63*(2), 126–133.

5

Performance Assessment

> Performance samples . . . yield a record of a highly complex behavior on tasks that approximate the conditions and resources the student normally encounters in the classroom or other "real-life" settings.
>
> —Teale, 1988

The children in a second-grade classroom are designing and writing the invitations to their parents to attend the fall open house at their school. In another school, teams of eighth-grade students are conducting a land use study in their county to recommend a location for a sewage treatment facility. Each team conducts the research and develops a report to be submitted to the county council. These assessments address complex capabilities and they also address the suggestions for authentic assessment described in Chapter 2.

These and other tasks, such as retelling a story one has heard and writing an essay, are examples of performance assessments. They are defined, open-ended tasks that require the student to organize information for a particular purpose, use language appropriately, and communicate with an identified audience.

Performance tasks emerged as a major form of assessment as part of the effort to develop curricula that focus on meaningful learning. A primary reason is that they can reflect the actual challenges faced by writers, business people, or community leaders (Wolf, LeMahieu, & Eresh, 1992; Wiggins, 1993). Discussed in this chapter are the defining characteristics of performance assessments, typical performance tasks in the classroom, and guidelines for developing and implementing performance assessments.

Overview

In one sense, any action taken by a student in relation to the curriculum is a performance, from answering teacher questions and documenting books read in a journal to reading a story the student has written. However, in the literacy classroom, performance samples "occupy a middle ground between the openness of observations and the restrictions of testing" (Teale, Hiebert, & Chittenden, 1987, p. 773). They are similar to observations in that they provide a record of complex behavior on tasks that provide the learner some choice in responding. Examples are constructing a story from a wordless picture book and writing an essay. However, performance assessments resemble tests in that they focus on predefined problems (p. 773).

Also, as assessments, performance tasks must meet four major requirements (see Table 5.1). First, as indicated in the examples, a performance assessment requires the demonstration of complex capabilities in applied or open-ended settings. That is, performance assessments are not intended to measure the acquisition of basic knowledge or a single skill (such as inferring the main idea of a piece of writing). Instead, they involve actual demonstrations that require the integration of particular processes, skills, and concepts (Delain, 1999, p. 110). An example is a child retelling a story he has listened to or read. This task informs the teacher about the child's ability to think about particular story elements, relate them to each other, and construct a coherent text (Morrow, 1990).

Second, performance assessments also focus on teachable processes, such as ways to elaborate episodes in a narrative with detail and selecting key episodes during retelling. That is, success on an assessment should not depend on student ingenuity in discovering an original way to address the stated problem. Third, a related requirement is that the assessment should inform the teacher of the student's strengths and weaknesses. Review of a student's response to a performance task should inform the teacher if, for example, the student understands the elements of a fictional narrative or if the student continues to struggle with plot development.

TABLE 5.1 *Requirements for Performance Tasks*

Requirement	*Example*
1. Assess complex capabilities	**1.** Retelling a story, writing a story about a series of four pictures, writing a persuasive letter to the principal about the need to reduce homework
2. Focus on teachable processes	**2.** Engaging the audience by orienting the reader to time and place and by foreshadowing upcoming events; using appropriate transitions to new paragraphs
3. Inform teachers about student progress and/or strengths and weaknesses	**3.** Emergent reading, brief original stories, persuasive essays, expository writing, retelling
4. Involve products or performances that are valued in their own right	**4.** Same as No. 3

Finally, the assessment should involve products or processes that are valued in their own right. Examples include writing stories, poems, and persuasive essays. This requirement (along with the first requirement) calls into question the suggested practice of requiring students to maintain a record of all works or books read with a commentary on each. First, such a record does not assess a complex capability. Second, the key question is what is the purpose of the record? If the purpose is to determine the extent of the student's reading, then interviews or monthly sweeps can determine this information. If the purpose is for students to evaluate books they have read, then tape recordings or periodic written summaries of reading selections are appropriate.

Other characteristics of performance assessments may vary. They may range from informal to formal in terms of the constraints on the task. That is, they may be (1) structured or unstructured, (2) preannounced or unannounced (Stiggins, 1987), and (3) embedded in ongoing classroom activities or separate assignments accompanied by directions. For example, the teacher may review samples of young children's emergent writing produced during the year, or, periodically, she may ask each child to write a story.

Further, the focus of the assessment may be the process by which the student completes the task, the product the student has developed (Nitko, 1996; Stiggins, 1987), or both. The choice of whether to evaluate a process or a product depends largely on the nature of the strategies or capabilities to be demonstrated (Messick, 1994). For example, in constructing meaning from text, the process of oral reading fluency may be the focus of the assessment. For other tasks such as reacting to a story one has read silently, the product, a reaction paper, may be the focus. In some areas, both the process and the outcomes are important. In the evaluation of a student's speech, for example, both the content outline (product of the student's research) and the delivery (process) are important.

This chapter discusses both formal and informal performance assessments. In preschool and kindergarten settings, performance assessments include assessing emergent literacy, children's retelling of stories read to them, and story construction from sequences of pictures. In the early grades and middle school, performance assessments include students' retelling of stories they have read and various types of writing tasks. Performance tasks in high school typically consist of essays and other types of writing in English classes and research reports in other subject areas. The chapter concludes with guidelines for developing and implementing performance tasks.

Assessing Emergent Literacy

The concept of emergent literacy, first introduced by Marie Clay (1966), reflects the belief that, in an educated society, legitimate literacy learning begins early in life (Teale, 1988). Further, children's early behaviors develop in predictable ways toward conventional literacy (Clay, 1966; Teale, Hiebert, & Chittenden, 1987). Of interest in preschool and kindergarten are children's emergent reading and writing, as well as the skills of listening comprehension and story construction. Assessment of these capabilities must be sensitive to the social and developmental characteristics of young children, particularly their level of attentiveness and ability to understand instructions. That is, for young students performance assessments should be informal and conducted in the context of classroom activities.

Emergent Reading and Writing

The term *emergent reading* refers to the phenomenon of a not-yet-literate child "reading" a book—to herself, siblings, dolls, or pets (Sulzby, 1985; Teale, 1988). In this activity, the child may be attending primarily to the pictures or the print and more or less forming a coherent story. The teacher obtains a performance sample of the child's emergent reading by asking the child to "read" a favorite storybook to her. By listening to the child's speech and observing his actions, the teacher can estimate the approximation of the child's activities to conventional literacy.

Sulzby (1985) has identified a developmental sequence of categories of emergent reading that may be applied to the child's performance. As indicated in Table 5.2, children typically progress through five broad phases from picture-governed to print-governed reading. The child's story narration gradually moves from page-specific brief comments to a sequential decontextualized narration with reading-like intonation.

Similar to reading, children typically have notions about the functions of writing when they enter school (Martlew, 1988). They often are aware of a few shop signs or street names and realize that marks on a page signify meaning (p. 91). Further, like the activity of reading, young children begin to "play around" with writing. The many forms of their writing illustrate parts of the concepts they are inferring about the process (Sulzby, 1990, p. 85).

TABLE 5.2   *Categories of Emergent Reading*[1]

Category	Description
1. Picture-governed, stories not formed **a.** labeling and commenting **b.** following the action	Speech is a response to each discrete page: "Doggie." "He big." "There he goes; gonna catch 'im."
2. Picture-governed, story formed; oral language-like	Story-like sequence can be inferred: "They looked all over the place, and then he writted a note to the king."
3. Picture-governed, story formed; oral and written language mixed	Parts inserted that sound like written language, intonation, wording, or both; story contains parts that are decontextualized "'And here's your lunch,' the mom said."
4. Picture-governed, story formed; written language-like	Story similar to original or verbatim-like; language is decontextualized and intonation is reading-like "His brother said, 'Nothing's gonna grow.' Then he, but he didn't give up. He kept on watering it."
5. Print-governed	Child may read known sight words, skipping other words

[1]Summarized from Sulzby (1985)

The forms of children's emergent writing include drawing as writing, scribbling, nonphonetic letter strings, copying of conventional print, and invented spellings. However, emergent writing does not develop according to invariant sequential stages. For example, children develop drawing as a form of writing quite early, but may continue to use it until age 6 or 7 (p. 91).

Of importance is that children's emergent writing functions to document composition or intention. That is, it is produced in response to a request to "write" or with the announced intention to "write" (Sulzby, 1990, p. 85). Further, although writing in kindergarten appears to be a robust behavior, children are likely to hide these capabilities if adults ignore or do not respond positively to their preliterate efforts (p. 93). They will, however, typically respond to an accepting teacher and a direct request to write a story (p. 93).

Chapter 3 introduced a checklist that may be used throughout several months to record the various forms of emergent writing observed when children are working in writing centers or during independent writing time. When the child writes a story in response to the teacher's request, either the checklist or a brief description of the forms used by the child may be used.

The teacher also may ask the child to read the story he or she has written. The forms of reading, similar to reading from print text, may vary. The types are conversational, oral monologue, oral/written mix, written monologue, and attending to the nonconventional print (Sulzby, 1990, p. 97). These categories are similar to the emergent reading categories in Table 5.2.

Samples of children's emergent writing accompanied by the teacher's notations on the writing and reading categories may be placed in a child's writing folder to document development over time. These samples and the teacher's comments also may serve as a resource for parent conferences (Teale, 1990).

Story Retelling and Story Construction

In addition to emergent writing and reading, children's capabilities in listening comprehension and story construction are aspects of developing literacy. The basis for assessing listening comprehension is the stories the teacher has read to the children several times, which the children later retell to the teacher.

Retelling. The activity of retelling refers to telling a story or reporting informational text in one's own words. However, it does not mean memorizing words and sentences from the written text (Morrow, 1989). The process involves reconstruction, which requires thinking about the particular story elements, relating them to each other, and arranging them in sequence. In this way, children build an internal representation of the story (p. 89).

As an assessment tool, retelling may be used in both kindergarten and the elementary grades. As indicated in Table 5.3, retelling addresses the child's literal recall of specifics, sense of story structure, and abilities to organize, integrate, and classify information implied in the story. Children's growth in these capabilities may be assessed throughout the year with story retelling.

TABLE 5.3 *Assessment Functions of Story Retellings[1]*

Function	Definition
1. Literal recall	Event sequence, facts and details, cause-effect relationships
2. Sense of story structure	Setting, theme, plot episodes, and resolution
3. Inferential abilities	Decisions about the organization, integration, and classification of information that is implied in the story

[1]Summarized from Morrow (1989); Morrow et al. (1986)

Retelling is a unique form of assessment. It differs from the ability to answer questions about the text (Leslie, 1993). First, unlike answering questions, retelling is heavily dependent on the student's schema or understanding of the type of text. Second, direct questions frequently include clues that indicate the answer (p. 25).

For young children, individual story recall following group storybook reading can reveal children's difficulties in reconstructing important information (Mason & Stewart, 1990, p. 170). For example, young children tend to tell everything, rather than selecting key events. Retelling also can indicate young children's understanding of story sequence and logical inference as well as their oral language development.

Prior to the retelling, the teacher should read storybooks several times and then ask children to retell or pretend-read the stories. Anecdotal notes or a checklist may be used to document the child's reconstruction of the story. This form of retelling assessment is referred to as oral-to-oral retelling. In a variation of this procedure, after the teacher has read a story a few times, the child draws a picture that represents the story. He or she then tells the teacher about the picture. This assessment format is referred to as oral-to-drawing retelling.

Selections for use with young children should have good plot structures with clear story lines that contribute to ease of retelling (Morrow, 1989). In addition, pre- and post-discussions and practice with prompting are essential in the classroom so that children feel at ease with the process. The use of flannel board characters and props, such as stuffed animals and puppets, assists in introducing the procedure to younger students during instruction (Morrow, 1989).

Story Construction. A related, yet different, capability is that of constructing a story from a sequence of pictures that illustrate a set of events. An example is a set of four to six pictures that illustrate going on a picnic. Another device that may be used is a wordless picture book. Children, using the pictures, their own background experience, and their understanding of story structure, construct a story about the pictures. The teacher may record anecdotal notes as the child shares the story with the class. In addition, discussion of the children's stories can illustrate the influence of their different backgrounds on the stories the children develop.

In summary, children exhibit reading- and writing-like behaviors that are precursors to conventional literacy. The various forms of both oral story reading and story writing may be documented for parent–teacher conferences and reporting student growth. The teacher also can obtain information about children's language development and story structure from post-listening retellings and story construction from wordless picture books.

Retelling in Elementary School

The prior section introduced oral-to-oral and oral-to-drawing retellings as methods for assessing young children's oral development of language and understanding of story structure. A third format, for children who can read, is print-to-oral retelling. That is, children read brief stories and then retell them to the teacher.

In the elementary school years, in addition to the development of oral language, knowledge of story structure, and comprehension, retelling also contributes to confidence in one's reading and writing (Morrow, 1990). For example, words, phrases, rhetorical devices, and text organization used by children in retelling stories find their way into the children's writing (Brown & Cambourne, 1987). This form of learning transfer is referred to as "linguistic spillover" (Brown & Cambourne, 1987).

Related to the issue of format for retellings is that elementary school children have learned to write. However, frequently asking them to write summaries of stories they have read may prove problematic. First, this alternative, unlike oral retelling, is less enjoyable for some students. Brown and Cambourne (1987) report that children said, "There was just too much to write down, and I got sick of it," and "I don't like trying to write down someone else's story" (p. 30). Second, the learner may recall and understand more than he is able to demonstrate in writing. Thus, this approach may not accurately reflect the child's knowledge. That is, the emphasis on writing can skew the evaluation process for some children (Hiebert, 1991, p. 515).

Guidelines for Assessment

Retelling should not be used as an assessment method until it has become an accepted facet of classroom instruction. This requirement is essential to ensure that children are relaxed and that the retelling reflects the extent of their capabilities. Also, retelling, that is, "telling what happened," is sometimes referred to as a "natural" form of language behavior. However, a careful selection of the material is important to ensure a fair assessment (Brown & Cambourne, 1987). Required are stories with predictable plot structures and vocabulary within the children's reading level.

When conducting the assessment, the teacher should first ask the child to retell the story as though he or she were telling it to a friend who has never heard it before (Morrow, 1990, p. 126). Also, if the teacher's evaluation addresses relating the story to one's personal experience, this suggestion should be included in the directions.

During the retelling, the teacher encourages students by showing interest, but does not provide prompts during the assessment. However, during pauses the teacher may ask,

"Can you think of anything else about the story?" or "You're doing very well. Can you continue?" (Morrow, 1989, p. 51).

Scoring Methods

One of two methods may be used to score the retelling. One option is to develop a checklist that includes the key information in the story or text and the skills the retelling should reflect (see Figure 5.1). During instruction, some teachers emphasize the importance of the child's generalizing beyond the text and relating the story to her own experience. In such situations, these features should be included in the checklist.

Morrow (1990) suggests assigning one point to each element. For characters and story elements, the child earns a percentage score that reflects the number recalled. For

---

FIGURE 5.1 *Checklist for Retelling*

Selection:_____

Child's name: _____   Date: _____

Setting

      time   _____

      place   _____

      (weather)   _____

Characters

      Major

      _____   _____

      _____   _____

      _____   _____

      Minor

      _____   _____

      _____   _____

      _____   _____

Theme (main character's primary goal or problem to be solved) _____

Story events (No.   )   _____

      No. recalled   _____

Resolution   _____

Sequence (mostly accurate) _____

---

example, mentioning two out of three episodes earns a score of .66. Also, the child should receive points for the "gist" of story elements. That is, saying "boy" instead of specifically naming "Sam," and "dog" for "Spike" are acceptable when naming story characters.

A different approach is to use a holistic scoring guide (Irwin & Mitchell, 1983). Specifically, a holistic guide assigns an overall rating that reflects the quality of the retelling on an identified continuum. Table 5.4 is an example in which the levels of proficiency range from 1 to 4. However, a disadvantage of the holistic method is that it cannot be applied while the child is retelling the story. The reason is the number of discrete elements that must be attended to by the teacher. Thus, the teacher must take notes during the retelling and tape record the child's performance. Then the scoring can be completed using this information.

Other Assessment Issues

Also important in the use of retelling in the classroom are validity, reliability, and the advantages and limitations of the procedure. First, as already stated, a validity concern is that the student should be relaxed so that the retelling can reflect the learner's capabilities. Second, a particular retelling is not a complete reflection of all the meaning created by the reader (Goodman, Watson, & Burke, 1987). Therefore, retellings should be conducted over time and tap different genres.

Further, several factors can influence the reliability of the inferences about story retellings (Morrow, 1990, p. 129). Within the child are factors such as the child's memory

TABLE 5.4 *Holistic Scoring Guide for Story Retelling*

4	*The student relates a complete, coherent rendition of the story with appropriate supporting details.* Setting is described; the main character's primary goal or problem to be solved is clearly explicated; major and minor characters and events are described, and the resolution is clear.
3	*The student relates a coherent sequence of events with some details, but omits one component* (e.g., settings, clear explication of main character's primary goal or problem to be solved, or lack of clear resolution).
2	*The student relates a skeletal, yet coherent, sequence of major events.* However, supporting detail is lacking; setting, if mentioned, lacks detail; minor characters and/or minor events are missing.
1	*Key information essential for the coherence of the story is missing.* The listener cannot determine the main character's primary goal or problem to be solved, or major story events are missing and/or are not correctly sequenced; setting description is inadequate or missing; no supporting details.

4 = highest level; 1 = lowest level

and awareness of the task. A factor associated with the task is the topic of the story. That is, children's interest and their responses may vary across topics.

Other task factors that can influence children's responses are text length and the extent of predictability of the story. Specifically, text length clearly should not exceed the child's capacity for recall and the text should be predictable. That is, it should not sequence story elements in an unfamiliar way. Further, teachers should ensure that children understand they are to tell the story to someone who is unfamiliar with the narrative. The reason is they will react differently if they think the "listener" is someone who knows the story.

Retellings are not responses to predeveloped questions that provide limited information about a student's understanding. Instead, one advantage is that retelling provides students with opportunities to organize and orally present their conception and understanding of a story. Instructionally, retellings are an important prelude to students' organizing and presenting their own independent reports on some topic. Second, for the teacher, retellings provide information about the student's ability to follow a story line and understand plot, theme, and characters. They also indicate how the student responds to a text. A disadvantage is that like other assessments that are a rich source of information, retellings are time consuming.

Summary

Retelling involves reconstructing key story elements, relating them to each other, and arranging them in sequence. Retelling should involve oral reproduction of the story, rather than writing, so that the student can adequately demonstrate his understanding. As an instructional strategy, retelling provides words, phrases, and organizational forms that children then apply in their writing (linguistic spillover).

The teacher should ask the student to retell the story as though she were telling someone who had never heard it before. Student performance may be recorded on a checklist that addresses the major story elements or a holistic guide that identifies levels of quality of performance.

Validity of the procedure depends on the student's comfort level and the use of several assessments. Influencing reliability are the topic of the story and factors within the child. Advantages of retellings include the opportunities for students to organize and present orally their understandings and the information provided to the teacher. A disadvantage is the time required to use the procedure.

Writing Assessments

In today's information society, literacy is an essential capability and writing is a key component. Individuals may be expected to organize information for reporting purposes, develop reports, and communicate in writing with others in the job setting. Writing also is expressive, and writing initiated in the early school years can assist students to express their thoughts, feelings, and impressions in new ways. Therefore, becoming proficient in different kinds of writing for different audiences is an accepted literacy goal.

The purpose of any writing assessment is to demonstrate the student's capabilities to communicate to an identified audience for a particular purpose. Assessments may document the emergence and gradual development of these capabilities or they may address the application of writing skills and strategies to different kinds of writing. Discussed in this section are demonstrating growth in developing the skills and strategies of writing, demonstrating the application of these capabilities to different kinds of writing, and cautions on the use of writing as an assessment.

Documenting Growth

One perspective on developing writing skills in the early grades organizes classroom activities within a framework referred to as the authoring cycle (Harste, Short, & Burke, 1988). The cycle progresses from uninterrupted reading and writing time through author's circle, self-editing, peer editing, publishing/celebrating authorship, invitations to write/ language strategy instruction, and then back to uninterrupted reading and writing (p. 55). During uninterrupted reading and writing time, children may write on anything they wish. Lists of ideas they develop as well as picture books and magazines are available as resources for ideas. Author's circle convenes when three or four students have a complete rough draft they wish to think about with other writers. In addition to providing feedback, the other writers help the author develop a sense of audience (p. 69).

This curriculum framework values first drafts as much as final drafts (Harste et al., 1988). Further, students soon have several rough drafts—some that are complete and others in process—because they are usually working on more than one piece at a time. Teachers maintain all drafts in the child's author folder, which serves as a cumulative record of published and unpublished work.

Evaluation, in this framework, addresses the emergence and development of writing capabilities represented by the various drafts. A single sheet of paper stapled to the inside front cover of the folder serves as the evaluation record. Noted are teacher comments on mechanics and strategies, accompanied by the date. Examples are "is using complete sentences" (mechanics) and "revised by inserting new information into an old paragraph, instead of tagging it onto the end" (strategy) (Harste et al., 1988, p. 66). Strategies also include anecdotal observations such as "self-edited rough draft before presentation in author's circle."

Advantages of these assessments are (1) they are embedded in ongoing classroom activities, and (2) the children have maximum choices as to the types of writing they undertake. A disadvantage can be ensuring that all author folders are reviewed frequently. The purpose of reviewing various drafts of children's stories, brief narratives, and other products is to document their growth in writing. Thus, one validity issue is what constitutes growth. That is, what capabilities represent development in writing proficiency? A second validity issue is the extent to which others contributed to the particular drafts undergoing revision. Here, anecdotal records on the input provided by other children in author's circle and outside editing can be helpful. Reliability addresses the consistency of the inferences about student capabilities; therefore, frequent review of the folders is important.

Developing Proficiency in Different Kinds of Writing

As students progress through school, they are expected to become proficient in different kinds of writing. Table 5.5 summarizes the major types suggested by the National Council of Teachers of English (Myers & Spalding, 1997). As indicated, they range from brief examples of expressive writing to formal research reports.

Opportunities to develop proficiency in different types of writing can begin in the elementary grades and progress to more advanced writing in the middle or high school years. For example, assessment of a fourth-grade student's writing may include a letter to

TABLE 5.5 *Major Types of Classroom Writing Assessments*

Type	Description	Importance	Examples
Expressive writing	Includes observations, thoughts, and reflections; may describe a scene or explore the significance of a person, object, or memory; requires emotional and/or personal engagement by the author (Myers & Spalding, 1997)	Does not adhere to the strict requirements of narrative, description, argument, and comparison/contrast; therefore, can allow young writers to use writing to develop fluency and to grow in their capabilities to perceive and reflect (Myers & Spalding, 1997)	Diaries, short compositions
Description or nonfiction narrative	Shares memories of someone in the writer's life or a personal experience	Provides experience in elaborating episodes, use of detail, and engaging an audience	Brief compositions, autobiographical incidents
Narrative, fiction	Interweaves plot, fiction, setting, and character to develop striking images	Provides experience in words to develop plot, setting, and character in the exploration of life issues	Incidents, brief stories
Persuasive argument	Addresses five questions: purpose (argument), who, what, why, possible objections from the other side, and counterarguments	Provides experience in marshalling evidence to support a position, appeal to an audience, and viewing an issue from a counterperspective	Letters, essays
Exposition	Marshalls factual information, observations, and conceptual descriptions to describe accurately a phenomenon of interest	Provides experience in researching, organizing, and presenting factual information	Brief paragraphs, research reports

persuade her teacher to reduce the amount of homework. In contrast, a high school student writes an essay setting forth the evidence to support his definition of tragedy in English literature. In the first instance, arguments pro and con are derived from the views of others about the role and function of homework. In the second example, the student draws from literature selections, such as Shakespeare's tragedies, to support his definition of tragedy and refute other likely perspectives.

In contrast, expository writing begins with basic facts about the topic of interest. In the early grades, performance samples may consist of simple paragraphs on topics such as snakes and turtles. In high school, the assessment of expository writing often takes the form of comprehensive research reports.

A key requirement for brief stories written in the early grades is that each must have a beginning, middle, and end. However, narratives and expository writing have specific composition requirements to be mastered by the students. For example, a narrative requires elaborating episodes through use of detail and engaging the audience in the recounted experiences. In contrast, expository writing requires conveying accurate information to the reader. Tompkins (1994), cited in Bear and Barrone (1998), described several points for the student to consider in expository writing. Included are to describe it, compare it to other things you know, analyze what it is composed of, and apply it by explaining what you can do with it. Of importance to assessment is that these points can serve as the basis for developing a guide to score the student's performance.

The unique characteristic of writing assessments is that they are tangible examples of the student's actual performance. This advantage contributes to their versatility in providing information for parent conferences, grading purposes, and communicating with other teachers. A disadvantage is the time involved in the initial planning. However, once designed, they may be used with subsequent groups of students.

Cautions in the Use of Writing in the Classroom

Because writing is integrated with reading in the classroom, a teacher may be tempted to over rely on students' written responses as an assessment tool. Obtaining written samples for a classroom of children is much easier than obtaining samples of their oral readings and retellings. Also, the ability to express oneself in writing is an important literacy goal.

However, problems occur with a reliance on written responses to assess purposes such as students' acquisition of items of content knowledge and their prior knowledge about a topic. First, stating one's knowledge about a concept or topic does not meet the requirement that performance assessments address students' complex capabilities.

Second, students' communication of their understanding is directly related to their capabilities to document that knowledge through written responses. That is, students often know more than they are able to translate into written paragraphs. Therefore, requiring a written account of information learned will underestimate the learning of most students.

This issue of response format is particularly problematic for second language learners (Pearson, DeStefano, & Garcia, 1998, p. 23). For them, in addition to writing, language dominance is a factor. For example, when Spanish bilingual students have the opportunity to respond to English texts in Spanish instead of English, their scores are higher on a range of tests (p. 24).

A third problem associated with a heavy reliance on writing for basic tasks is that writing can become a distasteful chore for the student. In other words, other formats should be considered when assessment of student comprehension of content is the goal. As indicated in Chapter 4, in introducing a new topic, assess students' prior knowledge through informal questioning. Also, tasks such as students' periodic evaluations of reading selections may be obtained through tape recordings. In one third-grade classroom, for example, children twice monthly tape recorded their evaluations of books and stories read during free time (Lamme & Hysmith, 1991).

Validity and reliability also are important issues in using writing assessments. As discussed in the following section, a clear statement of performance requirements, ample opportunity for students to develop the required capabilities, and adequate samples of student performance are essential to establishing validity and reliability of the assessments.

Summary

Becoming proficient in different kinds of writing for different audiences is an important literacy goal. A key role for writing assessments in relation to this goal is to document children's growth in mastering the processes of expressing oneself in writing. For this purpose, various drafts of students' writing projects are evaluated. Essential in this process is to review writing folders frequently. Important validity issues are the identification of capabilities that reflect growth and documenting the extent of input provided by other children or the teacher. A second important role for writing assessment is to document student progress in mastering different types of writing. These writing forms may range from brief examples of expressive writing to formal research reports. These types differ in the specific composition requirements the student must master. Expository writing, for example, includes basic facts whereas narratives require elaboration.

An advantage of written products is that they are tangible evidence of a student's performance and are useful in parent conferences. Although they require planning time, the assessments may be used with subsequent groups of children. Essential in establishing the validity and reliability of writing assessments are a clear statement of performance requirements, opportunities for students to develop their capabilities, and adequate samples of student work.

Because written products are easy to obtain, they may be misused. Relying on students' written responses to assess their prior knowledge of a topic or their content knowledge after instruction is not recommended. First, they do not meet the requirements for performance assessments. Second, students often understand more than they can communicate in writing. Third, an overreliance on writing as an assessment method can lead to students' dislike of writing.

Developing and Implementing Performance Assessments

Classroom observations and questioning can capture the moment-by-moment characteristics of students' engagement in literacy activities. In contrast, performance assessments are tasks or projects that require students to marshal several capabilities to accomplish a goal. That is, they require organizational as well as literacy skills. Second-graders who are designing and writing invitations to their school open house and eighth-graders conducting a land use study reflect this characteristic of performance assessments.

Development

Performance assessments, which often are culminating tasks, also are a direct outgrowth of instruction. Therefore, instructional preparations also should include planning for performance assessments. This approach identifies the important capabilities and strategies to be addressed during instruction, and it helps to ensure that performance assessments do not focus on trivial behaviors.

Essential Steps.   The essential planning steps are important in supporting the validity of a performance assessment. As indicated in Table 5.6, the first step is to establish a clear purpose. Specifically, what decision is to be made from the assessment? The decision, for example, to document student growth or calculate a student's grade, has implications for the types of situations that are best suited to the assessment (discussed in step 3).

Second is to identify the strategies, skills, and knowledge the student is to demonstrate. For example, in a persuasive essay the student should demonstrate the capability to marshal evidence in support of the writer's case and address counterarguments. In con-

TABLE 5.6   *Guidelines for the Development of Performance Assessments*

Steps	*Examples*
1. a. Establish a clear purpose for the assessment **b.** Specify the decision to be made from the assessment	**1. a.** Develop a persuasive argument; demonstrate prereading skills **b.** Document student growth, calculate a student's grade, identify priorities for instruction
2. Specify the strategies, skills, and knowledge the student is to demonstrate	**2.** Student is to develop a clear thesis statement, and include both examples and counterexamples from the literature, support the thesis statement and refute other views in a well-organized argument
3. Specify the opportunities by which the student demonstrates the performance	**3.** Ongoing work in the student's authoring folder; on-demand assessment to be completed in the classroom; assignment to be completed outside of class
4. Describe the task and subparts, if applicable	**4.** Planning sheet for a persuasive letter and final draft of the letter
5. Establish the dimensions or criteria for the performance and review the task	**5.** Children's stories should have a beginning, middle, and an end; narratives should engage the reader and elaborate episodes with detail
6. Develop a scoring guide	**6.** Discussed in Chapter 6

trast, if the capability is demonstrating prereading skills, the assessment is to capture the level at which the student is working at particular points in the school year.

Third, identify the opportunities by which the student is to demonstrate the performance. Options include ongoing activities in the classroom, on-demand assessments to be completed in the classroom, and assignments completed outside of class. As already stated, review of various drafts of the student's projects in her author's folder may provide the essential information to record growth. In contrast, if the purpose is to calculate a student's grade, then care should be taken that the student is not distracted, rushed, or otherwise inattentive when completing the work. Therefore, on-demand tasks may be needed.

Step four is to describe the task and the subparts, if applicable. For example, developing a persuasive letter may include the submission of (1) a plan that states the purpose, who (the audience), why (reasons), possible objections, and possible arguments, and (2) the final draft of the letter-argument (Myers & Spalding, 1997). Similarly, submissions of research papers by middle and high school students typically include their note cards.

The next step is to establish the dimensions of the performance. These dimensions, also referred to as criteria (Arter & MicTighe, 2001; Cooper, 1999; Stiggins, 1987; Wiggins & McTighe, 1998), elements (Wolcott with Legg, 1998), and traits (Spandel, 2001) are the central features of the performance or product. For example, the dimensions of a persuasive essay in which the student proposes his own definition of tragedy in English literature may include a clear statement of the definition (thesis), examples with support from literature selections, counterexamples and their weaknesses, well-organized ideas, and a clear writing style (Brookhart, 1993).

Identification of the specific dimensions of the task is particularly important for written papers. The reason is to ensure that the student who writes elegant prose but who does not address the subject does not receive a high evaluation (Brookhart, 1993, p. 235). Also important is that the performance dimensions should be consistent with instruction, and focus on the key aspects of the performance (Kuhs, Johnson, Agruso, & Monrad, 2001). That is, a dimension should not be named unless instruction specifically addresses that capability. For example, in evaluating a persuasive essay, the dimension "citation of sources," unless taught, would be excluded.

Performance tasks also should be reviewed to determine if they draw out the expected kinds of thinking (Brookhart, 1993, p. 234). For example, a sixth-grader who is using a thesaurus to "translate" an encyclopedia article into a research report is not evidencing the thinking skills expected by the teacher. Careful delineation of tasks and requirements can avoid such problems.

The final step is to develop an assessment guide for the performance assessment. This task is discussed in Chapter 6.

Developing Performance Dimensions during Instruction. Performance dimensions are characteristics or features of the performance or product that are important. They also are features that students should have an opportunity to develop during instruction. However, the terms "performance dimensions" or "performance characteristics" are abstract, and likely to be intimidating to students.

One way to develop students' understanding of performance dimensions is to engage them in the identification process. The idea of performance dimensions may be introduced by first asking students to brainstorm, for example, the characteristics of a good sandwich (Spandel, 2001, p. 141). Then the discussion can move to the performance assessment of interest. For example, the teacher may ask, "If you were watching a great skit based on *Where the Wild Things Are,* what would you see?"

In discussing the features of writing, however, students often focus on mechanics. One way to facilitate a focus on "thinking big" is to share samples of writing and discuss them (Spandel, 2001). This activity, repeated with different writing selections, can assist students in thinking about the less obvious characteristics of writing that are important. Eighth-graders who are about to conduct a land use study, as a result, may identify organization, extent of comparative data, and discussion of the implications of various sites for different purposes.

Also important, when dimensions are identified, is to incorporate the students' words as descriptors. For example, "good organization" may be accompanied by "a great opening to hook you," "easy to follow," and "builds to the good parts." Also, "powerful words" may be described as "you can picture it," and "Wow! the *best* way to say it" (Spandel, 2001, p. 152).

Developing performance dimensions in this way accomplishes several purposes. Among them are to make abstract terms meaningful by developing concrete descriptors, helping students to focus their work, and facilitating student investment in learning.

Implementation

Discussed in this section are the essential requirements for implementing performance assessments and their advantages and disadvantages. These requirements are important to support the validity of the assessment. First is to ensure that the student is not threatened by the assessment and has ample opportunity to demonstrate the capabilities required by the task. Retelling, for example, particularly when used with young children, should be a familiar exercise in the classroom.

Also important is that the directions should be clear and unambiguous so that the student does not make inadvertent errors. As stated earlier for retellings, children should be asked to tell a story they have heard as though they were telling a friend who has never heard the story.

Clear directions also can help the student understand the breadth of the task. An example of the directions for a paper on developing and supporting one's definition of tragedy in English literature is as follows:

> Define tragedy as a literary genre. You need not agree with other literary critics in your description of the characteristics of tragedy, but you must illustrate and support your thesis with tragedies you have read this year. Cite examples from *Macbeth, Hamlet, Waiting for Godot, Rosencrantz and Guildenstern Are Dead,* and one other work of your choice. (Brookhart, 1993, p. 237)

A third consideration is the provision of adequate resources for the task, one of which is time. For individual oral performance tasks, for example, the teacher must plan adequate time for all children in the class to complete the task. One approach is to use a portion of independent reading and writing time for three to four class days. Student development of written assessments that are to be graded also requires adequate class time or sufficient time that the student can complete the task along with other homework.

An equally important resource is the opportunity to learn. Originally identified as a requirement for high-stakes testing, this concept refers to the need for instruction to address the assessed capabilities. For example, writers experience particular difficulty in organizing the text when developing expository pieces (Harste et al., 1988). Unlike narrative texts, there is no story plot for them to follow (p. 269). Therefore, during instruction, teachers should have students (1) write the major ideas related to their topics on separate headings, (2) write ideas for expanding the major ideas on other cards, and (3) try out different organizations by arranging and rearranging the cards (p. 269). The teacher also should model this process and show the students a paper at each of these steps. Similarly, if the student is to search the Internet for information about a topic, then these skills, including ways to evaluate sites that purport to provide information, also must be addressed in instruction.

Finally, implementation should obtain more than one sample of student performance. Attention to this requirement, together with careful attention to the steps in Table 5.6, contributes to both validity and reliability of the assessment.

An advantage of performance assessments is that they can be opportunities for students to demonstrate complex capabilities in situations that resemble real-world tasks. Examples include young children's emergent reading and writing, story retelling, and the organization and construction of persuasive letters and research reports by older students. A disadvantage is the time required for planning and evaluation.

Summary

Key performance tasks for assessment purposes should be identified in advance to ensure that classroom instruction focuses on important capabilities. The first step in planning a performance assessment is to identify the decision to be made from the assessment, such as documenting growth. Second is to identify the strategies, skills, and knowledge the student is to demonstrate. Third is to identify the opportunities by which the student is to demonstrate the skills. Options include classroom activities, on-demand classroom assessments, and out-of-class assignments.

Step four is to describe the task and subparts, if applicable. Some writing projects, for example, include prior submission of an outline or writing plan. Step five involves establishing the dimensions of the performance. They are particularly important so that the student who writes elegant prose but does not address the topic does not receive a high evaluation. Finally, performance tasks are reviewed to ensure that they draw out the expected levels of thinking and an assessment guide is developed for the assessment.

Implementation issues include ensuring that the student is not threatened by the task, and providing clear directions and adequate resources for the task. Also important is ensuring that classroom instruction addresses the capabilities required for the task and obtaining more than one sample of student behavior.

Discussion Questions_____

1. Designating the task of correcting subject–verb agreement and other syntax errors in a typescript as a performance assessment violates which of the essential criteria?

2. What are the factors that can influence the validity and reliability of story retelling?

3. Spandel (2001) suggested introducing the concept of performance dimensions in the classroom by asking students to brainstorm the characteristics of a good sandwich. What are some other ways to introduce performance dimensions?

4. A teacher and his sixth-grade class are discussing expressive writing. What dimensions might they develop?

5. What does the concept *opportunity to learn* mean in relation to performance assessment?

6. What are the major validity and reliability concerns in the implementation of performance assessments?

References_____

Arter, J., & McTighe, J. (2001). *Scoring rubrics in the classroom: Using performance criteria for assessing and improving student performance.* Thousand Oaks, CA: Corwin Press.

Bear, D., & Barrone, D. (1998). *Developing literacy: An integrated approach to assessment and instruction.* Boston: Houghton Mifflin.

Brookhart, S. (1993). Assessing student achievement with term papers and written reports. *Educational Measurement: Issues and Practice, 12*(1), 40–47.

Brown, H., & Cambourne, B. (1987). *Read and retell.* Portsmouth, NH: Heinemann.

Clay, M. (1966). Emergent reading behavior. Unpublished doctoral dissertation. Aukland, New Zealand: University of Aukland.

Cooper, C. (1999). What we know about genres, and how it can help us assign and evaluate writing. In C. Cooper & L. Odell (Eds.), *Evaluating writing: The role of teachers' knowledge about text* (pp. 23–52). Urbana, IL: National Council of Teachers of English.

Delain, M. (1999). Equity and performance-based assessment: An insider's view. In S. J. Barrentine (Ed.), *Reading assessment: Principles and practices for elementary teachers* (pp. 109–112). Newark, DE: International Reading Association.

Goodman, Y., Watson, D., & Burke, C. (1987). *Reading miscue inventory.* New York: Richard C. Owen.

Harste, J. C., Short, K. G., & Burke, C. (1988). *Creating classrooms for authors.* Portsmouth, NH: Heinemann.

Hiebert, E. (1991). Teacher-based assessment of literacy learning. In J. Flood, J. M., Jensen, D. Lapp, & J. R. Squire (Eds.), *Handbook of research on teaching the language arts* (pp. 510–520). New York: Macmillan.

Irwin, P. A., & Mitchell, J. N. (1983). A procedure for assessing the richness of retellings. *Journal of Reading, 26,* 391–396.

Kuhs, T. M., Johnson, R. L., Agruso, S., & Monrad, D. (2001). *Put to the test: Tools and techniques for classroom assessment.* Portsmouth, NH: Heinemann.

Lamme, L., & Hysmith, C. (1991). One school's adventure into portfolio assessment. *Language Arts, 68*(8), 629–640.

Leslie, L. (1993). A developmental-interactive approach to reading assessment. *Reading and Writing Quarterly: Overcoming Learning Difficulties, 9,* 5–30.

Martlew, M. (1988). Children's oral and written language. In A. D. Pellegrini (Ed.), *Psychological bases for early education* (pp. 71–121). New York: John Wiley & Sons.

Mason, J. M., & Stewart, J. P. (1990). Emergent literacy assessment for instructional use in kindergarten. In L. M. Morrow & J. K. Smith (Eds.), *Assessment for instruction in early literacy* (pp. 155–175). Englewood Cliffs, NJ: Prentice Hall.

Messick, S. (1994). The interplay of evidence and consequences in the validation of performance assessments. *Educational Researcher, 23*(2), 13–22.

Morrow, L. M. (1989). *Literacy development in the early years: Helping children read and write.* Englewood Cliffs, NJ: Prentice Hall.

Morrow, L. M. (1990). Assessing children's understanding of story through their construction and reconstruction of narrative. In L. M. Morrow & J. K. Smith (Eds.), *Assessment for instruction in early literacy* (pp. 110–134). Englewood Cliffs, NJ: Prentice Hall.

Morrow, L. M., Gambrell, L., Kapinus, B., Koskinon, P., Marshall, N., & Mitchell, J. (1986). Retelling: A strategy for reading instruction and assessment. In J. A. Niles & R. V. Lalik (Eds.), *Solving problems in literacy: Learners, teachers, and researchers.* Thirty-fifth yearbook of the National Reading Conference. Rochester, NY: National Reading Conference.

Myers, M., & Spalding, E. (1997). *Standards exemplar series: Assessing student performance grades K–5.* Urbana, IL: National Council of Teachers of English.

Nitko, A. (1996). *Educational assessment of students* (2nd ed.). Englewood Cliffs, NJ: Prentice Hall.

Pearson, P. D., DeStefano, S., & Garcia, E. (1998). Ten dilemmas of performance assessment. In C. Harrison & T. Salinger (Eds.), *Assessing Reading 1: Theory and practice* (pp. 21–49). New York: Routledge.

Spandel, V. (2001). *Creating writers* (3rd ed.). Reading, MA: Addison-Wesley Longman.

Stiggins, R. (1987). Design and development of performance assessments. *Educational Measurement: Issues and practices, 6*(3), 33–42.

Sulzby, E. (1985). Children's emergent reading of favorite storybooks: A developmental study. *Reading Research Quarterly, 20*(4), 458–481.

Sulzby, E. (1990). Assessment of emergent writing and children's language while writing. In L. M. Morrow & J. K. Smith (Eds.), *Assessment for instruction in early literacy* (pp. 83–109). Englewood Cliffs, NJ: Prentice Hall.

Teale, W. H. (1988). Developmentally appropriate assessment of reading and writing in the early childhood classroom. *Elementary School Journal, 89,* 173–183.

Teale, W. H. (1990). The promise and challenge of informal assessment in early literacy. In L. M. Morrow & J. K. Smith (Eds.), *Assessment for instruction in early literacy* (pp. 45–61). Englewood Cliffs, NJ: Prentice Hall.

Teale, W. , Hiebert, E., & Chittenden, E. (1987). Assessing young children's literacy development. *Reading Teacher, 40,* 772–777.

Tompkins, G. (1994). *Teaching writing: Balancing process and product* (2nd ed.). Englewood Cliffs, NJ: Prentice Hall.

Wiggins, G. (1993). Assessment: Authenticity, context, and validity. *Phi Delta Kappan, 75*(3), 200–208, 210–214.

Wiggins, G., & McTighe, J. (1998). *Understanding by design.* Alexandria, VA: Association for Supervision and Curriculum Development.

Wolcott, W., (with Legg, S.) (1998). *An overview of writing assessment: Theory, research, and practice.* Urbana, IL: National Council of Teachers of English.

Wolf, D., LeMahieu, P., & Eresh, J. (1992). Good measure: Assessment as a tool of reform. *Educational Leadership,* 8–13.

6

Guides for Scoring Student Performances

> If you do not have a clear sense of the key dimensions of sound performance—
> a vision of poor and outstanding performance—you can neither teach students to
> perform nor evaluate their performance.
>
> —Stiggins, 1987, p. 37

One teacher, during her planning period, is evaluating audiotapes of children's story retellings. Using the holistic assessment guide in Table 5.4, she notes that Ron states the major events with supporting details. However, he does not mention the main character's primary goal, so she assigns a "3" to his retelling. Dale, in contrast, verbally sketches only an outline of the story with few supporting details, and she assigns a "2" rating. Another teacher, listening to children's retellings in the classroom, uses the scoring guide in Figure 5.1. She checks that Anne identifies "place" in the setting, names the major characters, two of the three major events, and the resolution of the story. However, other details of the setting, the two minor characters and the theme are missing. She makes a note to determine if Anne recalled these elements and did not include them or did not recall these aspects of the story.

As illustrated, the assessment guide, which consists of the key dimensions of the performance task, assists the teacher in evaluating students' performances on major tasks in a consistent manner. Discussed in this chapter are the three major types of assessment guides, guidelines for development, and issues in design and use.

Overview

The three major types of assessment guides are checklists, analytic rubrics, and holistic rubrics. In addition to evaluating student progress, all three types (1) provide information about student strengths and areas needing improvement, (2) assist in planning instruction, and (3) provide information for communicating with parents. However, they differ in the amount of detail they provide. Specifically, rubrics are designed to address the varying degrees of performance associated with a complex task (Airasian, 2000; Arter & McTighe, 2001; Spandel, 2001; Wolcott, 1998), whereas checklists simply indicate the presence or absence of key elements in a performance.

Checklists

As the name indicates, a checklist is a set of concrete, observable behaviors or task dimensions that are organized in a logical sequence. In addition to documenting the presence of important dimensions of a performance task, checklists, on occasion, may illustrate major milestones in a broad area of performance. The checklist illustrating the forms of children's emergent writing in Table 3.1 is an example. It documents changes in children's prewriting forms for several months.

Checklists for performance assessments list the key dimensions of the particular task. The teacher indicates the presence of observed dimensions by placing a check in the appropriate blank. On occasion, points also may be assigned. In the checklist for retellings in Figure 5.1, the child earns one point for each of the essential dimensions.

In addition to assisting the teacher, checklists can communicate classroom expectations to students. Examples are the checklists for point-of-view essays (Figure 6.1) and story writing (Figure 6.2). Of importance in Figure 6.2 is that the language is personalized for the second-graders and is easy for them to use as they review their work. Also, children use the checklist in Figure 6.2 as they review their work. Therefore, it includes some personal reminders in addition to explicit characteristics of the story. Examples are "Before writing, I thought about my story" and "I read my story to myself."

An advantage of checklists is that they are easy to construct and use. A limitation is that, unless carefully constructed, they may omit important dimensions or focus on trivial behaviors. A second limitation is that they do not differentiate levels of quality. The checklist for point-of-view essays, for example, does not indicate how well the student supports her position with statements of authorities. Further, the reasons the student provided for taking a position cannot be evaluated with the checklist.

FIGURE 6.1   *Checklist for Point-of-View Essays*

_____	Asserts a clear position on the issue
_____	Provides specific reasons for taking the position
_____	Supports position with personal experiences
_____	Supports position with statements of authorities
_____	References opposing views
_____	Sequences the argument in a logical step-by-step way

Summarized from Cooper (1999)

FIGURE 6.2   *Writer's Checklist for Second-Grade Students in Philadelphia Public Schools*

_____	Before writing, I thought about my story.
_____	I have a good title.
_____	My story has a good beginning.
_____	The sentences are in the right order to make sense.
_____	Each sentence begins with a capital letter.
_____	Each sentence has a punctuation mark at the end.
_____	People and place names have capital letters.
_____	I spelled the words correctly.
_____	My handwriting is legible.
_____	I asked to check my story.
_____	I read my story to myself.
_____	I fixed my story.

Analytic Rubrics

An analytic rubric may be viewed as a checklist in which a scale representing levels of performance and descriptors is attached to each dimension. They are appropriate when the quality of each dimension of a task is to be recorded. An example is the following dimension from the checklist for point-of-view essays.

Supports position with statements of authorities

0	1	2
No supporting statements	One or two brief statements	Two or more statements with clear links to the main thesis

As indicated in Figure 6.3, a complete analytic rubric consists of a scale and descriptors for each dimension. Higher numbers on the scale indicate higher qualities of the performance. Also important is that the descriptor associated with each numerical rating clarifies the meaning. In evaluating students' narratives, the teacher reviews student responses for each dimension and selects one of the numbers on the associated scale.

Figure 6.4 illustrates an analytic rubric for scoring the informational reports of middle school students. In this example, the scales are 0 to 2 or 0 to 3. In other words, the number of meaningful levels of quality indicates the range of the scale. For example, the levels for the title are none (0), attempted title (1), and a title that reflects the central idea of the paper (2).

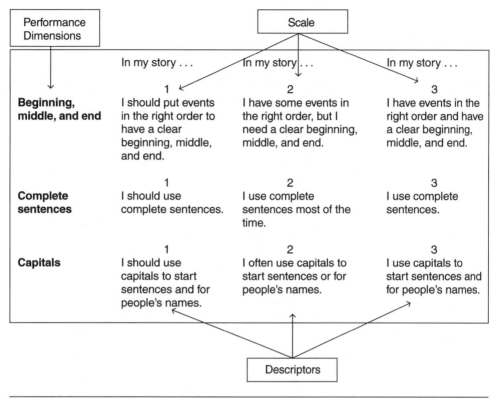

FIGURE 6.3   *Example of the Performance Dimensions, Scale, and Descriptors in an Analytic Rubric for Evaluating Third-Grade Narratives*

Figure 6.4 also illustrates the situation in which the dimensions of the task are not of equal importance. In such cases, weights are assigned to reflect the relative importance of each dimension. In this example, the title, introduction, conclusion, and neatness are less important, and each is weighted "3." In contrast, central idea is weighted "8" and supporting paragraphs are weighted "9." The total possible score for this task is 100 points. A student's work is evaluated by multiplying the rating assigned to each dimension by the respective weight and summing the weighted dimension scores.

A strength of analytic rubrics is the specific feedback provided to students. However, compared to holistic rubrics, analytic rubrics require additional time to review student work. The reason is that a separate decision must be made about each dimension in the analytic rubric.

Holistic Rubrics

In contrast to analytic rubrics, holistic rubrics evaluate a student's complex performance on a single scale. In the situation described at the beginning of this chapter, Dale's skeletal retelling of a story receives a "2," and Ron's more complex retelling receives a "3." In

FIGURE 6.4 *Example of the Dimensions, Scales, and Descriptors for an Analytic Rubric to Assess Informational Reports in Middle School*

Student Name: Meagan R   Date: February 18

Dimensions	Rating Scales				Weights	Scores
Title	0 No title.	1 Title attempted, but it does not summarize the central idea.	2 Title summarizes the central idea.		3	
Introduction	0 No introduction.	1 Introduction should be more interesting, and it should lead more directly to the central idea.	2 Introduction should be more interesting, or it should lead more directly to the central idea.	3 Interesting introduction that leads to the central idea.	3	
Central Idea	0 No central idea stated.	1 Central idea is unclear.	2 A clear central idea is stated.		8	
Supporting Paragraphs	0 No supporting paragraphs.	1 Paragraphs should provide details to support a central idea.	2 Paragraphs provide some details to support a central idea.	3 Paragraphs provide sufficient details to support a central idea.	9	
Conclusion	0 No conclusion attempted.	1 Conclusion does not summarize or bring closure.	2 Conclusion summarizes the paper or brings closure.	3 Conclusion summarizes and brings closure.	3	
Content	0 Content lacks accuracy.	1 Content contains some inaccuracies.	2 Content demonstrates accuracy.		4	
Style	0 No attempt to establish style.	1 An attempt was made to establish style by limited use of vivid vocabulary or varied sentence structure.	2 An attempt was made to establish style by limited use of vivid vocabulary and varied sentence structure.	3 Style is established by using vivid vocabulary and varied sentence structure.	4	

FIGURE 6.4 *Continued*

Student Name: Meagan R   Date: February 18

Dimensions	Rating Scales				Weights	Scores
Conventions: spelling, capitalization, punctuation, grammar, and sentence formation	0 The conventions of standard English are not applied and the errors interfere with the writer's meaning.	1 The conventions of standard English are applied in few instances and the errors interfere with the writer's meaning.	2 The conventions of standard English are applied some of the time; however, in some instances errors interfere with the writer's meaning.	3 The conventions of standard English are applied most of the time and errors do not interfere with the writer's meaning.	2	
List of Sources	0 No list of sources provided.	1 A list of sources provided that contains some of the required information.	2 A list of sources is provided that contains all the required information.		2	
Neatness	0 Format does not demonstrate neatness and attractiveness.	1 Format demonstrates neatness and attractiveness.			3	

other words, a holistic rubric provides only a summary evaluation of the student's overall proficiency.

Table 6.1 illustrates a holistic rubric developed from the dimensions of the analytic rubric in Figure 6.3. A teacher's decision to assign a performance level of 1, 2, or 3 to a student's narrative involves consideration of the dimensions "beginning, middle, and end," "capitals," and "complete sentences" concurrently. The closest match between the descriptors and the teacher's assessment of the narrative determines the performance level assigned to a paper.

Advocates of holistic scoring maintain that this form of scoring captures the interrelationships of all the dimensions of a performance. In using the holistic rubric, the premise is that the whole is greater than the sum of its parts. Describing the use of a holistic rubric to score students' retellings, Irwin and Mitchell (1983) wrote:

> . . . a retelling could be likened to a tapestry which, while composed of many different colored strands, can be properly viewed and appreciated only in its totality. Examination of any given section of tapestry yields only an accumulation of the components. Its richness—its essence—the very qualities which define it as a tapestry—must be experienced in terms of its total impression. (p. 393)

TABLE 6.1 *Example of a Holistic Rubric to Evaluate Narrative Writing of Third-Grade Students*

Level	Performance Descriptors
3	I have events in the right order and my story has a clear beginning, middle, and end. I use complete sentences in my story. I use capitals to start sentences and for people's names.
2	I have some events in the right order, but my story needs a clear beginning, middle, and end. I use complete sentences most of the time. I often use capitals to start sentences or for people's names.
1	I should put events in the right order to have a clear beginning, middle, and end for my story. I should use complete sentences in my story. I should use capitals to start sentences and for people's names.

However, a review of the rubric in Figure 6.5 reveals the tension between the ideal of a holistic rubric and practical applications. Used to score student narratives in the National Assessment of Education Progress (NAEP) (Greenwald, Persky, Campbell, & Mazzeo, 1999), the dimensions in the rubric are not interwoven at each score level, but presented as distinct characteristics.

One weakness of holistic rubrics is that they do not provide feedback to students on their specific strengths and the features of the performance that need improvement. Further, students who are struggling may become discouraged with a summary score that does not meet expectations. In the earlier example, Dale is likely to focus on the position of his score of 2 in the 4-point holistic scale. The positive feature, which is that he related a coherent sequence of events, is unlikely to be noticed. In contrast, an analytic scale would report a high score for relating the major ideas. In other words, the occasional positive mark on a checklist or a high rating on an analytic scale can provide some good news in addition to specific areas of challenge.

A second weakness is the difficulty in using holistic rating scales to plan instruction. Further analyses may be required to identify the specific performance dimensions that should be addressed in instruction.

Summary

Checklists and rubrics reflect the important criteria or dimensions that frame a teacher's review of a student performance on a complex task or a product. A checklist is a set of the key dimensions of a task and the teacher typically records the presence of observed dimensions. Analytic rubrics accompany each dimension with a scale and associated descriptors that represent the levels of performance. Holistic rubrics, in contrast, report performance on a single continuum. Levels of the dimensions are combined to reflect an overall performance, and the teacher considers all dimensions concurrently when determining a student's score.

Advantages of checklists are the ease of construction and use. A disadvantage is that they do not indicate quality of performance for the dimensions. In contrast, an advantage of

FIGURE 6.5   *Excerpts from Grade 8 Narrative Scoring Guide for the NAEP Writing Assessment*

6   Excellent Response

- Tells a clear story that is well developed and shaped with well-chosen details across the response
- Is well organized with strong transitions
- Sustains variety in sentence structure and exhibits good word choice
- Errors in grammar, spelling, and punctuation are few and do not interfere with understanding

5   Skillful Response

- Tells a clear story that is developed and shaped with details in parts of the response
- Is clearly organized, but may lack some transitions and/or have occasional lapses in continuity
- Exhibits some variety in sentence structure and some good word choices
- Errors in grammar, spelling, and punctuation do not interfere with understanding

$$\vdots$$

2   Insufficient Response (may be characterized by one or more of the following):

- Attempts to tell a story, but the attempt may be a fragment and/or very undeveloped
- Is very disorganized throughout the response OR too brief to detect organization
- Minimal control over sentence boundaries and sentence structure; word choice may often be inaccurate
- Errors in grammar or usage (such as missing words or incorrect word use or word order), spelling, and punctuation interfere with understanding in much of the response

1   Unsatisfactory Response (may be characterized by one or more of the following):

- Responds to prompt, but provides little or no coherent content OR merely paraphrases the prompt
- Has no apparent organization OR consists of a single statement
- Minimal or no control over sentence boundaries and sentence structure; word choice may be inaccurate in much or all of the response
- A multiplicity of errors in grammar or usage (such as missing words or incorrect word use or word order), spelling, and punctuation severely impedes understanding across the response

Greenwald, E., Persky, H., Campbell, J., & Mazzeo, J. (1999). *The NAEP 1998 Writing Report Card for the Nation and the States* (NCES 1999-462) Washington, DC: U.S. Government Printing Office.

analytic rubrics is the detailed information they provide. However, disadvantages include the time to construct and use them. Holistic rubrics, which focus on the totality of the performance, require less time to use than analytic rubrics. However, they are less useful in providing specific feedback to students and in planning instruction. The holistic score does not provide information to students about specific areas of strengths and weaknesses.

Of the three types of assessment guides, the checklist is likely the easiest for students to use in planning or reviewing their work. Holistic rubrics, because they combine several criteria in the description of each level, are less effective as a guide for student planning or review.

Guidelines for Development

Discussed in this section are the preliminary planning decisions and the steps in constructing checklists and analytic and holistic rubrics.

Preliminary Decisions

The initial decision, discussed in Chapter 5, is to consider the consistency of the performance dimensions with the nature of the task and the task directions. The other preliminary decisions are selecting a sequence for the dimensions and the type of assessment guide.

Sequencing the Dimensions.   The performance dimensions should be sequenced in a logical order (chronological, structural, or from general to specific). When the dimensions are substeps of a procedure, they are listed in the order that they are performed (chronological). An example is a search on the Internet. The dimensions are (1) generating search words, (2) launching the Internet program, (3) selecting a search engine, (4) initiating the search (entering the key search words and clicking the search button), (5) reviewing the selections, and (6) printing relevant materials (Kuhs, Johnson, Agruso, & Monrad, 2001).

In contrast, the dimensions of written products, such as reports and essays, may be arranged in a structural format or from general to specific. The structural format corresponds to the location in the document. As indicated in Figure 6.4, the sequence for an informational report is title, introduction, central idea, and supporting paragraphs, followed by particular features of the writing. An arrangement of dimensions from general to specific is most likely to be used when the dimensions are intrinsic characteristics of the performance. An example in writing is the set of dimensions referred to as organization, voice, word choice, sentence fluency, and conventions (Spandel, 2001).

Selecting the Type of Assessment Guide.   Two questions can assist the teacher in choosing the type of assessment guide. The first is, Which type of guide will be most beneficial for my students? Important in answering this question is that the guide should be fairly easy for the students to understand, and provide them with information as they complete the task. Following the assessment, the guide also should inform students of their strengths and weaknesses.

Central to the potential benefits of an assessment guide for students is their understanding of the information. Younger students, for example, are likely to understand a checklist, whereas older students can more readily work with a holistic or analytic rubric. For children, the amount of information should not be overwhelming, so a checklist may suffice. For older students, analytic and holistic rubrics provide additional descriptions that may clarify the dimensions for them. Finally, checklists and analytic rubrics provide explicit feedback on the particular dimensions, whereas the holistic rubric does not. If a holistic rubric is to be used, a teacher's notes that accompany the scale or a conference with the student can clarify the student's strengths and weaknesses.

The second question is What is the purpose of the guide? For example, one purpose is to provide information for further instruction. In this case, either a checklist or analytic rubric may be selected. That is, the blending of levels of performance in the composite score of the holistic rubric is less useful for identifying specific problems.

Also, there are times when a rubric is not needed. In the preliminary stages of writing, for example, the use of a detailed rubric can be self-defeating. Thus, students, particularly children, may use a checklist initially to review their work. As the task becomes more meaningful for students, and they become comfortable with the task, a more detailed rubric may be introduced.

Constructing Assessment Guides

Discussed in this section are the basic steps in constructing each of the types of assessment guides, the selection of verbal descriptors for analytic and holistic rubrics, and the identification of weights for analytic rubrics.

Basic Steps in Construction.   To construct a checklist, the teacher simply lists the dimensions critical to a performance with a space beside each (see Figure 6.1). Each dimension should be a clear description of a component to the task. For example, in the checklist for point-of-view essays (Figure 6.1), the dimensions include asserting a clear position on an issue and providing specific reasons for taking the position.

In contrast to checklists, analytic and holistic rubrics require the identification of levels of performance and the assignment of verbal descriptors and numbers to the levels. Construction of an analytic scale requires the review of each dimension in turn, determining the levels of performance that clearly can be differentiated for that dimension, and clarifying the meaning of each. The teacher begins the process by writing a brief description of an exemplary response for the first dimension. For example, an exemplary response for the dimension of style in Figure 6.4 states that the student uses vivid vocabulary and varied sentence structure. The next step is to write descriptors for the less-proficient performance levels for that dimension. For style, lower levels of the continuum refer to the limited use of varied vocabulary and/or varied sentence structure. This process is then repeated for each of the other dimensions.

Important is to identify meaningful levels that can be differentiated, not to establish the same number of levels across dimensions. For example, the analytic scale for an informational report (Figure 6.4) uses three levels for "central idea," and four levels to differentiate the quality of conclusions in the report. The final step is to assign a rating to each descriptor. The ratings for style, for example, range from 0 to 3.

The construction of a holistic rubric, in contrast, proceeds differently. Here, the task is to combine aspects of the dimensions into composite levels of performance. Each level in the NAEP writing rubric (Figure 6.5), for example, combines aspects of clarity, organization, variety in sentence structure and word choice, and conventions. The lowest level of the rubric, level 1, depicts a response that has little or no coherent content, lacks organization, reflects minimal control of sentence structure, and includes many mechanical errors that impede understanding. Level 5, in contrast, refers to a response that clearly tells a story, but the organization may lack transitions and/or well-established continuity, the sentence structure and word choices reflect some variety and appropriateness, and the mechanical errors do not impede understanding. In other words, the same dimensions are addressed in all the levels (Kuhs et al., 2001).

The first step in constructing a holistic rubric is to review the dimensions and write an exemplary response that reflects the entire set. The teacher then determines the number of levels that can differentiate a range of performance from very basic attempts to advanced understanding or achievement. Then a description that incorporates all the dimensions is written for each performance level. The final step is the assignment of numbers, categorical labels, or both to the descriptions. The Kentucky statewide assessment, for example, uses the categories of Novice, Apprentice, Proficient, and Distinguished (Strong & Sexton, 1996). The NAEP rubric uses both numbers and labels.

Selection of Verbal Descriptors in Analytic and Holistic Rubrics. A common consideration in both analytic and holistic rubrics is the identification of verbal descriptors for either the specific levels for each dimension (analytic rubric) or the composite levels in a continuum (holistic rubric). As indicated in Figure 6.6, one issue is whether the levels of performance should be described in quantitative and/or qualitative terms. When a quantitative differentiation is the focus, descriptors should address frequency, intensity, or number. For example, in a debate, the frequency with which students refute the arguments of the opposing team may be of interest. As shown in Table 6.2, a teacher who identifies frequency (a quantitative measure) as most important may use the terms "often," "occasionally," and "rarely" to distinguish between performance levels.

In other instances, a teacher may emphasize the qualitative aspects of a performance to differentiate between levels of student responses. In the debate example, instead of frequency of the refutations, the teacher may be concerned about quality and whether the team's rebuttals were generally "appropriate" or "irrelevant." A teacher may use these terms to describe two ends of the performance spectrum: "Students delivered appropriate rebuttals to opponents' arguments" and "Students' responses to their opponents' arguments were irrelevant." To define the middle of the performance spectrum, a teacher may blend the quantitative and qualitative aspects of the performance. In the case of the debate,

---

FIGURE 6.6 *Considerations in Selecting Verbal Descriptors*

1. Determine whether the particular dimension (analytic rubric) or level of composite performance (holistic rubric) is to be evaluated quantitatively and/or qualitatively.
2. Avoid inappropriate descriptors.
3. Review potential descriptors for appropriateness for the age level of the students.
4. Consider phrasing deficiencies or poor performance in language that identifies areas of improvement.
5. Identify potential extraneous dimensions that may influence the evaluation of student capabilities.

TABLE 6.2   *Examples of Quantitative and Qualitative Aspects of a Performance That Distinguish Levels in Rubrics*

Quantitative	
all/many/some/none	most/few
consistently/inconsistently	often/occasionally/rarely/never
extensive/limited	present/absent

Qualitative	
accurate/inaccurate	natural/stiff
active/passive	original/unique/clichéd/overused
appropriate/irrelevant	precise/vague
clear/logical/confused	specific/common/superficial
correct/incorrect	supporting/appropriate/irrelevant
fluent/smooth/choppy/monotonous	thorough/limited/sufficient/superficial
focused/broad	varied/repetitive

a descriptor may be "Students generally delivered appropriate rebuttals; however, sometimes responses to the opponents' arguments were irrelevant."

Also important, as indicated in Figure 6.6, is to avoid the use of vague descriptors, such as "poor," "weak," "good," "superior," or "excellent." Such descriptors are actually labels that provide little information about the qualities of the performance that contributed to the rating. Suppose, for example, the analytic scoring guide for informational reports had simply used the terms "missing," "weak," "good," and "superior" as descriptors. Students who received a "weak" rating would not know that the expectations for an introduction included an interesting opening that leads directly to the central idea.

Third is to review potential descriptors for age appropriateness. An example is the variations in the language for the dimensions of an informational report. For example, depending on the age of the students, teachers may use the term "main idea," "central idea," or "thesis statement" to indicate the statement that encapsulates the purpose of the paper. In middle school, the expectation may be that "A clear central idea is stated." In contrast, in high school, the expectation may be more detailed. The description may state "Thesis statement establishes the topic and organization of the paper. The language is clear and precise."

Age-appropriate language is essential when students are to use a rubric to assess their own work. The descriptors in the checklist in Figure 6.2 are examples written from the student's perspective in language that is appropriate for young children.

Fourth, particularly when developing rubrics for use in the early grades, consider phrasing the descriptors to suggest improvements instead of focusing on deficiencies (Kuhs et al., 2001). Students may be more receptive to language that suggests aspects of performance that may be improved rather than stating deficiencies. An example is the descriptor at the lowest level of the dimension "beginning, middle, and end" in the analytic rubric for narrative writing (Figure 6.3). The descriptor is "I should put events in the right order to have a clear beginning, middle, and end" instead of "I do not get events in the right order."

Finally, features that are extraneous to the critical dimensions can have an unintended influence on perceptions of student performance. Examples are handwriting (Chase 1968, 1979, 1986; Markham, 1976) and essay length (Breland & Jones, 1984; Grobe, 1981; Stewart & Grobe, 1979). A possible solution in these instances is to note on the teacher version of the assessment guide that these factors should not influence scores. This reminder makes it less likely that handwriting or essay length will unduly affect a student's score.

Identification of Weights in Analytic Rubrics.   A final issue in the development of an analytic rubric is whether the dimensions should be weighted (Brookhart, 1993). The weight for a dimension should be determined by its importance to the performance. For example, in a report, the central idea and supporting paragraphs are crucial elements (see Figure 6.4). Accordingly, these dimensions receive higher weights of 8 and 9, respectively, than the more peripheral dimension of "neatness," which receives a weight of only 3. Thus, the qualities that primarily affect a teacher's judgments about her students' ability to compose are those of thesis statements and supporting paragraphs. To the extent that the dimensions of central idea and supporting paragraphs were the focus of instruction and are crucial to composition, then the weightings result in scores that support accurate (valid) decisions about instruction and student performance.

Other factors that influence perceptions of writing quality include language mechanics (Chase, 1983; Marshall, 1967; Rafoth & Rubin, 1984; Scannel & Marshall, 1966) and spelling (Grobe, 1981; Stewart & Grobe, 1979). To appropriately consider these influences, a teacher should weight the scoring dimensions of language mechanics and spelling relative to their importance to the task. To continue the example of the rubric for informational reports, establishing a central idea and developing supporting paragraphs are critical dimensions for this task. They should be weighted most heavily in a rubric, whereas conventions should receive less weight in determining a final score.

On occasion, teachers use weights so that the points for a task may sum to 100. To design such a rubric, a teacher first considers the number of points that each dimension should contribute toward the 100 points. For example, in designing the rubric for informational reports, 27 points were assigned to the performance dimension of "supporting paragraphs." Then the highest possible rating for this dimension, 3, is multiplied by the appropriate weight, 9, to equal 27. Similarly, the remaining dimensions were reviewed to determine the portion of the 100 points to assign to each and the weight required to attain that number.

Weighting is not feasible for scales that include five or fewer dimensions. The reason is that some dimensions would be weighted 20 or higher out of 100 points. Such a procedure heavily penalizes students for even the slightest mistake. Another situation for which weights are inappropriate is in rubrics for young children because of the need to understand multiplication. However, simple integer-level weights, as illustrated in Figure 6.4, may be used with students who have mastered multiplication and understand the implications of weighted scores.

Summary

The first step in constructing an assessment guide is to arrange the identified dimensions in a logical order and select the type of guide to be developed. In contrast to checklists, which require only the inclusion of a space for documentation, analytic and holistic rubrics require the identification of levels of performance and verbal descriptors for the levels. To construct an analytic scale, the teacher reviews each dimension in turn, determining the appropriate number of levels, and selecting verbal descriptors for each. In contrast, to construct a holistic rubric, the teacher identifies broad levels of performance that address aspects of all the dimensions at each level.

A common consideration in the construction of analytic and holistic rubrics is the selection of verbal descriptors. Issues to be addressed in this process are whether the descriptors should be quantitative or qualitative, the avoidance of inappropriate descriptors, the use of age-appropriate language, whether to phrase deficiencies as areas that need improvement, and the identification of extraneous dimensions that may influence the teacher's evaluation.

An issue exclusive to analytic rubrics is whether the dimensions should be weighted in some way. Issues in the consideration of using weights are the need to assign greater importance to some dimensions of the task than others, and developing a rubric that sums to 100 points. However, weighting is not feasible for scales with five or fewer dimensions.

Issues in Design and Use

Three issues in the design and use of scoring guides are important in successful use in the classroom. They are (1) incorporating the language of checklists and rubrics into the classroom, (2) ensuring the accuracy of scoring, and (3) converting scores to grades.

Incorporating the Language of Scoring Guides into the Classroom

The potential of checklists and rubrics as learning tools for students can be achieved only if students understand their use and the role of performance dimensions. However, the term "performance dimension" is an abstraction and a complex concept for students to understand. Addressing this understanding is an important role for classroom instruction.

As discussed in Chapter 5, performance dimensions may be developed in discussions with students. However, this activity does not ensure that students can use them effectively. Particularly important is for the teacher to model their use and provide guided practice as students begin to use assessment guides to review their work. For example, the teacher may place an essay that the class had previously written as a group on a transparency on the overhead projector. She then talks through the steps in applying the guide to review the class essay. For those students who struggle with making the link between the dimensions in the guide and their own work, a teacher–student conference offers an additional opportunity to develop student understanding. The review of a student response with a checklist or rubric can focus the conference. Also, it is an additional illustration of the review process using the performance dimensions.

Another method for teaching the meaning of dimensions is for students to answer open-ended questions about their work and the performance dimensions. For example, if "style" were included as a dimension, responding to the questions shown in Figure 6.7 assists students to develop an understanding of this rather abstract dimension. The final step is for students to assign their work a rating based on their responses to the prior questions.

Providing visual reminders in the classroom environment also can assist students with their writing. For example, some teachers use posters to outline the stages of the writing process to help students incorporate those stages into their writing. Similarly, posters may illustrate performance dimensions relevant across reading or writing tasks, such as

FIGURE 6.7   *A Task to Develop Student Understanding of the Performance Dimension of "Style"*

Establishing Style

One of the qualities that we are developing in our writing is *style*. The questions below focus on the features of your historical fiction story that help to create a sense of style. Answer each question, then circle your rating for the "style" dimension.

1. Write at least three specific nouns that you used to help establish style in your story. Beside each specific noun list the general noun that you could have used (but wisely did not).

Specific noun	General noun
example: trout	fish

2. From your story give five examples of adjectives that describe nouns.

3. Write three action verbs that you used in your story.

4. List two examples of adverbs that describe verbs in your story.

5. We learned that writers use synonyms because reading the same word over and over again becomes boring. Give an example of a word and its synonym that you used in your historical fiction.

6. Write your most descriptive sentence.

7. Give one sentence from your story that has an introductory clause.

8. Think about your answers to the questions above and then use the scale below to rate your story for "style." Circle your rating.

Style	0	1	2	3
	No attempt to establish style.	An attempt to establish style by limited use of vivid vocabulary or varied sentence structure.	A better attempt to establish style by limited use of vivid vocabulary and varied sentence structure.	Style established by vivid vocabulary and varied sentence structure.

the dimensions outlined in the six-trait writing rubric. The poster may list a dimension, such as organization, and relevant statements. Examples include "My opening will hook you!" "I see just how all the parts fit together," "I know where I'm going," and "The ending really works!" (Arter & McTighe, 2001, p. 134). Used as instructional tools, these posters help students understand the concept of "performance dimensions" and apply those dimensions to their own work.

In summary, several activities can contribute to students' understanding of assessment guides. In addition to student collaboration in developing the dimensions, other activities are teacher modeling of their use followed by student practice, teacher–student conferences, open-ended questions related to the dimensions, and visual reminders in the classroom environment.

Scoring Student Performances

The importance of assessment guides is that they provide organization and clarity to the evaluation of student performance. However, even with the best of assessment guides, the teacher must guard against extraneous factors that can inappropriately influence the evaluation process. For example, if a teacher continues scoring student essays when she is fatigued, the likelihood of evaluating the last few essays more stringently is very high.

Two general guidelines are important in ensuring consistent evaluations. One, preparatory to evaluating student products, is to review the task directions and the assessment guide to align expectations with those communicated to the student. Second, during the scoring, revisit responses evaluated earlier to gauge the similarity of expectations across student responses.

In addition, some specific steps are needed to guard against other extraneous influences. One such influence is teacher knowledge of prior achievement that can inadvertently influence perceptions of a student's current performance. One example is the situation in which a student who typically writes very well may complete an essay that does not meet expectations. However, the teacher, on seeing the student's name on the paper, is prepared to read an above-average paper. The result, referred to as *halo effect,* is that difficulties or problems are not noticed, and the paper is scored more leniently than others in the class.

To avoid halo effect, a teacher may mask identities by asking older students to use student identification numbers, rather than names, on their papers. Younger students may write their names on the back of their papers or projects. Perhaps the most realistic method to control for this factor is to be aware of its influence and to remember to assign scores based on a match between the assessment guide and a student's performance on the task.

A similar situation can occur on essay questions in a test (Bracht, 1967, cited in Hopkins, 1998). That is, the student may write an exceptional answer to the first question, which establishes the mind-set in the teacher of above-average answers by the student on subsequent questions. To counter this problem, referred to as item-to-item carryover, the teacher first should evaluate question one for all the students in the class. Then, after a short break, he should evaluate question two for all the papers, and so on. Frequent reference to the assessment guide also will contribute to an appropriate evaluation.

Evaluating a set of answers in sequence or a stack of papers, however, can lead to the problem referred to as test-to-test carryover (Daly & Dickson-Markman, 1982; Hales

& Tokar, 1975; Hopkins, 1998; Hughes, Keeling, & Tuck, 1980). That is, after evaluating a series of exemplary responses, the teacher reads an essay answer or paper that meets the prestated expectations, but appears somewhat lackluster compared to the others. The tendency is for this response to be evaluated too stringently. To counter this tendency, the teacher should frequently refer to the scoring guide to determine if expectations are consistent with those expressed in the guide.

In sum, assessment guides provide organization and clarity that contribute to the consistency of teachers' evaluations of their students. However, assessment guides alone cannot control the extraneous factors that inappropriately influence the scoring of student performances. Essential in assuring consistent evaluations is teachers' awareness of extraneous influences in the scoring process and methods for eliminating those unwanted influences. Factors extraneous to the scoring of a student's current performance include the tendency to be influenced by a student's *past* performance in the class, the student's performance on a previous essay question on the same test, and the classmates' responses that immediately preceded the student's test. As discussed in this section, methods for controlling unwanted influences include reviewing the task directions and assessment guide in preparation for scoring, frequently referring to the assessment guide during scoring, and reviewing performances scored earlier to gauge the similarity of teacher expectations across student performances.

Converting Scores to Grades

Checklists and rubrics may be used to provide feedback to students to assist them in editing or revising their responses. At other times, a teacher may want to use a scoring guide to assign a grade to culminating projects or other performance tasks. Thus, the teacher will be faced with the issue of converting the information in the assessment guide to a grade. For checklists, the teacher may create a scale that associates the number of checks with a letter grade. For example, on the point-of-view essay (Figure 6.1), a teacher may require 6 checks for an A+ or A, 5 checks for a B+ or B, 4 checks for a C+ or C, and so on. The use of the plus (+) designation allows some flexibility for the teacher in deciding the level of performance reflected in the work.

The decision about the number of checks required for a grade should not be made arbitrarily. Instead, the teacher should review the performance dimensions and consider the number of dimensions the student must demonstrate to earn a particular grade. A task that is particularly demanding may require fewer checks to earn an A compared to the number required to earn an A on a less strenuous task. After the teacher has determined the number of checks for each grade, she should add a scale to the assessment guide that translates the number of checks to a grade. In assessing a student's point-of-view essay, the teacher completes the checklist, counts the number of checks, refers to the scale to determine the letter grade, decides whether to add the + designation, and then records the student's final grade (e.g., B+ or B) on the checklist.

In the case of analytic rubrics that use 100-point scales, no conversion is necessary if a teacher uses numerical grades. When letter grades are used, the rubric also should indicate the range of points associated with each grade. For example, 93 to 100 points may be an A, 85 to 92 a B, and so on.

Converting the ratings for analytic rubrics with few dimensions to grades can be achieved by defining a range of scores associated with each letter grade. For example, for the analytic rubric for third-grade narratives (Figure 6.3), a score of 8 may be required for an A on the task. That is, a narrative that receives an A is characterized by high levels of performance across the dimensions. One possible combination for an A requires that the student has events in the right order (a 3 rating), uses complete sentences most of the time (a 2 rating), and uses capitals to start sentences and for people's names (a 3 rating). The teacher then proceeds to determine the scores required for a B, a C, and so on. In this manner, a teacher may develop a scale that associates an A+ with 9 points, an A with 8 points, a B+ with 7, a B with 6 points, and so on. This scale should be added to the bottom of the rubric. If the rubric is shared with students as part of the task, then they know the critical dimensions of the performance and how they translate into grades.

In the case of holistic rubrics, the translation of a score to a grade may be achieved by associating each level of the rubric with a letter grade. To do so, a teacher considers the quality of performance that is described for each level to decide the appropriate letter grade (Arter & McTighe, 2001). In the holistic rubric for narratives written by second-grade students, the highest level may be associated with A or B, the middle level for C, and so on. The letter grade can be incorporated into the labels for the rubric (e.g., Advanced = A+ or A; Proficient = B+ or B) or a scale added to the bottom of the guide.

Several of the above methods result in letter grades; however, some students will want to know the translation of a letter grade into a numerical grade so that they can monitor their grade average. Letter grades from the rubrics can be converted to percentage grades that parallel those given on report cards (Arter & McTighe, 2001; Kuhs et al., 2001). One method to translate scores from assessment guides to numerical grades is shown in Table 6.3. Posting such a scale in the classroom communicates to students the meaning of the information in checklists and rubrics and helps them understand the method for converting the information into grades. The numerical grades can then be combined with grades from other assignments to calculate grades for report cards, a subject addressed in Chapter 10.

In summary, at some point a teacher may convert the information contained in a checklist or rubric to a grade. To convert checklist information to grades, the teacher

TABLE 6.3 *Example of a Poster to Translate Rubric Scores, Letter Grades, and Numerical Grades*

Rubric Score	Letter Grade	Numerical Grade
Advanced—4	A+	100
	A	96
Proficient—3	B+	92
	B	88
Basic—2	C+	84
	C	80

reviews the performance dimensions and determines the number of dimensions the student must demonstrate to earn a particular grade. Analytic rubrics are sometimes constructed on a 100-point scale in order to combine the score with other assignments for grading purposes. The teacher weights each dimension to determine the contribution of that dimension to the total of 100 points. In scoring, the students' earned points for each dimension are multiplied by the respective weight. In analytic rubrics without weighted dimensions, the teacher specifies the number of points for each grade. With holistic rubrics, the teacher associates each level of the rubric with a letter grade. A teacher should post a chart in the classroom that converts rubric scores and letter grades to numerical grades so that students can translate the former into the latter for purposes of averaging.

Discussion Questions

1. Identify the criteria you would include in an assessment guide to review a student production of a play that they have adapted from a historical fiction novel.

2. What features do checklists, analytic rubrics, and holistic rubrics have in common? What is a unique feature of each?

3. Which of the following would you use to document student contributions to the discussion about a novel in a literature circle—a checklist, analytic rubric, or holistic rubric? Would you use the information to provide student feedback, to assign grades, or to do both? Support your decisions.

4. What changes should be made to the analytic rubric for informational reports (Figure 6.4) to use it with elementary students?

5. How would you rephrase the language in the lowest level (1 Unsatisfactory Response) of the NAEP rubric in Figure 6.5 to suggest areas for improvement?

References

Airasian, P. (2000). *Assessment in the classroom: A concise approach.* Boston: McGraw-Hill.

Arter, J., & McTighe, J. (2001). *Scoring rubrics in the classroom: Using performance criteria for assessing and improving student performance.* Thousand Oaks, CA: Corwin Press.

Breland, H., & Jones, R. (1984). Perceptions of writing skills. *Written Communication, 1*(1), 101–109.

Brookhart, S. (1993). Assessing student achievement with term papers and written reports. *Educational Measurement: Issues and Practices, 12*(1), 40–47.

Chase, C. (1968). The impact of some obvious variables on essay test scores. *Journal of Educational Measurement, 5,* 315–318.

Chase, C. (1979). The impact of achievement expectations and handwriting quality on scoring essay tests. *Journal of Educational Measurement, 16,* 39–42.

Chase, C. (1983). Essay test scores and reading difficulty. *Journal of Educational Measurement, 20,* 293–297.

Chase, C. (1986). Essay test scoring: Interaction of relevant variables. *Journal of Educational Measurement, 23,* 33–41.

Cooper, C. (1999). What we know about genres, and how it can help us assign and evaluate writing. In C. Cooper & L. Odell (Eds.), *Evaluating writing: The role of teachers' knowledge about text and learning* (pp. 23–52). Urbana, IL: National Council of Teachers of English.

Daly, J., & Dickson-Markman, F. (1982). Contrast effects in evaluating essays. *Journal of Educational Measurement, 19*(4), 309–316.

Greenwald, E., Persky, H., Campbell, J., & Mazzeo, J. (1999). *The NAEP 1998 Writing Report Card for the Nation and the States* (NCES 1999-462) Washington, DC: U.S. Government Printing Office.

Grobe, C. (1981). Syntatic maturity, mechanics, and vocabulary as predictors of quality ratings. *Research in the Teaching of English, 15*(1), 75–85.

Hales, L., & Tokar, E. (1975). The effect of the quality of preceding responses on the grades assigned to subsequent responses to an essay question. *Journal of Educational Measurement, 12*(2), 115–117.

Hopkins, K. (1998). *Educational and psychological measurement and evaluation* (8th ed.). Needham Heights, MA: Allyn and Bacon.

Hughes, D., Keeling, B., & Tuck, B. (1980). The influence of context position and scoring method on essay scoring. *Journal of Educational Measurement, 17*, 131–135.

Irwin, P., & Mitchell, J. (1983). A procedure for assessing the richness of retellings. *Journal of Reading, 26*, 391–396.

Kuhs, T., Johnson, R., Agruso, S., & Monrad, D. (2001). *Put to the test: Tools and techniques for classroom assessment.* Portsmouth, NH: Heinemann.

Marshall, J. (1967). Composition errors and essay examination grades re-examined. *American Educational Research Journal, 4*, 375–385.

Markham, L. (1976). Influences of handwriting quality on teacher evaluation of written work. *American Educational Research Journal, 13*, 277–284.

Rafoth, B., & Rubin, D. (1984). The impact of content and mechanics on judgments of writing quality. *Written Communication, 1*(4), 446–458.

Scannell, D., & Marshall, J. (1966). The effect of selected composition errors on grades assigned to essay examinations. *American Educational Research Journal, 3*, 125–130.

Spandel, V. (2001). *Creating writers* (3rd ed.). Reading, MA: Addison-Wesley Longman.

Stewart, M., & Grobe, C. (1979). Syntatic maturity, mechanics, and vocabulary and teachers' quality ratings. *Research in the Teaching of English, 13*, 207–215.

Stiggins, R. (1987). Design and development of performance assessments. *Educational Measurement: Issues and Practices, 6*(3), 33–42.

Strong, S., & Sexton, L. (1996). Kentucky performance assessment of reading: Valid? *Contemporary Education, 67*(2), 102–106.

Wolcott, W. (with Legg, S.). (1998). *An overview of writing assessment: Theory, research, and practice.* Urbana, IL: National Council of Teachers of English.

7

Portfolio Assessment

How many times have you been asked by parents, friends, and relatives, "So, you teach preschool-aged children . . . what other than the ABCs and 123s do they learn?"

—Hanson & Gilkerson, 1999, p. 87

Prior chapters have discussed different types of assessments, including classroom observations, teacher questions, and performance assessments. In contrast, portfolios are meaningful collections of student work that are planned in advance to reflect identified learning goals.

Portfolios, which address the multifaceted nature of literacy development, can provide a comprehensive response to the question, "So, what do they learn?" In the preschool classroom, a child's portfolio may contain examples of his drawings, photos of him playing a character in a story, samples of his prewriting, and a teacher checklist that notes his socialization skills.

In contrast, Brian's portfolio in his sixth-grade writing class contains several drafts of an essay on the Civil War, a poem, a story about his brother, his journal in which he recorded his thoughts and ideas, and his written reflections on his progress as a writer. The essay drafts reflect Brian's increasing control over different aspects of composition. Together with the poem and the story, they indicate Brian's expressiveness and his sense of audience. Finally, his reflections indicate his awareness of the processes involved in writing, and his capabilities in self-evaluation.

Of importance is that the portfolio is not an "add-on" to other assessments, it is *the* assessment system. Also, as indicated by the preceding examples, portfolio entries will differ, depending on the purposes and goals for the portfolios. In the preschool classroom, the goal is to document the child's overall development. In Brian's classroom, the goal is to develop expressive writers who take responsibility for their learning.

Since the introduction of portfolios in the classroom in the 1980s, states and school systems have implemented them for other purposes. Therefore, in addition to the major characteristics of portfolios this chapter briefly describes the major types. Important issues for classroom teachers are developing the portfolio framework, attending to implementation, and developing student responsibility for learning. These topics also are discussed in this chapter as well as related assessment issues, including validity and reliability.

Overview

Formally defined, a portfolio is "a purposeful collection of student work that tells the story of the student's efforts, progress, or achievement in (a) given area(s)" (Arter, 1992, p. 1). Important for the classroom teacher is to understand the differences among the major types of portfolios and essential characteristics of portfolios for classroom use.

Five major types of portfolios that address somewhat different assessment purposes may be identified (Gredler, 1995). Summarized in Table 7.1, they are the original or learner-development portfolio, the growth portfolio, the documentation format, the showcase, and the evaluation or external portfolio. The first four formats are collections of student work that are directly linked to classroom activities. The external portfolio, in contrast, is a form of accountability. These portfolio types also range from most to least involvement of the student as a participant in either the selection of items for providing reflections in his or her work.

The learner-development portfolio originated in the mid-eighties through a funded project in imaginative writing in grades 6 through 12 (Camp, 1992). The new curriculum focused on assisting students to become "perceptive readers and engaged writers of poems and dialogues" (p. 63). Classroom activities emphasized learning and discovery, making choices, and taking risks (p. 61).

In the project curriculum, developing self-reflection was a major activity. As students drafted, revised, and reworked their pieces, they reflected "on the choices they had made as writers and the effect of those choices on the pieces written" (Camp, 1992, p. 63). Through dialogues with the teacher and the reflective process, students developed personal responsibility for their learning and became thoughtful evaluators of their own histories as learners (Wolf, 1989, p. 6). In this context, the portfolio served as an enabler in learning about the rich and complex processes of writing (Camp, 1992).

Currently, portfolios that incorporate a strong emphasis on learner reflections and developing self-awareness in students are referred to as diagnostic-reflective portfolios (Courtney & Abodeeb, 2001). A key characteristic is that the teacher develops diagnostic assessments of the student's learning and assists the student to develop goals. Students also learn to develop meaningful reflections on their progress in learning.

In contrast, the primary emphasis of the growth portfolio is to tell a story about the student's efforts. Poems, narratives, tape recordings of the student's review of books read, and/or tape recordings of class presentations are examples of student work that may be included. Students are involved in the selection of pieces for the portfolio, a process that occurs periodically during the year. Students' written reflections, while important, are not a central focus of the growth portfolio.

The documentation portfolio, unlike the other types, includes various kinds of information that may indicate student progress. Included are observations, checklists, anecdotal

TABLE 7.1 *An Overview of Types of Portfolios*

Type	Focus	Activities/Contents
Learner-development or diagnostic-reflective portfolio	Develop autonomous learners who develop standards and criteria for their writing and who become aware of the strategies and processes they use in learning (Camp, 1992)	Writing classroom is organized as a workshop in which students read their work aloud, listen to others' work, reflect on their own and others' writing, and engage in dialogues with the teacher. Portfolio entries change through the year as the student develops maturity and insight about his/her learning. Entries include writing samples, student reflections, and a "biography" of one finished piece, which is the story of the development of the piece.
Growth portfolio	Document student strengths and reflect growth over time	Portfolio entries are selected from the variety of classroom tasks. Analysis of earlier versus later work indicates growth. The contents may include journal entries, poems, narratives, tape recordings of class presentations, and student reflections. Teacher and student collaborate on the requirements for optional entries and discuss periodic student reviews of his or her progress.
Documentation portfolio	Provide a systematic ongoing record of student progress (Valencia & Calfee, 1991)	Portfolio entries include observations, checklists, anecdotal records, interviews, and classroom tests, as well as performance-based assessments (Valencia & Calfee, 1991, p. 337). Entries also may include periodic student reflections.
Showcase portfolio	Display a collection of student work assembled for a particular demonstration, such as a school fair	Portfolio contents include the student's best or favorite work. Entries are drawn from the student's class portfolio.
External portfolio	Gauge student progress to report to the general public or government agencies	Portfolio entries and dimensions for scoring typically are standardized; identified categories of student work (e.g., essay, letter to a pen pal) are not directly related to classroom activities. Cover sheets or other descriptions of the details of the assignment (e.g., assigned topic or free choice and number of revisions, if permitted) are included because reviewers may be unfamiliar with the context of the portfolio.

records, interviews, classroom tests, and performance-based assessments (Valencia & Calfee, 1991, p. 337). In one prekindergarten-to-grade-3 school, for example, the portfolio goes with the child from grade to grade (Lamme & Hysmith, 1991, p. 620). One difficulty with the documentation portfolio, however, is that it may contain an extensive amount of different kinds of information that may be difficult to evaluate.

Unlike the other types, a primary goal of both the showcase and the external portfolios is to speak to an audience beyond the classroom. The showcase portfolio, which reflects the student's best or favorite work, is prepared for gatherings such as school fairs and PTA meetings. The external portfolio, in contrast, is a form of external assessment. When prepared for school boards and other agencies, it functions as a summary of student performance.

Portfolios that go with the child to the next grade often are summarized in a brief descriptive or narrative report. However, evaluation of portfolios for external reporting typically relies on numerical scoring of the key dimensions. That is, either analytic or holistic rubrics, rather than descriptive or narrative summaries, are used. For example, levels 2, 4, and 6 on a 6-point holistic scale used by one group of teachers with writing portfolios are as follows:

> 6—work that is consistently high in quality; creativity or depth of content; work shows a real engagement by the writer. Writing is fluent, pieces are well developed, organization is appropriate for most selections, and work evidences a solid command of grammar and mechanics.
>
> 4—work is solid in quality; some content and some development; work shows some writer involvement. The organization is usually adequate; a few errors throughout.
>
> 2—work is generally weak; content is often shallow, and development is often weak. Writer involvement is negligible; grammar and mechanics errors throughout. Sentence structure is usually simplistic. (Wolcott, 1998, p. 54)

Developing the Portfolio Framework

The decision to implement portfolio assessment in the classroom may be made by individual teachers, the teachers in a particular subject area, a school, or a district. Typically, in the elementary and secondary grades, the decision is made by a group of teachers or a school. Because such a decision involves implementing a total system, planning is extremely important. Portfolio programs undertaken with careful thought beforehand are more meaningful than those established without this planning (Wolcott, 1998, p. 38).

Characteristics of Classroom Portfolios

In general, five characteristics differentiate classroom portfolios from folders that simply collect student work. Summarized in Table 7.2, they are (1) the dynamic nature of the system, (2) guidelines for selecting portfolio items, (3) the identification of the dimensions of the work that reflect student progress, (4) student participation in the selection of portfolio items, and (5) evidence of student reflection (Arter, 1992). A general purpose for these characteristics is to alter the view of students in which they value only particular

TABLE 7.2 *Characteristics of Classroom Portfolios*

Characteristic	Purpose
1. An ongoing assessment system; not a static collection	Allows the teacher to document the movement of children's growth (Hanson & Gilkerson, 1999)
2. Specification of guidelines for selecting portfolio contents	Build a shared understanding of expectations among teachers and students
3. Identification of criteria determining merit or student progress	Prevent the question, What does it all mean? after collecting a variety of student products
4. Participation of the student in selecting items for the portfolio	Develop student ownership in the assessment process
5. Evidence of student reflection	Develop self-aware learners who take responsibility for their learning

assessments administered at a particular point in time as evidence of achievement. In other words, portfolios illustrate the ongoing and varied nature of assessment and the relationship to learning.

As indicated in Table 7.2, the portfolio is not a static system. The class may be structured, for example, such that student work and reflections go into a "working portfolio." Then, periodically, the teacher and the student make selections for the final portfolio. However, this procedure does not mean that only the best pieces are selected. Instead, a range and variety of work are included. In one classroom, for example, in the last two weeks of each marking period (three times a year), children make their final selections for their portfolios from their ongoing work, and write their final reflections on their learning (Courtney & Abodeeb, 2001).

The importance of specifying guidelines for the selection of items for the portfolio and the identification of the essential dimensions that reflect student progress are twofold. One is to build a shared understanding about the nature of the tasks with students and with other teachers. Second, specifying the guidelines and the essential dimensions prevents the collection of a variety of student work in the absence of determining the meaning for summarizing student progress. Finally, involvement of students in the assessment process is a broad purpose for portfolio assessment. Student participation in selecting entries and learning to be self-reflective contributes to this goal.

In summary, five major types of portfolios may be identified that vary in the extent of student participation, the selection of portfolio items, and the centrality of student reflections on their learning. The five types are the learner-development (diagnostic-reflective), growth, documentation, showcase, and external assessment portfolios. In the classroom, five characteristics differentiate portfolios from other approaches to assessment. Included are the dynamic nature of the system and student involvement in the assessment process.

The purpose of establishing a framework is to reach agreement on important aspects of the portfolio without diminishing the individual voices of the teachers and students who are the participants (Paratore, 1995). Essential decisions include (1) identifying the purpose and goals for the portfolios, (2) identifying guidelines for the inclusion of items, and (3) identifying the key dimensions of portfolio items and the portfolio.

Identifying Purpose and Goals

Of importance is that portfolios should not be developed according to a rigid format. As indicated by the two examples at the beginning of this chapter, the exact nature of the portfolio system will differ, depending on the purpose, the curriculum goals, and the students.

Identification of the broad purpose is the first step for the grade-level teachers, the school, or the district (see Table 7.3). For example, among the possible purposes are to show growth or change over time, to trace the evolution of one or more projects/products, to document student strengths, to document achievement for alternative credit for coursework, and to show the process by which work is done as well as the final product (Arter & Spandel, 1992).

Without the identification of purpose, the portfolio is only a folder of student work. More important is that the nature of the purpose affects all the subsequent design decisions about the portfolio system (Arter, 1992, p. 1). For example, documenting student strengths implies the selection of portfolio pieces that illustrate particular capabilities. In contrast, showing growth over time requires demonstration of the evolvement of capabilities from the initial phases to emerging mastery.

Next is to identify the key goals for instruction that establish the focus for the portfolios (Johnson, Willeke, Bergman, & Steiner, 1997; Valencia, 1999). For example, the student learning goals selected by one group of teachers for the growth portfolios in the classroom were (1) interact with text to construct meaning, (2) choose to read a variety of materials, (3) communicate effectively through writing, and (4) engage in self-evaluative reflection (Valencia & Place, 1994, p. 139). Another group of teachers decided that the purpose for their use of portfolios was to evaluate children's performance in relationship to the district literacy benchmarks, which served as portfolio goals An example is composing oral or written summaries to support comprehension (Paratore, 1995, p. 72).

TABLE 7.3   *Steps in Developing the Portfolio Framework*

Steps	*Examples*
1. Identify (a) purpose and (b) goals for instruction	**a.** Show growth over time, to document student strengths **b.** Interact with text to construct meaning, develop expressiveness in one's writing
2. Select guidelines for the inclusion of items	Specify categories of items; identify core elements only and permit optional elements that reflect student interest
3. Identify the key dimensions of student work	Student identification of strengths and weaknesses (self-reflective summary); writing that reflects a sense of setting, character, and/or feelings, includes risk, engaging details, and a clear purpose (expressive writing)

Selecting Guidelines for Inclusion of Items

The second step is to develop guidelines for the inclusion of items in the portfolio. The portfolio can be highly structured in that the exact products can be specified. However, this approach is not recommended. To do so is to remove the option of student choice, which is an important aspect of the instructional impact of portfolios for students.

Guidelines may, for example, specify categories of items, such as an essay, a research report, a multimedia project, and so on (Arter & Spandel, 1992). This approach permits student choice on the particular work in each category. Some planning groups feel that some uniformity in portfolio contents from class to class and grade to grade is important. One group of teachers agreed to include a few core elements (a reading log, writing samples, and a monthly student self-reflection) and optional elements that reflect individual interests or unique performance (Paratore, 1995, p. 60). Two of the writing examples were (1) a piece in which students demonstrated their ability to describe an event, a character, or setting, and (2) a summary of their understanding of a reading selection.

In the area of writing, for example, in addition to some identified categories, teachers may specify the inclusion of the student's best work, a creative piece, and the student's favorite piece (Gillespie et al., 1996). The guidelines also may further specify that the portfolio may contain some student-selected, some teacher-selected, and some collaboratively selected materials (Gillespie et al., 1996).

Also of importance in planning the contents of a portfolio is to consider activities teachers have used during instruction to help students progress toward goals. An example is the use of story maps as part of the instruction on understanding story structure (Valencia, 1999). This same mechanism may be used to assess students' knowledge of plot after they complete a story (p. 115).

One danger to avoid in identifying items for the portfolio is an overreliance on written work. Some writing samples should, of course, be included. However, other methods also can provide evidence of growth. An example is audiotapes, particularly when the focus is organization of ideas, comparisons with other readings, and similar capabilities. In addition, too much dependence on writing can send the indirect message to students that growth can be measured only through writing (Gillespie et al., 1996, p. 488).

Identifying the Key Dimensions

Chapter 5 discussed the identification of essential dimensions or traits for the evaluation of performance assessments. Similar to that analysis, the identification of the key dimensions of the portfolio refers to the characteristics of the work that are valued. For example, in Brian's class, the identified dimension should reflect the goals of becoming an expressive writer and taking responsibility for one's learning. Portfolio dimensions may include (1) writing that (a) shows progress, (b) a sense of setting, character, and/or feelings, (c) establishes a clear purpose, and (d) includes rich, engaging details, and (2) student reflections that include self-identification of strengths and weaknesses. In another class, in which pursuing study of a student-selected topic is a goal, a key dimension may be evidence of developing expertise in that topic.

The purpose of identifying the key dimensions for evaluating the portfolio is twofold. One is to avoid the situation in which the teacher faces a stack of collected information and asks, What does it all mean? and How does this help me plan instruction?

Second, judgments are more likely to be fair, teachers are not vulnerable to criticisms of arbitrariness, and students are not left to guess the important requirements of tasks (Arter, 1992; Wiggins, 1988). Student familiarity with the dimensions also demystifies the evaluation process and can provide the foundation for students to develop their own self-reflection skills (Wolcott, 1998, p. 41).

In addition, the discussion and examination of dimensions by teachers engaged in implementing portfolios leads to developing "shared understandings of the important dimensions and characteristics of tasks" (Arter, 1992, p. 2). Valencia and Place (1994) noted that engaging in portfolio assessment required that they explore and, in some ways, alter their teaching. For example, if the purpose of the portfolio is to show growth over time, then the first question is What growth? (Gillespie et al., 1996). If a goal is to interact with text to construct meaning, what constitutes growth in this instance? Stated another way, identification of the dimensions answers the question, What do you want to learn about your students?

Summary

Developing a framework for the portfolio is essential so that the system will be meaningful for both teachers and students. The first step is to identify the general purpose and goals for the portfolio. A purpose, for example, may be to show growth over time, which requires demonstration of the evolvement of literacy capabilities. Goals, for example, may include learning to interact with text to construct meaning and choosing to read a variety of materials.

The second step is to develop guidelines for the inclusion of items in the portfolio. The guidelines may, for example, specify categories of items. Or, they may specify core items and allow optional elements that reflect individual interests or unique performance. One danger to avoid is an overreliance on written work, which sends the message that growth is not measured in other ways.

The third step is to identify the essential dimensions that indicate progress in learning. Examples are developing control over one's writing and developing expertise in a student-selected topic such as the Civil War battle at Gettysburg. This step is important to develop a shared understanding of tasks and their dimensions. Included in this step is the identification of the characteristics of a well-developed performance or product and the characteristics of a poor example.

Implementation Issues

Because the portfolio is the classroom assessment system, other questions should be addressed prior to implementation. They are the formats and procedures for key tasks and logistical issues.

Formats and Procedures for Key Tasks

The purpose of this discussion is twofold. First, in the case of core elements that are to appear in all portfolios, clarification of formats and procedures can ensure that all students have the same opportunities to develop their capabilities. For example, engaging in self-reflection can be a difficult task initially for students. Teacher agreement that all students likely require prompting questions to help them get started on their initial self-reflections ensures that some students will not be left to struggle, perhaps frustratingly, with this new task. For example, one selected procedure specified a set of key questions useful in encouraging students to use the portfolio to reflect on their learning. Examples include, What was your favorite thing to read? What would you like to read next? What would make you a better reader? (Valencia & Place, 1994).

Second, the discussion can clarify the rationale for including particular tasks in the portfolio and may lead to changes in the requirements for some tasks. For example, a goal in one elementary school was that students develop an interest in reading. Discussion of the plan to have first-graders submit weekly logs led to changing the requirement to that of a two-week sweep each semester (Valencia & Place, 1994). This change provided the needed information without relying on an arduous chore for the children.

Logistical Issues

Three types of logistical decisions are important in preparing to implement portfolio assessment. They are (1) determining ownership of and access to the portfolio, (2) organization and location of portfolios, and (3) allowing needed time for portfolio activities.

Determining ownership is not a trivial decision because several groups may maintain that they have a need for information in the portfolio. Potential audiences include parents, counselors, administrators, and next-grade teachers (Arter & Spandel, 1992, p. 78). Also important is that students feel a sense of ownership because the portfolio is an extension of themselves. They may not feel comfortable about including personal thoughts about their writing, for example, if portfolio information is open to anyone who asks.

Decisions about organization may be made by the planning group or the individual teacher. For example, portfolio contents may be organized chronologically, thematically, or by genre. Further, evaluative comments may accompany or be attached to the work, or student work may be placed in one section with evaluations in another. One second-grade classroom maintains a diagnostic section in each portfolio that includes anecdotal records, checklists, running records, and reading interviews (Courtney & Abodeeb, 1999).

Although teachers typically make the decision about the organization of the portfolio, students may be involved in the choice of portfolio containers. One option is expandable file folders that can be fastened. They are functional and durable; however, they are expensive. Other options include cardboard boxes, pizza boxes, and double grocery bags (for strength) with the top edges folded down. Placement on a table at the back of the room allows students access to them during individual work periods. Numbering the portfolios also facilitates student access and return of the portfolio to the proper location. In addition, all student work placed in the portfolio should be dated.

Some teachers and students use technology to both store work and organize the portfolio (Edyburn, 1994; Salend, 1998). Videocassettes record students sharing their portfolios, scanners enter work on a computer diskette or laser disk, and photo CD technology records pictures (Salend, 1998, p. 38). Others use the Grady Profile, a hypermedia-based system to create electronic portfolios, which can include sound, graphics, text, and video

(Edyburn, 1994). The Grady Profile also provides a template for teachers and students to enter work samples or test scores (Wolfe, 1999). Other software programs, such as Hyperstudio, permit users to create their own templates (Wolfe, 1999).

Finally, managing portfolios in the classroom requires refocusing so that classroom time can be allocated differently (Tierney, Carter, & Desai, 1991, p. 7). When implemented, portfolios change the relationship of the student to the assessment process. Students participate in the assessment process through collaborating with the teacher in selecting items for the portfolio and by learning to reflect on and evaluate their learning. These activities are discussed further in the following sections.

In summary, identifying formats and procedures for core elements in the portfolio ensures that all students have the same opportunities to develop their capabilities. The discussion also can clarify the rationale for including tasks in the portfolio.

In addition, three types of logistical decisions are important in preplanning. They are determining ownership and access to the portfolio, determining the organization and location of the portfolios, and planning for the needed time for portfolio activities. Time is required for students to collaborate with teachers and to learn to reflect on and evaluate their learning.

Developing Student Responsibility for Learning

One expectation for the use of portfolios is "active student engagement in learning and student responsibility for and control of learning" (Arter & Spandel, 1992, p. 36). This expectation may vary across age levels and settings, depending on the extent that students are expected to set personal goals, reflect on and evaluate their learning, and select pieces for inclusion in their portfolios.

However, students are accustomed to the teacher informing them when they are making progress toward externally imposed standards. Therefore, portfolios, in and of themselves, will not lead to student self-understanding (Gomez, Graue, & Block, 1991, p. 627). Instruction must address taking responsibility for one's own learning as well as evaluating one's performance (Gillespie et al., 1996; Paulson, Paulson, & Meyer, 1991). Key issues in successful implementation are introducing the portfolio, student goal setting, and reflecting on one's progress.

Introducing Portfolios

First is to allow time for the preparatory steps in implementing portfolios. Included are logistical arrangements and introducing the portfolio concept to students. The idea of "doing portfolios" cannot be introduced without careful discussion (Wolcott, 1998, p. 38) because one purpose of portfolios is to change students' views of learning and assessment (see Table 7.4). In one classroom, a high school art student shared her art portfolio with the class. Items included work in different media (sculpture, line drawings, watercolors, and works in progress). During the presentation, she shared her goals and her reflections on each work and the collection (Tierney et al., 1991, p. 80).

TABLE 7.4   *Issues in Developing Student Responsibility for Learning*

Issue	*Requirements*
1. Introducing portfolios	Allow time with several examples and discussion so that children understand the concept of shared goals, reasons for selection of portfolio items
2. Assisting students to set goals	Allow time for discussion of goals, including examples of things the children might want to work on
3. Assisting students to develop self-reflective skills	Separate the concept of self-reflection on one's work from overall beliefs of goodness and self-worth; allow extensive time and teacher collaboration for development, provide teacher modeling of reflective language and practice by the children

In a second-grade classroom, the teacher began by reading *Grandma's Scrapbook* to the class and they discussed the ways the children in the story changed and grew (Courtney & Abodeeb, 2001, p. 15). The class then discussed how they could document the ways they grow during the year. The teacher also asked students who had literacy portfolios from the previous year to bring them in and share them with the classmates.

The opportunity to examine examples of portfolios and ask questions about the process is very important. Further, multiple discussions and reassurances about portfolio procedures and goals may be needed. One first-grade teacher, for example, structured portfolio mini-lessons (Vizyak, 1999), addressing first the contents of student-managed portfolios and reasons for item selection. The students' first selections were primarily their best work. Subsequent mini-lessons explored other reasons for item selection, such as something that took a long time (effort), something you have learned (growth), and something that was challenging (risk taking).

Student Goal Setting

Learning to set goals is not an easy exercise for students. Young children, because they think in concrete terms, often suggest such goals as "getting more recess" and "coloring." They also suggest goals related to self-worth, such as "being good" (Benson & Smith, 1998, p. 173).

Children may set either implicit or explicit goals. Implicit goals typically emerge in conferences with the teacher in which the children identify things they want to work on (concrete activities). Examples are "I want to work on writing better opening paragraphs" and "I would like to write better sentences."

Explicit goals, in contrast, are an aspect of the diagnostic-reflective portfolio. The teacher's role is to assist children in this process (Courtney & Abodeeb, 2001, p. 36). In one second-grade classroom, the children first brainstormed their concept of a goal. For example, one response was that "a goal is something you practice, practice, and practice until you get good at it and then you have a new goal" (p. 36).

The teacher then asked the children to discuss things they might want to work on or get better at. She and the class then talked about things they might do when they were working on their goals. They then incorporated this information into sample specified goals. Examples included "Get better at reading by putting in words that fit, make sense, and sound like language," "Improve reading by reading at home and school," and "Improve my writing by reading my drafts out loud and then changing them" (p. 37). The teacher then worked with the children individually to assist them in setting three specific goals to work on.

Some children are able to consciously work on their goals. Others, however, need assistance. For example, the teacher may say, "What is something you said you wanted to work on while you were reading? Can you show me an example before you start reading today?" (Courtney & Abodeeb, 2001, p. 37). Another example is "What else do you want to do to make this the way you want it?" (Potter, 1999, p. 13). However, the teacher should not overwhelm children with a set of questions, but should provide prompts to assist children in their thinking.

Reflecting on Progress

Developing meaningful guidelines for selecting and analyzing one's work requires instruction and practice. Recall the writing classes described earlier in the chapter that first introduced the learner-development portfolio. Two months of oral reflections on one's own work and that of others was needed to develop student investment in the assessment process and readiness to proceed to written reflections. In addition, time is needed for teachers and students to review work as well as for teacher–student conferences.

Helping young children become involved in goal setting and evaluating their learning is consistent with a child-centered approach to learning (Potter, 1999). However, addressing these tasks without dampening children's optimism and their zest for learning is a challenge (p. 211).

Teachers face three major concerns in assisting children to develop self-reflective skills (Potter, 1999). First, their level of cognitive development leads them to rely on concrete or egocentric goals and criteria (p. 211). For example, one child selected a piece about his dog because "it is about my dog and I like my dog" (Vizyak, 1999, p. 146). When asked to choose their best work, children may pick the longest paper (concrete criterion), or state "I wrote good" (Benson & Smith, 1998, p. 177). The latter is simply a restatement of the task. Other initial reflections were "I chose this piece because I worked hard on it" and "When I read this I feel good" (Courtney & Abodeeb, 2001, p. 41).

Second, children tend to think of themselves very positively; they view themselves as "paragons of virtue" (Harter, 1996). Thus, they have difficulty in understanding that their work can have positive and negative features (Potter, 1999). Third, young children do not distinguish areas of achievement and behavior. They believe that assessment of achievement represents their overall worth. "Goodness" is viewed as working hard, behaving well, and meeting the expectations established by adults (p. 211). From this perspective, adult criticism of the child's work can have negative consequences such as a belief that it is impossible for the child to improve (p. 212).

Also, because young children expect to meet adult standards, sharing in the process of assessment is a wholly new concept for them. Teachers have reported that many of the children looked "dumbfounded" at the prospect (Benson & Smith, 1998). Some initially viewed it as a trick (p. 177).

Teacher modeling of ideas and suggestions for selecting work for the portfolio is essential. For example, one teacher, who was writing a story about penguins, talked about sequencing and story elements. She illustrated the beginning, middle, and end of the story and explained that the children should look for their stories that have a great beginning, middle, and end (Benson & Smith, 1998, p. 17).

Also important is teacher modeling of reflective language, teacher–student conferences, whole class discussions, and practice by the children (see Table 7.4). Questions as cues also are helpful. Examples include "What did you do to help yourself get better at _____?" and "How do you make sense while you are reading?" (Courtney & Abodeeb, 2001, p. 40). In other words, "getting students to pull together, reflect, review, share, and evaluate the portfolio will take time" (Tierney et al., 1991, p. 8).

Summary

Portfolios, by themselves, will not lead to student self-understanding. Important in the success of portfolio assessment are the activities implemented to introduce portfolios, assisting students in setting goals, and activities to assist students in learning to reflect meaningfully on their work. Introducing the concept of portfolios includes opportunities to examine examples, and to engage in discussions about portfolios.

Goal setting and reflecting on one's progress as a learner are difficult tasks for young students. Identifying aspects of their performance they wish to improve can assist students in developing goals. Three concerns in assisting children to develop self-reflective skills are their level of cognitive development which leads them to rely on concrete or egocentric criteria, their difficulty in understanding that their work can have positive and negative aspects, and their belief that assessment of achievement represents their overall worth. Important activities in assisting students to become self-reflective include teacher modeling of ideas and suggestions for selecting work for the portfolio, modeling reflective language, teacher–student conferences, and the use of questions as prompts for thinking.

Related Assessment Issues

Other issues important in the classroom implementation of portfolio assessment are fairness, validity and reliability, and advantages and limitations of portfolios.

Fairness

One expectation of portfolio assessment is that it can provide opportunities for less traditionally skilled students to develop their capabilities (Wolf et al., 1991). One study indicated, for example, that the poor writers in a group of fifth-graders improved to the level of average writers when portfolios were instituted. One contributing factor was likely the ample time provided students to complete their work (Simmons, 1990).

The flexibility of portfolio assessment also allows students to demonstrate their capabilities in different ways. Special needs children who have difficulty with writing, for example, may tape record their reflections and their story summaries.

Validity and Reliability

Educators face four validity issues in the implementation of portfolios. First, validity is assumed to be inherent in the "authenticity" of the portfolio (Calfee & Perfumo, 1993, p. 535). However, technical support for the claim of validity has yet to be developed. The first needed step is an analysis of the concepts of growth and development. Currently, different teachers reviewing the same classroom portfolio are likely to make different inferences about the student's capabilities (Valencia & Place, 1994). Also needed are strengthening the linkages to curriculum and instruction and developing effective techniques for analysis, interpretation, and reporting (Valencia & Calfee, 1991, p. 238).

Second, in the absence of a framework for the focus of the portfolio, the assessment can be misleading (Arter & Spandel, 1992). One possible problem with the portfolio is that the included work may not be representative of the student's knowledge. For example, a composite school portfolio with samples from different teachers does not reflect typical instruction if it includes only the best samples from the best teachers (Arter & Spandel, 1992).

Third, criteria used to evaluate student portfolios may not reflect the most relevant dimensions of the major purpose. If mechanics are weighted as more important than expression and fluency, for example, then an insightful portfolio may not be evaluated as positively as a portfolio characterized by flat writing that uses punctuation accurately. In other words, statements about a student's capability to compose are misleading if heavily influenced by a consideration of mechanics.

Fourth, the role of assessment is to provide information about the individual student's capabilities. However, current curriculum reforms recommend small-group collaboration, classroom discussions, peer reviews, and the use of other resources such as idea-based webs. These circumstances raise the question, Whose work is this? (Gearhart & Herman, 1998, p. 43). The individual teacher, who knows the students through working with them daily, often can clarify this situation. In contrast, these circumstances become a challenge when a student's portfolio is used to communicate to outside audiences. That is, the extent of support varies across assignments, students, and classrooms, compromising the validity of inferences about the work of an individual student. Data from two large-scale studies, for example, indicated wide variations in classroom revision policies, and weak relationships between portfolio scores and on-demand assessments. Suggested solutions include documenting the contributions of others and requiring only the use of non-assisted writing in large-scale assessments.

Reliability of inferences from portfolios is compromised if decisions are based on too few samples of student work in limited contexts. Therefore, adequate planning in advance on the scope of portfolio contents and the situations to be sampled is essential.

Advantages and Limitations

A key feature of portfolio assessment is that it can portray the richness and complexity of student learning. This feature leads to two major advantages. One is that the portfolio can chronicle student development and growth over time. Comparison of books or stories read early in the year with later selections, for example, can indicate that the student is choosing to read more complex text.

A second advantage is that portfolios facilitate communication with parents. Teachers are able to show parents the specific skills the student has mastered and illustrate these skills in the context of meaningful writing (Benson & Smith, 1998, p. 176). As noted at the beginning of this chapter, preschool teachers stated that portfolio assessment helps them answer the often-asked question, "So what do children learn other than the ABCs and 123s?" (Hanson & Gilkerson, 1999, p. 81).

A characteristic of portfolios as an assessment approach is flexibility. Portfolios can accommodate a variety of student products, teacher observations, and other information. A third advantage, associated with this feature, is that portfolios are inherently adaptable for children with special needs. When the purpose of an assessment task, for example, is to document the student's thinking, students who have difficulty with writing may produce oral book summaries or other reflections that are tape recorded for the portfolio.

A fourth advantage of portfolio assessment is the potential influence on curriculum, instruction, and decision making. This influence emerges as teachers work with each other in developing frameworks for portfolios in their classrooms. That is, initiating portfolio assessment requires answers to questions about the rationale for pursuing a particular emphasis in the curriculum. Teachers also have reported more emphasis on the writing process as a result of using portfolios and greater awareness of gaps in students' skills (Benson & Smith, 1998, p. 178).

Finally, students can learn the skills of self-assessment. Through teacher modeling, class discussions, and teacher–student conferences, students can learn to thoughtfully assess their strengths and identify areas for improvement.

Three limitations of portfolio assessment may be identified. Perhaps the biggest obstacle to the use of portfolios is the time required for planning, implementation, and evaluation (Wolfe, 1999). Portfolios do contribute to an increased workload for the teacher. Providing release time for teachers for organization and planning meetings, curriculum development, and networking with teachers who have expertise in portfolio development is important for effective implementation.

Another limitation is the concern about unreliability, inconsistency, and inequity across classrooms (Valencia, 1999). First, the flexibility and nonstandard format can be a disadvantage if the assessment purpose is not determined in advance (Carpenter, Ray, & Bloom, 1995). However, identification of purpose is not a guarantee that appropriate tasks and sufficient assessments are included in the portfolio to make decisions about growth and development. That is, questions have been raised that two or more persons may not evaluate portfolio contents in similar ways (e.g., Arter & Spandel, 1992; McDonald, 1993).

Third, portfolio assessment actually may interfere with teaching and learning. This problem can occur in one of three ways. First, too much time may be allocated to management tasks, such as decisions about selection and documentation (Snider, Lima, &

DeVito, 1994). Second, implementation may negatively affect student originality and student attitudes. Third is the lack of closure on assignments, given the logistics of keeping track of students' various efforts (Gillespie et al., 1996).

Summary

Issues that can affect the inferences about student capabilities based on portfolios are fairness, validity, and reliability. In terms of fairness, the intent of portfolios is that their flexibility can provide opportunities for less traditionally skilled students to develop their capabilities. Validity issues associated with portfolios are the lack of data on the concepts of growth and development, the importance of a framework for the portfolio, the importance of relevant dimensions for portfolio tasks, and the influence of peer and other assistance on assessment of student capabilities. Reliability depends on sufficient samples of student work across various contexts.

Advantages of portfolio assessment include chronicling changes in student capabilities over time, facilitating communication with parents, flexibility for children with special needs, the potential influence on curriculum and instructional decision making, and student development of self-assessment skills.

The major obstacle to implementing portfolios is the increased workload for the teacher. Other limitations are concerns about unreliability, inconsistency, and inequity across classrooms, and the potential to interfere with teaching and learning, given the logistics of implementation.

Discussion Questions

1. The external portfolio differs from the other types of portfolios in that the entries and dimensions for scoring are standardized. Why are they structured in this way instead of representing particular classroom emphases and interests?

2. Compare the advantages and disadvantages from the perspective of the teachers, the parents, and students for the following: (a) specifying categories of items for the portfolio, or (b) specifying core elements and permitting optional choices.

3. Why is determining ownership of and access to the portfolio important?

4. A group of fourth-grade teachers selects the literacy goal of "interacting with texts to construct meaning." What are some likely dimensions of student work that reflect progress in achieving this goal?

5. What are the key issues in establishing the validity and reliability of portfolios for classroom use?

References

Arter, J. A. (1992). Portfolios in practice: What is a portfolio? Paper presented at the annual meeting of the American Educational Research Association. San Francisco: April.

Arter, J. A., & Spandel, V. (1992). Using portfolios of student work in instruction and assessment. *Educational Measurement: Issues and Practices, 11*(1), 36–44.

Au, K. (1994). Portfolio assessment: Experiences at the Kamehameha Elementary Education Program. In S. W. Valencia, E. H. Hiebert, & P. Afflerbach (Eds.), *Authentic reading assessment* (pp. 103–126). Newark, DE: International Reading Association.

Benson, T. R., & Smith, L. J. (1998). Portfolios in first grade: Four teachers learn to use portfolio assessment. *Early Childhood Education Journal, 25*(3), 173–180.

Calfee, R. C., & Perfumo, P. A. (1993). Student portfolios: Opportunities for a revolution in assessment. *Journal of Reading, 36*(7), 532–537.

Camp, R. (1992). Portfolio reflections in middle and secondary classrooms. In K. B. Yancey (Ed.), *Portfolios in the writing classroom* (pp. 61–79). Urbana, IL: National Council of Teachers of English.

Carpenter, C. D., Ray, M. S., & Bloom, L. A. (1995). Portfolio assessment: Opportunities and challenges. *Intervention in School and Clinic, 31*(1), 34–41.

Courtney, A. M., & Abodeeb, T. L. (1999). Diagnostic-reflective portfolios. *Reading Teacher, 52*(7), 708–714.

Courtney, A. M., & Abodeeb, T. L. (2001). *Journey of discovery*. Newark, DE: International Reading Association.

Eccles, J. S., & Midgley, C. (1989). Stage-environment fit: Developmentally appropriate classrooms for early adolescents. In C. Ames & R. Ames (Eds.), *Reading on motivation in education: Vol. 3. Goals and cognitions* (pp. 139–186). New York: Academic.

Edyburn, D. L. (1994). An equation to consider: The portfolio assessment knowledge base + technology = The Grady Profile. *LD Forum, 19*(4), 35–37.

Gearhart, M., & Harmon, J. L. (1998). Portfolio assessment: Whose work is it? Issues in the use of classroom assignments for accountability. *Educational Assessment, 5*(1), 41–55.

Gillespie, C. S., Ford, K., Gillespie, R. D., & Leavell, A. (1996). Portfolio assessment: Some questions, some answers, some recommendations. *Journal of Adolescent and Adult Literacy, 39*(6), 480–491.

Gomez, M., Graue, M., & Block, M. (1991). Reassessing portfolio assessment: Rhetoric and reality. *Language Arts, 68*(8), 620-628.

Gredler, M. (1995). Implications of portfolio assessment for program evaluation. *Studies in Educational Evaluation, 21*(4), 431–437.

Hanson, M. F., & Gilkerson, D. (1999). Portfolio assessment: More than ABC's and 123's. *Early Childhood Education Journal, 27*(2), 81–86.

Harter, S. (1996). Developmental changes in self-understanding across the 5 to 7 shift. In A. J. Sameroff & M. M. Haith (Eds.), *The five to seven year shift: The age of reason and responsibility* (pp. 207–236). Chicago: University of Chicago Press.

Hobbs, R. (1993). Portfolio use in a learning disabilities resource room. *Reading and Writing Quarterly: Overcoming Learning Difficulties, 9*, 249–261.

Johnson, R. L., Willeke, M. J., Bergman, T., & Steiner, D. J. (1997). Family literacy portfolios: Development and implementation. *Window on the World of Family Literacy, 2*(2), 10–17.

Koretz, D., Stecher, S., Klein, S., & McCaffrey, D. (1994). The Vermont Portfolio Assessment Program: Findings and implications. *Educational Measurement: Issues and Practice, 13*(3), 5–16.

Krest, M. (1990, Feb.). Adapting the portfolio to meet student needs. *English Journal,* 29–34.

Lamme, L., & Hysmith, C. (1991). One school's adventure into portfolio assessment. *Language Arts, 68*(8), 629–640.

McDonald, P. (1993). Three pictures of an exhibition: Warm, cool, and hard. *Phi Delta Kappan, 74,* 480–485.

Meyer, C., Shuman, S., & Angelo, N. (1990). NWEA white paper on portfolio data. Lake Oswego, OR: Northwest Evaluation Association.

Moss, P., Beck, J., Ebbs, C., Matson, B., Muchmore, J., Steele, D., Taylor, C., & Herter, R. (1992). Portfolios, accountability, and an interpretative approach to validity. *Educational Measurement: Issues and Practice, 11*(3), 12–21.

Paratore, J. R. (1995). Assessing literacy: Establishing common standards in portfolio assessment. *Topics in Language Disorders, 16*(1), 67–82.

Paulson, L., Paulson, P. R., & Meyer, C. (1991). What makes a portfolio a portfolio? *Educational Leadership, 48*(5), 60–63.

Potter, E. (1999). What should I put in my portfolio? Supporting young children's goals and evaluations. *Childhood Education, 75*(4), 210–214.

Purves, A. (1993). Setting standards in the language arts and literature classroom and the implications for portfolio assessment. *Educational Assessment, 1*(3), 175–200.

Salend, S. J. (1998). Using portfolios to assess performance. *Teaching Exceptional Children, 31*(2), 36–43.

Simmons, J. (1990). Portfolios as large-scale assessment. *Language Arts, 67*(3), 262–268.

Snider, M. A., Lima, S. S., & DeVito, P. J. (1994). Rhode Island's literacy portfolio assessment project. In S. Vallencia, E. H. Hiebert, & P. P. Afflerbach (Eds.), *Authentic reading assessment* (pp. 71–88). Newark, DE: International Reading Association.

Tierney, R. J., Carter, M. A., & Desai, L. E. (1991). *Portfolio assessment in the reading-writing classroom.* Norwood, MA: Christopher Gordon.

Valencia, S. (1999). A portfolio approach to classroom reading assessment: The whys, whats, and hows. In S. J. Barrentine (Ed.), *Reading assessment: Principles and practices for the beginning teacher* (pp. 113–117). Newark, DE: International Reading Association.

Valencia, S., & Calfee, R. (1991). The development and use of literacy portfolios for students. *Applied Measurement in Education, 4*(3), 333–346.

Valencia, S., & Place, N. A. (1994). Literacy portfolios for teaching, learning, and accountability: The Bellevue Literacy Project. In S. Valencia, E. H. Hiebert, & P. Afflerbauch (Eds.), *Authentic reading assessment: Practices and possibilities* (pp. 134–156). Newark, DE: International Reading Association.

Vizyak, L. (1999). Student portfolios: Building self-reflection in a first-grade classroom. In S. J. Barrentine (Ed.), *Reading assessment: Principles and practices for elementary teachers* (pp. 135–138). Newark, DE: International Reading Association.

Wiggins, G. (1988). Rational numbers. Toward grading and scoring that help rather than harm learning. *American Educator, 12*(4), 20–25, 45–48.

Wolcott, W. (with Legg, S. M.). (1998). An overview of writing assessment: Theory, research, and practice. Urbana, IL: National Council of Teachers of English.

Wolf, D. (1989). Portfolio assessment: Sampling student work. *Educational Leadership, 46*(7), 35–39.

Wolf, D., Bixby, J., Glenn, J., & Gardner, H. (1991). To use their minds well: Investigating new forms of student assessment. In G. Grant (Ed.), *Review of research in education*, Vol. 17 (pp. 32–73). Washington, DC: American Educational Research Association.

Wolfe, E. W. (1999). How can administrators facilitate portfolio implementation? *High School Magazine, 6*(5), 29–33.

8

Special Needs in the Classroom

> With the expansion of inclusive education, the need for effective evaluation that focuses on the authentic performance of diversified learners becomes even more critical.
>
> —Jochum, Curran, & Reetz, 1998, p. 284

"Hey, look what I did, I'm smart!" exclaimed an 11-year-old student with mental retardation to a classroom visitor (Ezell, Klein, & Ezell-Powell, 1999, p. 453). His teacher reported that, a year earlier, the boy was a passive learner and would not have enthusiastically approached a visitor about his work. She attributed the change to the implementation of portfolio assessment which provided him with opportunities to develop self-determination skills. That is, the active participation in discussing and choosing portfolio pieces contributed to pride in his work and a sense of ownership.

The 11-year-old boy in this example is one of the children identified as learners with special needs. Specifically, the term *special needs* refers to any of a variety of intellectual, social, and physical characteristics that have implications for literacy instruction. For example, a child may be from a home where English is not spoken, or she may have a diagnosed learning disability that affects her learning.

Discussed in this chapter are two broad categories of special needs students and the implications for assessment. They are students from different cultural and language backgrounds and those with developmental disabilities.

Language and Cultural Differences

The children in classrooms today represent a variety of language and literacy backgrounds and cultural expectations. Knowledge of the cultural mores and customs and communication patterns of these children can assist the teacher to construct more effective assessments (Sattler, 2001, p. 636).

Language Orientation

Two broad categories of language orientation that have implications for literacy assessment and instruction may be identified. They are students whose native language is not English and those who speak nonstandard English.

English as a Second Language.   Census and other data indicate that the number of non-English native speakers in U.S. classrooms is increasing. Garcia (2000) notes that 9.9 million children, 22 percent of the school-age population, live in homes in which the family speaks a language other than English (p. 813). Moreover, some school districts resemble a virtual United Nations. Students in the San Jose Unified School District, for example, speak fifty languages and public school students in Arlington, Virginia, speak 509 languages, including Farci and Khmer (Dunn, 1993, p. 38). In today's classroom, the languages of the traditional immigrants to the United States (western Europe, Russia, China, and Mexico) are joined by the languages of Thailand, Vietnam, eastern European countries, and others.

The children speaking these various languages may be either new to this country or the children of immigrants who speak another language in the home. Further, they vary in their literacy capabilities. The children may not yet speak English or may not be fluent in English and are referred to as *English as Second Language Learners (ESL)*. They may not read or write in any language, or they may already read and write in at least one language. Students who are not sufficiently fluent in English to perform academic tasks successfully are sometimes referred to as *Limited English Proficient (LEP)* students (Tompkins & Hoskisson, 1995, p. 517). Special programs instituted for these children are referred to as ESL or *ESOL (English for Speakers of Other Languages)*.

Other children, in contrast, may be bilingual. They speak English fluently at school and their native language at home. Although some Hispanic American children are equally fluent in both English and Spanish, some have difficulty in both languages. They may use an intricate mixture of English and Spanish (Sattler, 2001, p. 544). Included are borrowing English vocabulary to complete utterances initiated in Spanish, anglicizing words, and maintaining Spanish word order in English.

For many years, immigrant children were simply placed in classrooms in the belief that they would learn to speak English because it was spoken around them. The problem with this practice was formally recognized in a 1974 Supreme Court decision. The ruling stated that simply providing students who do not understand English with the same textbooks and curriculum as other students effectively excludes them from a meaningful education (Rubin, 1997, p. 71). The court ordered school districts to provide assistance in learning English, but it did not specify the methods to be used.

In addition to becoming proficient in English, children who are nonnative speakers face other challenges. One is that attitudes, beliefs, values, foods, customs, and language conventions of their native language may conflict with the social and academic structure of the classroom or school (Spinelli, 2002, p. 126). For example, in some cultures, the school environment is much more formal than in schools in the United States. Students from European or Asian cultures, for example, view U.S. schools as chaotic, and may conclude that the informality indicates permission to misbehave (Tompkins & Hoskisson, 1995, p. 516). They also often lack the prerequisite cultural knowledge to understand topics and themes in their readings.

Another challenge is that the children's parents and family members may have different expectations for the nature of language learning in the classroom. For example, one group of immigrant Mexican families did not understand the focus in U.S. classrooms on knowing the alphabet. They thought a far more important goal was knowing the sounds of key syllables (Valdes, 1996).

Nonstandard English.   There is no single "pure" form of English. Instead, English speakers use dialects that vary across geographic areas, ethnic backgrounds, and socioeconomic levels (Tompkins & Hoskisson, 1995, p. 523). Two major characteristics define a dialect. One is that a dialect is "a structured subsystem of a language, with definite phonological and syntactic structures" (Rubin, 1997, p. 68). Second, a dialect is spoken by a group of people "united by their speech as well as by factors such as geographic location and/or social status" (Rubin, 1997).

Although there is no "pure" form of English, the dialect of book, newspaper, and magazine authors and television commentators is referred to as *standard English (SE)*. This dialect meets the criteria stated in Webster's dictionary for standard English. Specifically, it is (1) substantially uniform, (2) well established by usage in the formal and informal speech and writing of educated individuals, and (3) is widely recognized as acceptable wherever English is spoken (Rubin, 1997, p. 67). Other dialects that are variations of standard English are referred to as *nonstandard English (NSE)*. Students who rely on nonstandard speech patterns in 20 to 30 percent of their conversation are typically referred to as NSE speakers (Labov, 1970).

Of particular importance in the classroom is that children who speak a dialect of English are not inferior, nor is their dialect inferior. In prior years, students who spoke a version of nonstandard English were viewed as lacking in language ability. However, dialects are not disorders and speaking a dialect is not an indicator of an inability to learn complex rules. Research by linguists indicates that dialects are not accumulations of errors in standard English (Rubin, 1997, p. 68). Instead, dialects are highly structured systems with rules for pronunciation, grammar, and syntax. Of importance for assessment is that speech differences reflecting a dialect are not indicators of an inability to process language meaningfully or interact with others.

Implications for Assessment

The native language or English dialect spoken by a student has implications for classroom assessment in three areas. They are communication styles, syntax and phonology, and verbal and nonverbal knowledge.

Communication Styles.   Languages and dialects are manifestations of different cultures that have their own rules for the social uses of language. As illustrated in Table 8.1, differ-

TABLE 8.1 *Assessment Implications of Communication Styles of Other Cultures*

Communication Style	Example	Assessment Implications
Pacing	Preference for waiting to respond: Native Americans, Asian Americans	Does not mean resistance or lack of knowledge
	Interrupting others: Native Hawaiians (Kiefer & DeStefano, 1985; Sattler, 2001)	Not a sign of rudeness; demonstrates involvement
Response patterns	Children rely on one-word utterances: Amish, Native Americans (Kiefer & DeStefano, 1985)	Does not mean lack of knowledge; reflects the belief that children should be seen and not heard (Kiefer & DeStefano, 1985)
	Lack of eye contact: Amish, Native American, and Japanese cultures	Does not indicate inattentiveness, rudeness, or lack of intelligence (Sattler, 2001); reflects respect
Interrogation patterns	The asking of direct questions may be viewed as rude: Asian Americans, Native Americans (Sattler, 2001)	Lack of response to direct questions does not necessarily mean lack of knowledge

ences between these cultures and mainstream Euro-American culture can lead to inappropriate inferences about students' attitudes toward learning and their literacy capabilities. In one classroom, for example, the teacher complimented an African American child on the picture he was drawing. Later, referring to the child's lowering of his head and nonresponse, the teacher described the boy as a "sneaky child" (DeStefano, Pepinsky, & Sanders, 1982). She based this inference on his nonresponse to the compliment and his consistent involvement in playground conversations with the other children. However, in the child's microculture, his response to the adult (the teacher) was a sign of respect.

Other differences in communication patterns include preferences for waiting to respond to questioning, one-word or minimal utterances in response to direct questions, and lack of eye contact. For example, direct questions are basically unpleasant for Hawaiian children. In that culture, adults use direct questions primarily in disciplinary situations (Kiefer & DeStefano, 1985, p. 164).

Lack of understanding of these and other communication patterns can lead to inappropriate inferences, such as rudeness, inattentiveness, and lack of student knowledge. In one middle-class second-grade classroom, for example, the Amish children seldom volunteered to speak. When directly questioned, they responded with silence or barely audible one-word utterances (Kiefer & DeStefano, 1985). Halfway through the year, the teacher discovered that, at home, these children were expected to be seen and not heard. Further, their primary language was a form of German, not English. Similarly, in other classrooms, the requirement to answer teacher-controlled questions for which the answer already had been found was foreign to the Native American culture of some students (Erickson &

Mohatt, 1982, p. 140). However, these instances of no or minimal response do not indicate an unwillingness to participate in the classroom.

Culture clash also can occur when children respond as they would in their culture, but their reactions conflict with classroom expectations. For example, in some African American cultures, responding "Yes, yes," or "Right on" signals that listeners are following the speaker's point (Kiefer & DeStefano, 1985, p. 163). Instead of disciplinary action, ways to ease the children into classroom expectations are needed.

Finally, communication patterns also influence students' story retelling and writing. Some children, for example, with an "oral style" approach to communication and symbol use, approach telling narratives and writing quite differently from children with a "literature style" (Wolf et al., 1988, p. 149). Instead of indicating a lack of understanding, documentation of their approach indicates a need for instruction in a different approach. That is, they are inexperienced in the ways U.S. schools expect them to verbalize their thoughts (Pinnell & Jagger, 1991).

Syntax and Phonology. All languages and dialects reflect a particular phonology and complex structural rules. These characteristics initially lead to pronunciation and sentence structure errors in standard English. A common syntactic difference with standard English is the nonuse or differential use of "to be." Asian students, for example, may say "I warm" for "I am warm," and African American students may use the shortened form instead of "I'm warm" (Kiefer & DeStefano, 1985; Rubin, 1997). Further, African American students may say "she busy" or "she be busy" for "she is busy" (Tompkins & Hoskisson, 1995, p. 524).

A common phonological difference is the deletion of the final consonant or consonant cluster. Examples include "tes'" for "test" (Black English) and "Janet blouse" for "Janet's blouse" (Chinese) (Kiefer & DeStefano, 1985; Rubin, 1997). Other differences include, for example, (1) the greater number of vowels in English than in Chinese, (2) vowels that are difficult for the Spanish speaker, such as *bit* and *but,* and (3) English sounds that do not appear in Spanish (Rubin, 1997).

However, these variations should not be taken as evidence that the student is unable to learn the appropriate English patterns. They provide information to the teacher about the types of difficulties faced by speakers of other languages and dialects.

Verbal and Nonverbal Knowledge. The languages or dialects spoken by different individuals reflect particular cultures and microcultures. That is, in addition to certain communication styles and language rules, a particular language or dialect represents shared beliefs, values, and customs. Differences between cultures or subcultures can affect classroom instruction in two ways. One is differences in the meanings of nonverbal signals and verbal expressions. For example, the crooked finger gesture that indicates "come here" in U.S. culture is considered obscene by the Chinese (Kiefer & DeStefano, 1985).

For speakers of nonstandard English, a potential area of difficulty is that teachers may not know expressions used by the children. Also, the teacher's expressions may have different connotations for students (Rubin, 1997). In addition, similarities between dialects can also lead to misunderstandings because teachers and students may assume they understand each other when they do not. For example, a Britisher's statement, "It's in the boot" refers to the trunk of a car, not footwear.

A second concern is that children who speak different dialects or languages very likely lack sufficient background knowledge about subjects, topics, or themes to undertake classroom readings. Garcia (2000), in her review of reading research, reports several studies that indicate differences between English monolingual children and bilingual children in their background knowledge of topics in second-language texts. The studies indicated that the bilingual children had less cultural knowledge of the topics and knew significantly less of the English vocabulary in the test passages.

Specific Assessment Needs

Important initially for nonnative speakers of English is to determine their language proficiency. Then, in the classroom, particular areas of assessment are important for both ESL students and dialect speakers (see Table 8.2).

Assessment of Entry-Level Language Proficiency.   The purpose of this task is to determine the extent of additional assistance the child may need, such as enrollment in an ESL or ESOL program, placement with a bilingual teacher, or the assistance of a bilingual school volunteer or peer tutor. Most of the available tests assess Spanish and English for students whose primary language is Spanish. However, the Basic Inventory of Natural Language (Herbert, 1983) is a formal procedure for the collection of language samples in 32 languages. Samples are scored for fluency, complexity, and average sentence length (McLoughlin & Lewis, 1990). Another test is the Bilingual Verbal Ability Tests (BVAT) (Munoz-Sandoval, Cummins, Alvado, & Ruef, 1998). Individually administered, this test consists of three subtests of the Woodcock-Johnson-Revised (1989) Test of Cognitive Ability. It has been translated into fifteen languages (Sattler, 2001). The test addresses picture vocabulary, oral vocabulary, and verbal analogies. Each item is first administered in English and failed items are readministered in the student's native language. Although not standardized in each language, the test can provide information about a student's proficiency in more than one language (p. 648).

TABLE 8.2   *Implementing Key Assessment Tasks for ESL, LEP, and NSE Speakers*

Assessment Task	*Purpose*	*Examples*
Entry-level language proficiency	Determine extent of assistance for the child	Bilingual Verbal Ability Tests (BVAT), demonstrating action words
Background knowledge about upcoming topics	Identify gaps in child's understanding of key concepts and words	Picture naming, child's explanations in native language
Understanding of text readings	Evaluate text comprehension	Oral summarization of text, native language summarization
Emerging capabilities in English	Document increasing competence in English	Portfolio, observations

Informal assessment strategies also may be used to determine a child's receptive vocabulary in English. Receptive vocabulary refers to the words that the child can understand. For second-language learners, receptive knowledge is greater than the knowledge that individuals can produce orally or in writing. To assess receptive vocabulary, the teacher first presents a set of pictures or objects and names one of them. The child is directed to point to the identified item or picture (McLoughlin & Lewis, 1990). The child also may be asked to demonstrate action words ("Show me 'jump'") or prepositions ("Put the ball behind [or in front of] the apple") (p. 417). A child's expressive vocabulary may be assessed by asking him to label pictures or objects, describe objects or events, or tell a story (p. 417).

Some children, however, enter the classroom with little or no knowledge of English (referred to as *L2* students to designate English as the second language). Observation, or "L2 learner watching" is the key to discovering their emerging understanding of English (Genishi, 1989). The difficulty is that, at first, there may be little to hear and see because the child may be a non-English speaker who says nothing for weeks (p. 510). The task for the teacher is to (1) observe carefully, looking for signs of understanding or confusion, (2) engage the child in conversation, even when the responses are nonverbal, and (3) keep conversations going as long as possible, recording any signs of the child's learning.

Three Needed Areas of Assessment in the Classroom.   For ESL dialect speakers, one important assessment focus is the students' background knowledge about topics and concepts addressed in upcoming reading selections. As discussed in Chapter 4, the learner's background knowledge is a major predictor of his or her success in constructing meaning through text. Further, the differences between bilingual and monolingual English speakers in cultural knowledge and vocabulary indicate the need for particular attention to the relevant knowledge of ESL students prior to undertaking new themes or readings. In addition to U.S. holidays and customs, such as Halloween and Thanksgiving, students may lack knowledge about other topics such as mummies in ancient Egypt. Also important for students with limited English proficiency is ensuring that they understand the words used to describe and explain key concepts and ideas. The child's naming pictures that illustrate key ideas and explaining concepts in her native language are ways to identify gaps in the child's knowledge.

A second area of assessment that requires attention is assessing students' understanding of text they have read. Bernhardt (2000) notes that measures typically used for this purpose are not appropriate when English is not the student's primary language. For example, the cloze test, described in Chapter 9, cannot assess passage integration, which is essential to the construction of meaning. Further, recall in English confounds the student's comprehension with his or her ability to write in the second language. That is, understanding and receptive vocabulary in a second language are greater than an individual's ability to write words and sentences in that language (Au, Mason, & Scheu, 1995; Pearson, DeStefano, & Garcia, 1998).

One assessment option is to permit the student to summarize the text orally with the opportunity to use words from the student's native language when needed. Another, when possible, is to permit summarization in the student's native language, with the assistance of an interpreter. Students frequently show greater comprehension of English text when they are permitted to respond in their language (Pearson et al., 1998).

A third assessment area is that of documenting students' capabilities in English literacy as they develop. Two methods that are well suited to this task are portfolios and observations. Portfolios can reflect the current emphasis in ESL programs on language function, constructing meaning, and the process of learning (Moya & O'Malley, 1994). Professional ESL educators often have used a variety of formal and informal assessments; portfolios provide a system that combines multiple assessments and interprets them as an integrated unit (p. 17). The flexibility of portfolios is particularly useful for the ESL classroom in which children's primary languages and their levels of English proficiency differ. The reason is that portfolios permit individualization in terms of lesson goals and content. They are also useful in the regular classroom for the same reason. Also important is the use of observation to identify a student's difficulties or breakthroughs during classroom activities. Examples include inattentiveness and nods that indicate comprehension. These observations may be recorded through the use of anecdotal records or checklists as discussed in Chapter 3.

Summary

Two broad categories of language orientation that have implications for literacy assessment are students whose primary language is not English and those who speak nonstandard English. Children who speak another language may not yet speak English or may not be fluent and are referred to as English as Second Language Learners (ESL). Those who are not sufficiently fluent to understand academic tasks are sometimes referred to as Limited English Proficient (LEP) students. Among the challenges faced by ESL students are learning about different customs, and, on occasion, different expectations for learning in the classroom.

In contrast, speakers of an English dialect who rely on nonstandard speech patterns in 20 to 30 percent of their conversations are typically referred to as NSE speakers. Of importance in the classroom is that a dialect is not a language disorder and speaking a dialect does not indicate an inability to learn complex language rules.

Implications for assessment for these students include communication styles, syntax and phonology, and verbal and nonverbal knowledge. The importance of the communication styles of children from different language backgrounds is that their conventions should not be interpreted as indicating negative attitudes, lack of knowledge, or misbehavior. Similarly, pronunciation and syntax errors that reflect the child's primary language or dialect should not be taken as evidence that the child is unable to learn patterns of English speech. Finally, differences in verbal and nonverbal knowledge can lead to misunderstandings in the classroom. Also, the children's lack of background knowledge of both text topics and vocabulary can lead to serious problems in comprehending reading material.

An initial task for the school or district is to determine the language proficiency of students whose native language is not English. The purpose is to determine the extent of additional assistance the child needs. Both standardized tests and informal assessment strategies may be used. For example, pictures and objects may be used to determine receptive vocabulary and careful observation by the teacher can identify the non-English speaker's first uses of English.

In the daily life of the classroom, three areas of assessment are important. First is assessing children's background knowledge prior to their undertaking reading selections.

Second is adequately assessing students' comprehension of texts they have read. However, researchers indicate that the cloze test and recall in English are inadequate for this purpose. When possible, summarization in the student's native language will be more accurate. Third, two assessment methods particularly appropriate for documenting children's developing capabilities in English are portfolios and observations. Portfolios can accommodate individualization of lesson goals and observations can capture student's difficulties and new understanding during classroom activities.

Developmental Exceptionalities

Children whose native language is not English or who speak a nonstandard English dialect have particular learning needs in the classroom. Other children have mental, physical, or emotional characteristics that affect their learning. Prior to the 1970s, many of these children were not enrolled in school programs. The enactment of Public Law (PL) 94-142 mandated requirements for the education of children with particular disabling conditions.

Subsequently amended and renamed the Individuals with Disabilities Act (IDEA), the legislation requires identification programs, a special education, related services for students with particular disabilities, and inclusion in educational accountability systems. The legislation also specifies placement in regular classrooms, whenever possible. At present, most students identified as eligible for special services receive some instruction from regular classroom teachers and an increasing number are fully integrated into regular class settings (Meyen, 1996, p. 16). Discussed in this section are the types of developmental exceptionalities, the legally required Individual Educational Program (IEP) for students receiving federally mandated services, implications for classroom assessment, and the potential role of portfolio assessment.

Types of Developmental Exceptionalities

Developmental exceptionalities include several characteristics that affect a student's potential for learning. At one extreme is the category referred to as gifted and talented. Although a standard definition of giftedness is lacking, the term typically refers to individuals who have demonstrated high performance or potential in general intellectual ability, specific academic aptitude, or creative or productive thinking. In contrast, other exceptionalities contribute to students' learning difficulties.

Mental Disabilities.   Included in this category are mental retardation, students referred to as *slow learners*, and students identified as learning disabled. PL 94-142 defines both mental retardation and learning disabilities and mandates special services for students in these categories. Slow learners, however, are not addressed in the legislation.

Both mental retardation and the term *slow learner* are defined in terms of the student's I.Q. score. Intellectual performance that is two standard deviations or more below the mean of an I.Q. test defines mental retardation. For example, on the Wechsler Intelligence Scale, students identified as mentally retarded score at 70 or below.

Slow learners are students with I.Q. scores that are low but within the normal range. Further, these students do not have specific learning disabilities that can be diagnosed by present methods. Thus, they are not eligible for special education services. However, low achievers make very slow or inconsistent progress in reading (Mason & Au, 1986, p. 294). Also, some may appear to be more inattentive or restless than other students and many have difficulty in following directions and completing work. Further, although many slow learners can decode words fairly well, they typically cannot read with enough efficiency to understand and remember the material (Brophy, 1996, p. 65).

The category of learning disabilities, in contrast, refers to individuals with fairly normal intelligence who have severe learning problems. Federal legislation defines a specific learning disability as a disorder in one or more of the basic psychological processes involved in understanding or using language (spoken or written). Included are an imperfect ability to listen, think, speak, read, write, spell, or perform mathematical calculations (*Federal Register,* 1977). Standardized intelligence and achievement tests and assessments in other areas are used to determine eligibility.

Students identified as learning disabled are almost half (45%) of those identified with handicaps to learning and are the largest group (over 2 million) (U.S. Department of Education, 1991). Most of the students have difficulties in processing letters and symbols in print text and many also are unable to produce legible handwriting.

Emotional or Physical Impairments.   An emotional or behavioral disorder (formerly referred to as "emotional disturbance") includes any of several behaviors that (1) occur over a long period of time to a marked degree and (2) affect educational performance. Included are aggressive or acting-out behaviors (e.g., disobedience, tantrums, and destructiveness of property), immature or withdrawn behavior, chronic fearfulness, and sadness or depression (Edwards & Simpson, 1996, p. 258). Factors that determine an emotional or behavioral disorder include frequency, intensity, duration, and age-appropriateness of the behaviors (Hunt & Marshall, 1994). For example, continuous activity and exploration are typical of 2-year-olds, but not of sixth-graders (McLoughlin & Lewis, 1994, p. 248).

Physical disabilities that affect learning include hearing and visual impairments. The most pervasive effect of hearing loss is on language development (Mayer, 1996). Although individuals who are deaf or hard of hearing as a group have normal intellectual abilities, their academic achievement tends to lag one to three years behind their hearing peers (Hunt & Marshall, 1994, p. 356). The problem lies with their lack of mastery of the English language.

On occasion, teachers identify potential hearing loss through observation of their students. A child who seems to be straining to push himself closer to the speaker, speaks either very softly or very loudly, has difficulty following simple oral directions, and has difficulty pronouncing words may have a hearing problem (Rubin, 1997). The child should be checked for possible hearing loss.

Visual impairment refers to the condition in which the individual's educational performance is affected even with correction. Depending on the extent of the disability, the student may require large-print materials and felt pens. If the student is blind, he or she may require materials in Braille. Students who are visually impaired may have difficulty in developing some concepts such as colors. A low-incidence disability, approximately one student in a thousand is visually impaired and receives special services (Silberman, 1996, p. 353).

Disabilities in the Classroom.   Most students with disabilities that affect their learning may be described as mildly handicapped. They are mildly retarded, learning disabled, or mildly behaviorally disordered. Children within these categories tend to display similar characteristics that have implications for instruction and assessment (p. 185). They have difficulties in attending to key information in tasks, generalizing across similar situations, solving abstract problems, and remembering information. They also have difficulties in developing and using special skills and in evaluating their own performance. Children with these problems are typically diagnosed after experiencing repeated failure in school tasks (Hallahan & Kauffman, 1994).

Developing an Individual Education Program (IEP)

The IEP is a detailed instructional planning document. It is prepared for the student receiving federally mandated services or who has an identified learning disability. The IEP is a written commitment of the resources essential for the student's needs. The document is prepared by a multidisciplinary team that includes the student's teacher, one or both parents, a supervisory representative, such as the principal, and evaluation personnel (Bateman, 1992).

The IEP consists of several components. First is the student's current level of performance, annual goals, and short-term objectives. Information on the student's current performance level should address his or her unique needs that special services are to address and should be stated in concrete terms. An example is that Bobby (a third-grader) reads second-grade material at the rate of twenty to thirty words per minute with five to eight errors and comprehends very little (Bateman, 1992).

Similarly, the annual goals and short-term objectives should be clearly stated. An example of an annual goal is demonstrating six to eight months' gain in reading as measured by the Woodcock-Johnson Psychoeducational Battery. The short-term objectives stated in the IEP bridge the gap between the student's current performance levels and the annual goals. That is, they are teachable subcomponents of the goals and they describe specific, observable, and measurable activities (*Federal Register,* 1981). An example is "to read paragraphs at the third-grade level at eighty to one hundred words per minute with zero to two errors" (Bateman, 1992).

The extent of participation in the regular classroom, the extent of special education and related services, and the duration of services are identified next. The duration is usually one year; services typically are initiated within a few days of the IEP meeting and are projected for the remainder of the school year.

The IEP concludes with the evaluation procedures and schedules that determine whether the short-term objectives are being achieved. For example, the team may specify the completion of behavioral charts on the incidence of disruptive behavior in the classroom during the year. In language arts, the IEP may specify teacher observation of a student's oral responses for an objective that states the student can answer concrete factual questions on brief stories. For an objective that specifies reading at a particular grade level with few errors, the evaluation may specify the administration of an informal reading inventory.

In summary, the IEP is an individualized plan that identifies the student's current performance level and specifies annual goals, short-term objectives, types of services, and the methods of evaluating achievement of the short-term objectives.

Implications for Assessment

The IEP is developed for students receiving federally mandated services for a developmental exceptionality. It serves as a guide for both resource room teachers and the regular classroom teacher in planning instruction and assessment. In addition to the assessments identified in the IEP, observations and anecdotal records provide opportunities for the teacher to develop information about student engagement in classroom tasks and progress in literacy.

Of particular importance in planning assessments for both low achievers and students with developmental exceptionalities is to allow sufficient time for the completion of assessment tasks. That is, students may require additional time because of their slow work pace, difficulty in processing information, or visual motor problems (Spinelli, 2002). Also, students with physical impairments may require more time to write, type, or dictate their responses (p. 145). Sufficient time also can reduce anxiety, which is often a problem for students with learning difficulties.

A second concern is to plan assessments so that information on the student's capabilities is not dependent on a particular format. The issue is that of validity. For example, a student may understand a reading passage, but have difficulty with writing. Therefore, when the goal is to assess comprehension, students who have difficulty writing may be interviewed by the teacher. Also, student reactions to stories they have read may be tape recorded or documented in teacher interviews. Further, when the goal is composition, students may use a computer to develop a short story. Students with visual or hearing problems may require a computer with adaptive devices.

The Potential Role of Portfolio Assessment

Educators who have addressed the role of portfolio assessment for students with developmental exceptionalities have identified both advantages and cautions to be observed in implementation.

Advantages. Four advantages are identified for portfolio assessment with special needs learners. First, the portfolio can demonstrate progress throughout the year toward attaining objectives in the student's IEP (Hobbs, 1993, p. 251). Second, the portfolio encourages collaboration among the members of the interdisciplinary team (Jochum et al., 1998; Hobbs, 1993). Individual teachers, for example, noted that the resource room portfolio helped them in mainstreaming the children in their classrooms (Hobbs, 1993).

Third, portfolios promote communication between teachers and parents (Salend, 1998). Parents state that they want information on their child's academic progress, some indication of the child's capacity, and information about the child's ability to apply learning to new situations (Hobbs, 1993, p. 240). Portfolios, which can include the child's screening and placement assessments, teacher's anecdotal notes on student's independent work, and samples of student work can address these questions. Parents and teachers also describe the portfolio as useful in planning the student's IEP because the portfolio pieces are concrete examples of skill development (Ezell et al., 1999).

A fourth advantage, identified in surveys and interviews of twenty-seven teachers, is the positive influence on student learning (Ezell et al., 1999). The opportunity to practice setting goals and making decisions led to students' pride in their work and increased learning. One student, for example, remarked, "I did this today. Tomorrow I'm going to learn more. Will you be back to see me?" (p. 460). Goal setting also provides students the opportunity to set a purpose for their writing, a new experience for students with written language disabilities (Wansart, 1988). When students write with a purpose, the skill that they develop begins to have meaning for them (p. 317).

Further, a contributing factor to increased learning is likely the opportunities provided for students to repeat classroom work. That is, reviewing the portfolio and sharing the work with different audiences helps to compensate for the students' deficits in short-term memory (Ezell et al., 1999).

Cautions in Implementing Portfolio Assessment.   The complexity of higher academic standards represented by authentic assessment tasks may be beyond the capabilities of some students with disabilities. That is, many proposed authentic tasks are long-term projects that require planning, independence, and relying on references and other resources. Special learners, however, often have difficulty with these tasks (Choate & Evans, 1992). Portfolio goals, however, are flexible and should be appropriate for the individual student. Thus, careful planning during the development of the IEP is needed so that appropriate goals are set for special needs learners.

Also of importance in using portfolios with special needs students is to ensure that the portfolio requirements are implemented appropriately. For example, many students with learning disabilities have difficulty with writing skills. Therefore, beginning writers might use drawings and simple words to respond to prompts for self-reflection. As their writing skills develop, they might use one- and two-sentence reasons to respond to structured prompts. Examples of prompts include "This piece shows my improvement in . . ." and "I want this in my portfolio because . . ." (Jochum et al., 1998).

Scoring rubrics also should be carefully constructed. For example, one writing rubric for a first-grade student ranged from 1 to 3 on content, organization, and mechanics. Level 1, for mechanics stated, "draws pictures to convey meaning, and may dictate some words to be written down." The level 3 standard was "Includes 3 sentences or more with a purpose and some details" (Jochum et al., 1998, p. 289). In other words, target tasks and evaluations must ensure appropriateness and relevance for individual students (Choate & Evans, 1992).

Summary

Developmental exceptionalities include several intellectual, physical, or emotional characteristics that affect a student's potential for learning. Included in the category of mental disabilities are mental retardation, slow learners, and students identified as learning disabled. Other disabilities affecting student learning include emotional or behavioral disorders and visual and hearing impairments. All but slow learners are designated through federal legislation to receive additional educational services.

Most of the children in the classroom with learning problems are mildly handicapped. They have difficulties attending to key information in tasks, solving abstract problems, and remembering information. Students who receive federally mandated services also have Individual Educational Programs (IEPs). Typically planned for one year at a time, the IEP documents current performance level, annual goals, short-term objectives, methods of evaluation, and types of educational services (regular classroom and/or special education).

In the classroom, both low achievers and students with disabilities may require additional time to complete assessment tasks. Also, tasks should be designed so that demonstration of adequate performance is not dependent on a particular response format.

Some educators have noted the importance of portfolios in the assessment of students with learning problems. In addition to addressing IEP objectives, portfolios encourage collaboration among members of the interdisciplinary team and facilitate communication with parents. They also can serve as a positive influence on student learning through opportunities for goal setting and revising the work in the portfolio. Of importance in implementing portfolios for students with special needs is to establish requirements that are achievable by the learner and to construct scoring rubrics that are relevant to the student's learning needs.

*Discussion Questions*_____

1. What are two general ways that culture clash in communication patterns in the classroom can lead to inappropriate inferences about students? What are some ways that culture clash can be identified?

2. What is the purpose of assessing the English proficiency of nonnative speakers when they enter school?

3. Why should an assessment of vocabulary knowledge for nonnative English speakers readminister missed items in the student's native language?

4. What is the difference between the designation of slow learner and that of mental retardation?

5. The statement, "The student can write a meaningful paragraph of at least three sentences" is likely which component of the student's IEP?

*References*_____

Au, K. H., Mason, J. M., & Scheu, J. A. (1995). *Literacy instruction for today.* New York: HarperCollins.

Bateman, B. (1992). *Better IEPs: How to develop legally current and educationally useful programs.* Longmont, CO: Sopris West.

Bernhardt, E. B. (2000). Second-language reading as a case study of reading scholarship in the twentieth century. In M. L. Kamil, P. B. Mosenthal, P. D. Pearson, & R. Barr (Eds.), *Handbook of reading research. Volume III* (pp. 791–812). Mahwah, NJ: Lawrence Erlbaum.

Brophy, J. (1996). *Teaching problem students.* New York: Guilford Press.

Browder, D. M. (2001). *Curriculum and assessment for students with moderate and severe disabilities.* New York: Guilford Press.

Choate, J. S., & Evan, S. S. (1992). Authentic assessment of special learners: Problem or promise? *Preventing School Failure, 37*(1), 6–9.

DeStefano, J., Pepinsky, H., & Sanders, T. (1982). Discourse rules for literacy learning in a classroom. In L. C. Wilkinson (Ed.), *Communicating in the classroom.* New York: Academic Press.

Dunn, W. (1993, April). Educating diversity. *American Demographics,* 38–43.

Edwards, L., & Simpson, J. (1996). Children with behavior disorders. In E. L. Meyen (Ed.), *Exceptional children in today's schools* (3rd ed., pp. 251–279). Denver, CO: Love Publishing.

Erickson, F., & Mohatt, G. (1982). Cultural organization of participation structures in two classrooms of Indian students. In G. Spindler (Ed.), *Doing the ethnography of schooling* (pp. 132–175). New York: Holt, Rinehart, & Winston.

Ezell, D., Klein, C. E., & Ezell-Powell, S. (1999). Empowering students with mental retardation through portfolio assessment: A tool for fostering self-determination skills. *Education and Training in Mental Retardation and Developmental Disabilities, 34*(4), 453–463.

Federal Register (Part IV). (1977, August). Washington, DC: U.S. Government Printing Office.

Federal Register. (1981, January). Washington, DC: U.S. Government Printing Office.

Frazier, D. M., & Paulson, F. I. (1992). How portfolios motivate reluctant writers. *Educational Leadership, 49*(8), 62–65.

Garcia, G. E. (2000). Bilingual children's reading. In M. L. Kamil, P. B. Mosenthal, P. D. Pearson, & R. Barr (Eds.). *Handbook of reading research. Vol. III* (pp. 813–834). Mahwah, NJ: Lawrence Erlbaum Associates.

Genishi, C. (1989). Observing the second language learner, *Language Arts, 66*(5), 509–513.

Hallahan, D. P., & Kauffman, J. M. (1994). *Exceptional children.* Boston: Allyn & Bacon.

Herbert, C. H. (1983). *Basic inventory of natural language.* Monterey, CA: Publishers Test Service.

Hobbs, R. (1993). Portfolio use in a learning disabilities resource room. *Reading and Writing Quarterly: Overcoming Learning Difficulties, 9,* 249–261.

Hunt, N., & Marshall, K. (1994). *Exceptional children and youth.* Boston: Houghton Mifflin.

Jochum, J., Curran, C., & Reetze, L. (1998). Creating individual educational portfolios in written language. *Reading and Writing Quarterly, 14,* 283–306.

Kiefer, B. Z., & DeStefano, J. S. (1985). Cultures together in the classroom: "What you sayin'?" In A. Jagger & M. T. Smith-Burke (Eds.), *Observing the language learner.* Urbana, IL: National Council of Teachers of English.

Labov, W. (1970). *The study of nonstandard English.* Urbana, IL: National Council of Teachers of English.

Mason, J. M., & Au, K. H. (1986). *Reading instruction for today.* Glenview, IL: Scott-Foresman.

Mayer, M. H. (1996). Children who are deaf or hard of hearing. In E. L. Meyen (Ed.), *Exceptional children in today's schools* (3rd ed., pp. 315–350). Denver, CO: Love Publishing.

McLoughlin, J. A., & Lewis, R. B. (1994). *Assessing special students* (4th ed.). Columbus, OH: Merrill.

Meyen, E. L. (1996). Educating exceptional children. In E. L. Meyen (Ed.), *Exceptional children in today's schools* (3rd ed., pp. 1–50). Denver, CO: Love Publishing.

Moya, S. S., & O'Malley, J. M. (1994). A portfolio model for ESL. *The Journal of Educational Issues of Language Minority Students, 18,* 13–36.

Munoz-Sandoval, A. F., Cummins, J., Alvarado, C. G., & Ruef, M. (1998). *Bilingual Verbal Ability Tests.* Itasca, IL: Riverside.

Pearson, P. D., DeStefano, L., & Garcia, G. E. (1998). Ten dilemmas of performance assessment. In C. Harrison & T. Salinger, T. (Eds.), *Assessing reading I. Theory and practice* (pp. 21–49). New York: Routledge.

Pinnell, G. G., & Jagger, A. M. (1991). Oral language: Speaking and listening in the classroom. In J. Flood, J. M. Jensensen, D. Lapp., & J. R. Squire (Eds.), *Handbook of research on teaching the language arts* (pp. 691–720). New York: Macmillan.

Rubin, D. (1997). *Diagnosis and correction in reading instruction.* Boston: Allyn & Bacon.

Salend, S. J. (1998). Using portfolios to assess student performance. *Teaching Exceptional Children, 31*(2), 36–43.

Sattler, J. (2001). *Assessment of children: Cognitive applications* (4th ed.). San Diego: Jerome M. Sattler, Publisher, Inc.

Silberman, R. K. (1996). Children with visual impairments. In. E. L. Meyen (Ed.), *Exceptional children in today's schools* (3rd ed., pp. 351–398). Denver, CO: Love Publishing.

Spinelli, C. G. (2002). *Classroom assessment for students with special needs in inclusive settings.* Upper Saddle River, NJ: Merrill/Prentice Hall.

Tompkins, G. E., & Hoskinsson, K. (1995*). Language Arts: Content and teaching strategies* (3rd ed.). Englewood Cliffs, NJ: Merrill/Prentice Hall.

U.S. Department of Education. (1991). *Thirteenth annual report to Congress on the implementation of the Individuals with Disabilities Education Act.* Washington, DC: U.S. Government Printing Office.

Valdes, G. (1996). *Con repeto. Bridging the distances between culturally diverse families and schools: An ethnographic portrait.* New York: Teachers College Press.

Wansart, W. L. (1988). The student with learning disabilities in a writing process classroom. *A Case study. Reading, Writing, and Learning Disabilities, 4,* 311–319.

Wolf, D., Davidson, L., Davis, M., Walters, J., Hodges, M., & Scripp, L. (1988). Beyond A, B, and C: A broader and deeper view of literacy. In A. D. Pelegrino (Ed.), *Psychological bases for early education* (pp. 123–152). New York: Wiley.

9

Diagnostic Oral Reading Assessments

. . . the process by which a reader identifies words cannot be fully explained by traditionally defined word recognition skills. In many, or most cases, what a reader produces orally is a result of the use of meaning, the anticipation of meaning, or of syntactical clues.

—Johns, 1982, pp. 25–26

Linda is reading aloud a brief text about a swing. She says "I like the swing. I shall ke— get off it—on it. The swing will—No! wa—want—No! won't up and down" (Clay, 2001, p. 33). Linda's action indicates her awareness that the text contains a particular message. Further, she uses both meaning and syntax clues in her reading. Although she fails to correct her use of "won't" for "went" in the second sentence, she engages in problem-solving actions during her reading.

The importance of this and other diagnostic assessments is that they are a rich source of information about the knowledge and strategies that students use in relation to reading. This chapter discusses oral assessments that provide information about students' difficulties in reading and methods for identifying texts at appropriate reading levels for students.

Assessing Reading Strategies

Readers who make good progress address print text in an integrated way to construct meaning. In contrast, poor readers may have any of several difficulties. Among them are an inability to hear the separation of words in a spoken sentence, attending to only the final sounds of words, or an inability to relate their other knowledge about letter sounds and words as cross-checks on each other, or to get the messages conveyed by print (Clay, 2001). Two assessment methods are discussed in this section that provide the teacher information about the ways that readers address unfamiliar text. They are running records and miscue analysis.

Running Records

The purpose of the running record is to determine the ways that children can direct their knowledge of letters, sounds, and words to understand the messages in the text (Clay, 2000). For example, readers correct some of the errors they make without prompting. They pick up cues from sentence structure or meaning, or the visual cues of letters or letter sequences (Clay, 2001). The running record assists the teacher in inferring, from children's self-corrections and their comments, the information in the text they are addressing (p. 22). That is, it provides an opportunity to observe children's difficulties in monitoring and correcting their performance.

The running record is appropriate for the acquisition stages of reading and should be used by the end of the first year of school (Clay, 2001). Ideally, it should be used with all children in the class. If that is not possible, then the teacher should implement the procedure with the lowest 50 percent of the readers (Clay, 2001).

Materials. The focus of a running record is to capture all the child's actions that can assist the teacher to determine how the student is making decisions during reading (Clay, 2000, p. 7). To obtain a complete picture of the child's thinking, performance should be recorded for three levels of text (using little books with 200 to 300 words). These reading levels, based on the individual child's performance, are easy (the child's reading accuracy is 95 to 100 percent), instructional level (90 to 94 percent reading accuracy), and hard (80 to 89 percent reading accuracy). In practice, an easy text often is one the child has read successfully in the past (or a similar text) (Clay, 2001). An instructional level text may be one already introduced to the class, but the child must engage in problem solving to read at the designated accuracy level. The purpose of selecting such a text is to determine how well the child orchestrates the reading behaviors she controls in a situation in which she knows the text meaning (p. 22). Of importance is that the teacher should avoid preprinted texts from publishers because they cannot capture children's diverse problem-solving actions.

The three levels of text difficulty provide the teacher with insights into different aspects of reading strategies (Clay, 2001). They are as follows:

- Easier text: how the child orchestrates effective reading
- Instructional text: how the child processes information and solves problems
- Difficult text: how and when breakdowns in effective processing occur

Administration. The task is to record everything the child says and does while trying to read a book selected by the teacher (Clay, 2001). About two hours of initial practice for the teacher is a good beginning. Also the teacher will notice more as her ear becomes attuned to children's reading behaviors and the coding becomes more familiar (p. 24).

To obtain accurate information, the oral reading activity should be as relaxed as possible. The teacher should sit next to the child and explain that he wants to listen to the child read. Beginning with an easy text, the teacher should invite the child to read this book to him. Also, the teacher should explain that he will be writing down some things to better understand the child as a reader (Clay, 2000, p. 6). To obtain information about the child's strengths and weaknesses, a reading of 100 to 200 words from each of the three levels of text is needed (p. 24). This procedure efficiently captures children's reading behaviors.

Coding.   To record the child's oral reading behaviors, the teacher uses either a blank sheet of paper or a page divided into columns with the text typed triple-spaced in the left column. The types of reading behaviors the teacher records are each word that is correctly read, all attempts at a word, the child's self-corrections, nonresponses, and teacher provision of a word (Clay, 2001).

Table 9.1 illustrates the coding for these behaviors. As indicated, a checkmark (✓) identifies all words the child reads correctly. Also, recorded are misread words, all attempts at a word (with the correct text written below the attempts and/or the self-corrections), all self-corrections, and the words not read (items 2 through 5, Table 9.1).

TABLE 9.1   *Examples of Coding in Running Records*

Example	*Explanation*
1. Words read correctly (✓)	
Text: Bill ran all the way home.	All 6 words were read correctly
Record: ✓ ✓ ✓ ✓ ✓ ✓	
2. Misread word	
Text: home	Child read "home" as "house"
Record: <u>house</u> home	
3. All attempts at a word	
Text: home	
Record: <u>h—/house</u>	Child attempted the word, and then read it as
home	"house"
4. Self-corrections	
Text: home	The child first said "house" and then
Record: <u>house/SC</u>	self-corrected (SC), reading "home"
home	
5. No response	
Text: He fell asleep.	Child failed to read "asleep" in the sentence
Record: ✓ ✓ ———	

A child's repetition of a word may be coded R, but this event is not counted as an error. Also important is that the teacher should respond to a child's appeal for assistance by saying "You try it" (Clay, 2001, p. 27). The appeal is coded A. Then, if the child does not respond (coded as "_____"), the teacher's provision of the word is recorded (T).

On occasion, the child may become so confused that teacher assistance is indicated. First, the teacher should say, "Try that again" (Clay, 2001, p. 27). Brackets should be placed around the muddled phrase, and it should be coded TTA (p. 27). This attempt should be counted in the scoring as one error. Then the new attempt at the sentence is coded.

Scoring.   To score the running record, count the number of errors made by the child. However, self-corrections are excluded because the child, using information in the sentence structure or meaning, replaced the incorrect word.

During the reading, a child's insertions add errors and he can have more errors than the number of words in a line (Clay, 2001, p. 29). The following sentence is an example.

> *Text:*   The sad little girl sighed.
> *Child:*   The sad (-----) girl cried and cried and cried.
> *Scoring:* ✓ ✓ ✗ ✓ ✗ ✗ ✗ ✗ ✗   (6 errors)

Of importance, however, is that the lowest score for a page is zero; the child does not receive a minus score.

The purpose of counting the reading errors is to calculate the child's accuracy rate. It is the ratio of errors to running words. For example, 10 errors out of 140 words is a ratio of 1 to 14, or a 93 percent accuracy rate. The accuracy rate assists the teacher to identify children who are ready to work with more difficult material, those who are working on material that is too difficult for them, and those children who need more of the teacher's attention (Clay, 2000, p. 26). For example, a ratio of 1 to 9 or less indicates that the child tends to lose the meaning of the text (Clay, 2000). In contrast, a ratio of 1 to 14 indicates the reader may be ready for more difficult material.

Also important is the child's self-correction rate; efficient self-correction is an important skill in reading (Clay, 1985, p. 22). To calculate this rate, determine the ratio of the number of self-corrections to the sum of the child's errors and the self-corrections. (This sum reflects the number of the child's chances to make errors in that reading.) For example, suppose the child self-corrected four times and made twelve errors. Her self-correction rate is one in four (four out of sixteen [12 + 4]).

A self-correction rate of one in three to five chances for error is good; however, one in twenty is very poor (Clay, 1985). The absence of self-correction in a record with errors is a danger signal. The child may be unaware of the need to determine a precise message from the text, be unaware of available cues, lack the knowledge to use cues, or does not try to solve the problem (p. 22).

Interpretation.   The process of interpretation includes two key activities. First is to determine the type(s) of information that the child relied on in her word selection. Also important in this analysis is to rely on only the child's behavior up to the error (Clay, 2001, p. 31).

One source of information is sentence meaning. Even if the reading is inaccurate, if it makes sense, then the child is likely applying her knowledge of oral language to her reading (Clay, 1985, p. 21). Next, is the reading grammatical? If not, one possibility is that the child's "personal grammar" does not include these structures. Finally, does the child make use of visual cues?

The possible factors that the child relied on when the error was made are coded as follows: M = meaning or text message, S = structure (syntax) of the sentence prior to the error, and V = visual information from the print. For example, reader substitution of "possed" in the phrase "posed in front of the mirror" would be coded "VS." That is, the print symbols and the sentence structure seem to be the basis for the error. In contrast, substitution of "bedroom" for "room" in "going to his room" would be coded MS. The error is consistent with both the sentence structure and the meaning.

The teacher should then review the pattern of errors. For example, one child may be relying primarily on the visual print information with some attention to sentence structure, but seems unaware of the lack of meaning in her reading. The child should be encouraged to recognize when the meaning of a sentence is lacking. Another child, however, may rely on meaning and sentence structure, but be unaware of his discrepancies with the printed words. Attention to sound/symbol correspondences or expanding the child's vocabulary of sight words may be needed.

The second major interpretative activity is to review the reader's self-corrections. A self-correction occurs when the reader realizes that information in the text indicates something is wrong (Clay, 2001, p. 32). In analyzing the child's self-corrections, the teacher first reviews the error. The purpose is to determine the information the child was using when the error occurred. For example, a child erroneously may say "bike" for bicycle when he is reading because the word makes sense in the sentence. Then the teacher considers the additional information that led to self-correction. In the above example, the child may look at the word again and correctly say "bicycle." The source of information for the correction is likely visual cues—"bicycle" is longer than "bike" (Clay, 2001).

Although the child's self-corrections may be inefficient, they are a sign of progress. The child is aware of the existence of cues and that the text conveys a precise message. In contrast, the child who is unaware of her errors and makes no effort to self-correct is in difficulty (Clay, 2001, p. 32). She is either unaware of the role of text, unaware of the existence of cues, or unable to use the cues.

Advantages and Limitations.   An advantage of running records is that they can identify approaches to reading that are not readily identifiable by other means. For example, two children may have approximately the same accuracy rate, but approach print text in different ways. Another advantage is that running records can identify potential problems in children's processing approaches early, at a time when they are more readily corrected.

Like other diagnostic procedures that provide detailed information, administration and interpretation of running records can be time consuming. Another disadvantage is that valid and reliable scoring and interpretation are dependent on the teacher's ability to record all the errors accurately. That is, poor observation reduces the number of recorded errors, inflating the accuracy score and decreasing reliability.

In summary, running records determine the ways that young children use letters, sounds, and words to understand text. This information is obtained for 200- to 300-word stories that are at the child's reading levels of easy, instructional, and difficult. The three types of information obtained in the scoring and analysis are accuracy rate, the types of errors, and the self-correction rate. Interpretation of the reader's errors and self-correction can indicate particular difficulties.

Miscue Analysis

The running record was developed for use with young children to determine the extent to which they monitor and correct their reading performance and their strengths and difficulties. In contrast, miscue analysis is appropriate for other age levels. The major purpose is to analyze students' oral reading in order to plan specific reading programs and to organize reading programs for groups of students (Y. Goodman, Watson, & Burke, 1987, p. 7).

The term *miscues* refers to the unexpected responses a reader makes to text (K. Goodman, 1973). The term was introduced to remove the negative connotation of words such as *error* and *mistake* and to emphasize the belief that reading is not random behavior (Y. Goodman et al., 1987, p. 5). Instead, miscues indicate readers' logical predictions about the text, based on their general knowledge and experience and their knowledge about language. Miscue analysis involves coding students' word substitutions during oral reading, followed by the students' retelling of the passage.

Materials Selection and Preparation.   Selection of appropriate material for miscue analysis is important to obtain information that helps explain the student's reading problems. Table 9.2 lists the selection criteria. First, the text should be at least 500 words in length because students tend to self-correct the miscues that don't make sense after the first 200 words.

Second, the text should be neither too easy nor too difficult for the reader. If the material is too easy, the student will make few, if any, miscues that change the meaning. If the material is too difficult, the student will be unable to make sense of the syntax and semantics in an integrated way. The features in step four in Table 9.2 (predictable language and structure, concept load, and relevance) are particularly important because they influence the difficulty of the text for the reader. Unique style, breaks in the traditional sequence of events, and information that is not relevant add to the reader's difficulty in predicting and, therefore, increase the reading difficulty (Y. Goodman et al., 1987, p. 40).

Concept load refers to the amount of new information for the reader and relevance refers to the importance of aspects of the story to the reader's personal life. For example, suppose you were required to read a technical article on the artifacts of the Ming dynasty. The high concept load would require you to reread many sentences. Further, the meanings of some sentences would not be clear because of the prior knowledge required for the passage.

Relevance also influences concept load. For example, a story about the aerodynamic problems faced by the Wright brothers has relevance for the student whose hobby is airplanes. However, the story likely represents high cognitive load for the student who has no

TABLE 9.2 *Guidelines for the Selection of Material for Miscue Analysis[1]*

1. Material (fiction or nonfiction) selected for reading should be unfamiliar, unpracticed, and contain at least 500 words.

2. Material should challenge readers' strategies, but should permit the reader to proceed independently.

3. The text should be complete and cohesive, such as a story, poem, or article, and be both interesting to the student and well written.
   a. fiction—have a plot and story line
   b. nonfiction—develop at least one concept or completely describe an act or event

4. Features to consider in selecting material are (a) predictability of the language and overall structure, (b) concept load of the content, and (c) relevance of the material for the reader (p. 40).

5. Materials should show readers' strengths and their development over time.

[1]Summarized from Y. Goodman, Watson, & Burke (1987)

interest in this topic. A general rule is to strike a balance among these factors. That is, if the format is not predictable, then the information should be well known to the student (Y. Goodman et al., 1987, p. 40).

Procedure.   The atmosphere during the procedure should be informal and friendly. The student may be encouraged to leaf through the text to determine length and whether or not she has previously read or heard the story (Y. Goodman et al., 1987, p. 43). The student should be told that she will be asked to retell the story after reading it aloud.

The student reads directly from the original text. The teacher records miscues on a typescript of the material in which line length, spelling, and punctuation are identical to the original. The student's oral reading also should be tape recorded (Y. Goodman et al., 1987). The reading time typically is 15 to 30 minutes, depending on the characteristics of the reading and the complexity of the material.

After the reading begins, it should be stopped for only two reasons. One is very few miscues in the first few paragraphs. The teacher should compliment the student and ask him or her to read a different (i.e., more challenging) passage. The other reason for stopping is a student's inability to read independently. However, slow or choppy reading is not sufficient evidence to discontinue the exercise (Y. Goodman et al., 1987, p. 43). In the case of a discontinued read, the teacher should thank the student and decide whether he should read another selection.

Following the oral reading, the teacher thanks the student and asks him to retell the passage. One purpose for the retelling is to determine if the student who has read a passage with few miscues has failed to comprehend the meaning. Another purpose is that the student's construction of meaning is enhanced through the presentation of his perceptions and ideas and testing them with an audience (Y. Goodman et al., 1987, p. 44). To document the retelling, the teacher should have an outline of the passage. She also may record anecdotal notes. Y. Goodman et al. (1987) also recommend that, when the student is finished, the teacher should ask open-ended questions to stimulate further retelling (p. 46). An example is Why do you think (character mentioned by the student) did that?

Coding. The reading miscue procedures developed by Y. Goodman et al. (1987) are detailed and sophisticated. The process also can be costly in terms of time (Hiebert, 1991). Marzano, Hagerty, Valencia, and Distefano (1987) suggest using a modified miscue procedure. They recommend coding word substitutions, insertions, and omissions because these reader responses provide the most information about the student's reading processes (p. 99). In other words, they recommend excluding corrected words, word reversals, and repetitions.

As illustrated in Table 9.3, substituted words are written above the printed word in the teacher's typescript of the reading. Also, the teacher may choose to identify a student's dialect substitutions. Example 1b illustrates the coding for the substitution of "like" for "liked" and "bes" for "best." Words in the text omitted by the reader are circled (example 2) and insertions are written above the text, indicated with a caret (^) (example 3).

If the teacher also chooses to document word reversals, they are easily recorded. See the transpositional marking in example 4. Y. Goodman et al. (1987) further suggest that

TABLE 9.3 *Examples of Coding in Miscue Analysis[1]*

Example	*Explanation*
1. Word substitutions	
a. Text: Where is Ramos?	Student substitutes "that" for "where"
That	
Record: ~~Where~~ is Ramos?	
like⒟ bes⒯	
b. Text: She liked dolls best.	Student uses dialect words "like"
Record: She liked dolls best.	for "liked" and "bes" for "best"
2. Omissions	
Text: He left the book at home today.	The omitted phrase is circled
Record: He left the book(at home)today.	
3. Insertions	
Text: . . . put the box on the side	
in	
Record: . . . put the box on the ^side.	Insertion indicated with a (^)
4. Reversals	
Text: His two best friends were . . .	
Record: His two⌐best friends were . . .	Transposition line indicates reversals

[1]Summarized from Goodman et al. (1987)

corrections also may be coded. Suppose, for example, that Yuli says "head" for "heard" and then corrects herself. The teacher codes the text as follows:

He © head heard the dog bark.

The coding indicates the misstated word, accompanied by © to indicate the self-correction.

The teacher first notes the miscues during the student's oral reading. Later, she re-plays the tape to check for accuracy in the coding.

Interpretation.   The next step, interpretation, focuses on the sentence within the story or article (Y. Goodman et al., 1987, p. 116). Specifically, three questions are asked about each sentence and the answer "Y" for "yes" or "N" for "no" is noted in the right margin. The first question asks if the sentence, as produced by the reader, is syntactically accept-able. That is, does it sound like language and does it fit the grammatical structure of the sentence?

The second question addresses the semantic acceptability of the reader's altered sen-tence. That is, does the miscue "fit" within the sentence? For example, reading "*Tomor-row* I am going to fish in Grandpa's pond" for "*Today* I am going to fish in Grandpa's pond" does result in a semantically acceptable sentence.

Third, has the changed sentence semantically altered the meaning of the story? In the prior example, suppose the story was about the activities a boy is planning to com-memorate his grandfather's birthday that day. The substitution of "tomorrow" in the sen-tence about fishing changes the meaning.

Applying this questioning to example 1a in Table 9.3 yields Y, Y, N. The produced sentence is syntactically acceptable because the question, "That is Ramos?" is grammati-cally correct. The miscue also is semantically acceptable within the sentence, but the al-tered sentence does not fit the story. The subsequent sentences mentioned several possible locations where Ramos might be.

The percentage of sentences marked Y and N (of the total number of sentences) for each category may be calculated. Proficient readers are those who produce structures that are syntactically and structurally acceptable most of the time (Y. Goodman et al., 1987). Also, their substitutions are usually moderately similar to the text graphically (e.g., "there" for "where"). Moderately proficient readers also may produce acceptable struc-tures most of the time, but their reading may be slow and they have a tendency to rely extensively on letter/sound information. They also tend to correct miscues that are seman-tically acceptable. In contrast, nonproficient readers rely on sounding out letters, syllables, and words (Y. Goodman et al., 1987, p. 147). However, less than half of their miscues produce sentences that are syntactically and semantically acceptable or that do not result in meaning change.

Retrospective Miscue Analysis (RMA).   Appropriate for students from the upper el-ementary grades through adulthood, retrospective miscue analysis also records word sub-stitutions during oral reading (Y. Goodman, 1999). However, this approach differs from other oral reading procedures in that the reader is a partner with the teacher in determining the source of each word substitution. The role of RMA is "to move the reader toward understanding and valuing his or her own knowledge of language instead of giving up on ever being able to read proficiently (Moore & Aspegren, 2001, p. 494).

After the oral reading and documentation of the reader's miscues, the teacher has two choices. In the first option, if the reader lacks confidence or seems not be successful, the teacher may preselect the miscues for initial discussion with the student (Y. Goodman, 1999, p. 143). The teacher sets up a series of sessions in which five to seven miscues are selected. The initial miscues discussed are those that indicate the reader is using strategies that support his or her construction of meaning. Subsequent sessions then address the miscues that disrupted meaning. For each instance, the teacher and student explore the likely reasons for the miscue.

Table 9.4 illustrates questions that help guide the discussion. As indicated, the questions move from the miscue itself to the rationale for selection and the relationship to the reader's understanding of the text. That is, RMA invites the reader to view mistakes as attempts to construct meaning rather than failures to learn (Moore & Aspegren, 2001, p. 494).

The other option, for students who are considered to be average or better readers, is to involve them in the examination of the whole reading. The student listens to the tape recording and follows along with the original text. The teacher and student discuss the likely reasons for a miscue, and whether the substitution altered the syntactic or semantic meaning.

Over time, through discussions of the miscues, students "demythify" the reading process (Y. Goodman, 1999). They may believe, for example, that good readers know every word and can remember everything they read (p. 142). Also, they may learn that they are better readers than they think they are, that all readers miscue and transform the material they read in making meaning (p. 142), and that reading involves more than sim-

TABLE 9.4 *Guiding Questions in Retrospective Miscue Analysis*

Focus	*Questions*[1]
Nature of the miscue	Does the miscue make sense? Or sound like language?
Reader action	Did you self-correct? Should the miscue have been corrected?
Text–miscue comparison	Does the word in the material look like the substitution? Does it sound like it?
Rationale for the miscue	Why did you make the miscue?
Relationship of the miscue to text meaning	Did the miscue affect your understanding of the material?
Rationale for the reader's conclusion	Why do you think so? How do you know?

[1]Summarized from Goodman (1999)

ply trying to remember the words. The teacher also helps readers understand that high-quality miscues that do not change the syntactic and semantic pattern of the text are often indicators of sophisticated reading (p. 145). The shifts in personal views of one's reading are referred to as *revaluing* and can, according to Y. Goodman (1999), lead to greater reading proficiency.

Unlike the running record, neither miscue nor retrospective miscue analysis makes use of materials at different levels of reading difficulty for the student. Therefore, the validity and reliability of the analysis is dependent on the careful selection of material that is challenging for the reader, predictable, and relevant for the reader. Otherwise, the procedure may yield an inaccurate analysis. A disadvantage of the procedure is the time required for administration, and, for retrospective miscue analysis, the discussion. An advantage is developing an understanding of the reader's approaches to constructing meaning from text.

Summary.   Miscue analysis, like the running record, identifies the word substitutions made by a reader while processing text information. Material selected for miscue analysis should be unfamiliar, contain at least 500 words, and be a complete text with predictable language and structure. The selection also should be relevant for the reader.

A miscue procedure suggested for the classroom documents word substitutions, insertions, and omissions. Interpretation of the miscues involves answering three yes/no questions about each sentence. Calculation of the percentages of sentences that are syntactically and semantically appropriate leads to an identification of proficient, moderately proficient, and nonproficient readers.

Retrospective miscue analysis, in contrast, engages the reader as a partner in determining the source of word substitutions. It is appropriate for the upper elementary grades through adulthood. The purpose of discussing the miscues with the student is to demystify the reading process and lead to revaluing by the student, which can lead to improved reading proficiency.

Determining Reading Levels

Livia is a child whose preschool experience differed greatly from those of the average school entrant (Clay, 1993). He was more than seven years old before he had an opportunity to learn to read. By his fourth year in school he was reading competently at the level of children in their third year of school (p. 13). His rate of progress after he began reading was about average. Livia needed reading material and instruction at his level so he could continue to make progress. If he received material that was too difficult, he would be working at a frustration level. More important, Livia would be likely to lose reading skill because he would not be practicing his already-acquired skills in smooth combination (Clay, 1993, p. 13).

Two methods for assisting teachers to select reading materials at the appropriate level for students are discussed in this section. They are informal reading inventories (IRIs) and the cloze procedure.

Informal Reading Inventories (IRIs)

The abbreviation IRI is a generic term that refers to several measures of reading which include both oral and silent reading of graded passages. Although the term *informal* implies that the teacher constructs the inventory, several commercially published assessments are available.

A major function of an IRI is to "help determine the child's level of independence, instruction, frustration, and capacity" (Rubin, 1997, p. 166). This information helps the teacher match the child with the levels of books he or she reads. That is, the central purpose of an IRI is to establish the optimal level of text difficulty that can stimulate growth when the student is working with the guidance, support, and instruction of the teacher (Pikulski, 1990, p. 516). IRIs can be very useful in the classroom, including content subjects, because teachers frequently underestimate the difficulty of textual materials that children are attempting to read (Pumfrey, 1985). Some educators indicate that as many as 50 to 70 percent of students are placed with books that are too difficult for them (Johns, 1982, p. 3).

A second function is to provide information about a student's strengths and weaknesses in reading so that the teacher can plan an appropriate reading program for the student (Rubin, 1997, p. 166). A third function is to provide feedback to the student on his or her reading behavior. That is, the student can develop an awareness of her comprehension strengths and weaknesses, and the reading level appropriate for her (p. 168).

Procedure. The IRI is an individually administered assessment. The components typically consist of (1) lists of twenty to twenty-five words from each reader level (usually preprimer to eighth grade), (2) oral and silent reading passages at each reader level, accompanied by (3) factual, inferential, and word meaning questions (Rubin, 1997).

The student begins by orally reading the word list at two grades below his or her current grade placement. Reading continues until he makes the number of errors specified in the manual for the IRI (Marzano et al., 1987). As the student reads the passages, the teacher records the miscues. In addition to substitutions, omissions, and insertions, Marzano et al. (1987) suggest that repetitions, partial words, and phonics attempts should be recorded. (The commercially developed inventories differ somewhat in the types of miscues that are recorded.)

If the student orally reads the passage at the independent level (only one uncorrected miscue in 100 words) or the instructional level (no more than five uncorrected miscues in 100 words), the teacher asks the comprehension questions for the passage. The student then reads the silent passage at the same grade level and the teacher asks the related comprehension questions (Rubin, 1997, p. 167).

The student then proceeds to passages at the next grade level, and continues until he or she reaches the frustration level (miscues exceed 10%). Sometimes a student makes so many word recognition errors during oral reading that she is reading near her frustration level. In this case, the teacher should read passages aloud to the student and ask the related comprehension questions. This procedure assists the teacher to determine the student's listening comprehension or listening capacity (p. 167).

In addition, Emmett A. Betts (1946), the developer of the reading levels, identified a buffer zone between the instructional and frustration levels (Rubin, 1997). The buffer zone is identified as 91 to 94 percent word recognition and 51 to 74 percent comprehension. When a child's performance is in this zone, the teacher must decide whether or not to continue the assessment. If the child exhibits signs of frustration, the assessment should be discontinued.

Scoring and Interpretation.   In an IRI, the child's reading performance is compared to an established mastery standard. That is, the child is not compared to his or her peers. IRIs typically define three levels of reading. As indicated in Table 9.5, they are independent, instructional, and frustration levels. They are defined by the number of miscues in oral reading and the extent of the student's comprehension. The independent level is one at which the child reads library books; reference books for projects also should be at this level (Rubin, 1997, p. 168). In contrast, the instructional level is the one at which teaching occurs, and the frustration level should be avoided. Also important is that students may have reading levels that span from one to three reader levels (Rubin, 1997, p. 169). Students' background information, interests, and experience influence their performance in particular content areas. For example, a student's frustration level may be grade 4, with an instructional level of 2 to 3, and an independent reading level at first grade. This information indicates that the student should be instructed with materials that are one to two grades below his chronological age (Marzano et al., 1987, p. 82).

The student's reading of both the word lists and the oral passages also can provide useful diagnostic information (Marzano et al., 1987). For example, words that are recognized immediately indicate the student's sight vocabulary. Also, like miscue analysis, identification of students' miscues in the word lists and reading passages can indicate the students' particular difficulties.

TABLE 9.5   *Student Reading Levels on IRIs[1]*

Level	Description
Independent	No more than one uncorrected miscue in each 100 words with 90% comprehension. For oral reading, the student should read with good rhythm with appropriate phrasing. In silent reading, the student does not subvocalize or use lip movements.
Instructional	Accurate pronunciation of at least 95% of the words (no more than five uncorrected miscues in 100 words) and at least 75% comprehension on both oral and silent reading. The student also should read with good rhythm, with attention to phrasing and punctuation.
Frustration	Miscues exceed 10% with comprehension around 50%. The reader has difficulty anticipating meanings and may exhibit frustration by frowning, restless movements, and irregular breathing.

[1]Summarized from Marzano et al. (1987) and Rubin (1997)

Advantages and Disadvantages.   An advantage of commercially published IRIs is that the teacher is not required to determine the starting point for reading the graded passages. Placement is based on the student's oral reading of a graded word list. Limitations of IRIs are (1) some comprehension questions are not labeled accurately because they can be answered without reading, and (2) they do not describe strengths and weaknesses of the student's comprehension (Mason & Au, 1986). Also, although IRIs state similar definitions for the instructional level, they differ in the criteria (Pikulski, 1990). These differences have led to questions about the validity of the assessments. Mason & Au (1986) suggest that IRIs can be useful informal measures of children's reading because they include both word recognition and comprehension. They can provide clues as to appropriate levels of reading material for the student, but they should not be used to establish the student's reading performance.

Cloze Procedures

The term *cloze procedures* refers to reading passages with some deleted words. They are informal tasks that provide information about students' interactions with reading material. The task for the reader is to determine the missing words from the surrounding context and write them in the appropriate blanks. Wilson Taylor (1953), who developed the procedure, tentatively selected the term *cloze* to indicate a connection with the concept of closure in Gestalt psychology (Harrison, 1980, p. 85). For example, we tend to see a circle with gaps in the circumference as a closed figure. Although the process is different in reading, a reader completes the sentence pattern for each deleted word.

The original purpose of the cloze procedure was to determine whether particular textual material was within a student's reading ability. When used for this purpose, every fifth (or seventh) word in the text is deleted (referred to as the conventional or random deletion procedure). To successfully comprehend a text, the student should provide 60 percent of the omitted words (Harrison, 1980, p. 90).

In the classroom, however, the random deletion of words is unlikely to provide useful instructional information to the teacher. Nevertheless, one of the aspects of reading performance that differentiates good and poor readers is the capacity to make use of partial information (Harrison, 1980, p. 85). When adapted for classroom use, the cloze procedure can assess the student's ability to use grammatical (syntactic) and meaning (semantic) cues to complete the missing parts of a message. To accomplish this purpose, particular types of words in a passage are omitted (the rational selection procedure). Examples include pronoun antecedents and semantic relationships. The beginning of a passage to address pronoun antecedents, for example, is as follows:

> Maria and Lucy like to visit _____ Uncle Alex. _____ liked his stories about the countries _____ visited as a U.S. sailor.

Instead of a focus on a particular word type, Kemp (1987) suggests that the omitted words should sample most parts of speech and be balanced throughout the text. That is, omitted words should be those that students can provide if they use the syntactic and semantic clues in the text.

To provide sufficient information for the teacher, the selected passage should be 200 to 250 words in length with equal-length blanks for 25 to 50 omitted words (Pikulski & Tobin, 1982). To administer the procedure, the teacher should explain that the task is to fill in as many of the missing words as possible and that each blank represents one word. Also important is to tell students to read through the entire sentence to obtain clues about the missing word.

The utility of the cloze procedure is, first, it can identify particular problems with words that the student may have. An example is a habitual association of "for" with "from." It also can serve as an excellent vehicle for discussions with struggling readers about language, words, syntactic patterning, scanning, prediction, self-monitoring, and self-correction (Kemp, 1987, p. 163).

Two factors influence the student's performance on the cloze procedure. One is the student's understanding of language and semantic and syntactic clues. The other influence is the difficulty and/or ambiguity of the text. To the extent that the sentences are too complex for the student or are ambiguous, the procedure will not be a valid or reliable indicator of the student's capabilities.

An advantage of the cloze procedure is that it can be administered quickly and efficiently to several students at a time or to the class. A disadvantage is that it cannot make the same detailed diagnostic observations as individually administered instruments.

Summary

The procedures discussed in this chapter address some of the likely processing problems of struggling readers. The running record, which should be used by the end of the first year of school, documents children's errors in oral reading in texts identified as easy, instructional, and hard for the child. Scoring and analysis of the child's errors indicate the accuracy rate, the pattern of errors, and the self-correction rate. A self-correction rate of one in three to five chances for error is good, but one in twenty is very poor.

A similar procedure, miscue analysis, documents the reader's word substitutions and, following the oral reading, asks the student to retell the passage. Important for obtaining accurate results is to select reading material that is predictable, challenging, and relevant for the reader. Following the oral reading, the teacher determines if each sentence is semantically and syntactically acceptable and if the reader has changed the meaning. Nonproficient readers, for example, sound out syllables and words and do not produce acceptable sentences. In retrospective miscue analysis, the teacher and student discuss the student's likely reasons for miscues. One purpose is, over time, for the reader to develop a different view of reading and improve in reading proficiency.

In contrast, the general purpose of informal reading inventories is to establish levels of text difficulty for the reader that are referred to as independent, instructional, and frustration levels. Miscues also are recorded. However, informal reading inventories should not be used to establish the student's reading performance.

The cloze procedure, which uses passages with omitted words, was developed originally to identify text difficulty for a student. However, in the classroom, the teacher should omit particular types of words from passages, such as pronouns or prepositions, to examine possible syntactic and semantic difficulties. Using a 200- to 250-word text with deletions, the teacher can determine the extent to which the reader can make use of partial information.

Discussion Questions

1. What is the definition of an instructional level text in relation to running records? How does this definition differ from the informal reading inventories?

2. Why is calculating the child's self-correction rate important in implementing running records?

3. What are the features of a text that influence the difficulty of the text for a reader?

4. What is the major attitudinal goal of retrospective miscue analysis?

5. What function do IRIs and the cloze procedure share?

References

Betts, E. A. (1946). *Foundation of reading instruction*. New York: American Book Company.

Clay, M. (1985). *The early detection of reading difficulties* (3rd ed.). Portsmouth, NH: Heinemann.

Clay, M. (1993). *An observation survey of early literacy achievement*. Auckland, New Zealand: Heinemann.

Clay, M. (2000). *Running records for classroom teachers*. Auckland, New Zealand: Heinemann.

Clay, M. (2001). *An observation survey of early literacy achievement*. Auckland, New Zealand: Heinemann.

Goodman, K. (1973). Miscues: Windows on the reading process. In K. Goodman (Ed.), *Miscue analysis: Applications to reading instruction* (pp. 3–14). Urbana, IL: ERIC Clearinghouse on Reading and Communication Skills and the National Council of Teachers of English.

Goodman, Y. (1999). Revaluing readers while readers revalue themselves: Retrospective miscue analysis. In S. J. Barrentine (Ed.), *Reading assessment* (pp. 140–151). Newark, DE: International Reading Association.

Goodman, Y., Watson, D., & Burke, C. (1987). *Reading miscue inventory*. Katonah, NY: Richard C. Owen.

Harrison, C. (1980). *Readability in the classroom*. New York: Cambridge University Press.

Hiebert, E. (1991). Teacher-based assessment of literacy learning. In J. Flood, J. M. Jensen, D. Lapp, & J. R. Squire (Eds.), *Handbook of research on teaching the language arts* (pp. 510–520). New York: Macmillan.

Johns, J. L. (1982). The dimensions and uses of informal reading assessment. In J. J. Pikulski & T. Shanahan (Eds.), *Approaches to the informal evaluation of reading* (pp. 1–11). Newark, DE: International Reading Association.

Kemp, M. (1987). *Watching children read and write: Observational records for children with special needs*. Portsmouth, NH: Heinemann.

Marzano, R. J., Hagerty, P. J., Valencia, S. W., & Distefano, P. P. (1987). *Reading diagnosis and instruction: Theory into practice*. Englewood Cliffs, NJ: Prentice Hall.

Mason, J. M., & Au, K. (1986). *Reading instruction for today*. Glenview, IL: Scott, Foresman, & Co.

Moore, R. A., & Aspegren, C. (2001). Reflective conversations between two learners. *Journal of Adolescent and Adult Literacy, 44*(6), 492–503.

Pikulski, J. J. (1990). Informal reading inventories. *Reading Teacher, 43*, 514–516.

Pumfrey, P. D. (1985). *Reading: Tests and assessment* (2nd ed.). Kent, England: Hodder & Stoughton.

Rubin, D. (1997). *Diagnosis and correction in reading instruction*. Boston: Allyn & Bacon.

Taylor, W. L. (1953). Cloze procedure: A new tool for measuring readability. *Journalism Quarterly, 30*, 415–433.

10

Reporting Student Progress

What is needed is a reporting system that yields a more accurate and rich profile of the student's accomplishments.

—Wiggins, 1994, p. 34

At the end of the grading period, Jamelah's first-grade teacher is preparing a report to send to the child's parents. The teacher writes that at the beginning of the year Jamelah was printing random letters to which she attached her own words, and now has progressed to writing that conveys her ideas clearly. The teacher continues, "She writes with purpose and includes simple details. She uses spaces between words and some capitals and periods. I would expect her to continue to add more details to her writing along with a clearer sense of beginning, middle, and ending" (Hogan, 1995, p. 29).

In the narrative, the teacher conveys a sense of Jamelah's progress during the course of the year. For example, the child has progressed from printing random letters to writing that clearly communicates her meaning. The teacher also provides suggestions for improvement in Jamelah's writing skills.

Of course, the teacher cannot possibly communicate every piece of work or item of information about a student to parents and others. As indicated by the preceding example, the information in any report of student progress is a subset of the teachers' knowledge of students' literacy development (Afflerbach & Johnston, 1993). That is, any method of reporting is some type of summary of student work. The narrative about Jamelah reflects the teachers' professional responsibility "to make meaning from the work and present facts, judgments, and prescriptions in a user-friendly form" (Wiggins, 1994, p. 30).

In the following sections, the chapter describes various methods for reporting student progress and then reviews the strengths and weaknesses of each. The chapter concludes with a discussion of procedures for summarizing the information for the different types of reports.

Methods for Reporting Student Progress

A variety of methods may be used to report student development in the language arts. Included are grades, checklists, rubrics, teacher narratives, portfolios, and parent conferences (see Table 10.1). Among the purposes they fulfill are informing parents of their child's progress, providing information for educational planning, and providing information for administrative decisions.

Grades

Grades are summaries of student achievement reported as letters (e.g., A, B, C, D, F; P = Pass, F = Fail; O = Outstanding, S = Satisfactory, U = Unsatisfactory) or numbers (e.g., 95, 88). An advantage of grades is their familiarity to parents, teachers, and college admission committees. Parents, for example, view them as important in understanding their child's progress (Strickland & Strickland, 2000, pp. 129–130). In addition, grades facilitate administrative decisions about student eligibility for promotion, qualification for honors classes or special needs programs, and participation in athletics (Thorndike, Cunningham, Thorndike, & Hagen, 1991). Further, letter grades often play a key role in college admissions and the awarding of scholarships.

Although familiar to parents and others, a grade provides little specific information for parents or teachers on the successes and problems experienced by students. In addition, the meaning of grades varies from teacher to teacher. Some teachers focus solely on evidence of achievement, whereas others consider student effort, ability level, and growth (Cizek, Fitzgerald, & Rachor, 1995/1996; Cross & Frary, 1999). Some authors recommend the modification of grading systems to address varied dimensions such as achieve-

TABLE 10.1   *Methods for Reporting Student Progress*

Reporting Methods	*Description*
Grades	Numerical and alphabetic symbols used to summarize a student's performance
Checklists	Lists of key student characteristics and capabilities that are checked when accomplished
Rubrics	Narrative descriptions of integrated student characteristics and capabilities accompanied by a scale
Narratives	Written descriptions of student's capabilities and characteristics
Portfolios	A systematic collection of evidence of student capabilities and characteristics that is organized by the student and teacher
Conferences	Dialog between teacher, student, and parent about a student's development

ment, effort, growth, and ability (Frisbie & Waltman, 1992; Guskey, 2002; O'Connor, 2001; Tomlinson, 2001; Wiggins, 1994). One proposed modification uses both letter grades and numbers. Specifically, "A" reflects excellent growth, "B" very good growth, and "C" some growth and 1 indicates a student is working above grade level in the subject, 2 designates grade level achievement, and 3 indicates below grade level (Tomlinson, 2001, pp. 14–15).

Some authors, however, take issue with reporting grades on factors such as effort. Kohn (1994) states, "A low grade for effort is more likely to be read as 'You're a failure at trying.' On the other hand, a high grade for effort combined with a low grade for achievement says 'You're just too dumb to succeed'" (p. 41). Brookhart (1994) described her experience in a school district in which effort was evaluated as 1 for outstanding, 2 for average, and 3 for low. Her fellow teachers cautioned her that any combination other than A1, B2, C2, D3, F3 could create uncomfortable situations for the teacher and the school. For example, A3 (i.e., earning an A with low effort) created the possibility of a parent asking, "What kind of teacher are you—my child gets an A without even trying in your class?" (p. 297). Further, F1 (i.e., failing with outstanding effort) could result in a parent asking "What kind of teacher are you—my child tries hard and still fails in your class?" (p. 297).

Checklists

As discussed in Chapter 6, checklists and rubrics provide information to the teacher and student about performance on particular classroom tasks. Checklists also can summarize a student's progress during a reporting period by addressing the development of key skills, strategies, and attitudes in the language arts. When used for this purpose, the checklist reflects a teacher's review of the evidence of student performance (e.g., anecdotal notes, observation guides, written products) for the reporting period. One writing checklist, for example, includes capabilities such as "self-selects topics," "uses expansive vocabulary," "experiments with style," and "uses revision strategies" (Hogan, 1995, p. 27). Developed for classrooms with nonnative English speakers, the report contains a column for reporting progress in the student's primary language and a column for progress in the student's secondary language.

Checklists, on occasion, use such terms as *not yet, developing,* and *achieving* to report student progress. For example, in Ann Arbor, Michigan, teachers developed a checklist report that listed specific student outcomes in the language arts and other subject areas (Sperling, 1994). Accompanying each are phrases that provide specific examples of the outcome. In the section on writing, the outcome *Responds to writing shared by a peer* is accompanied by phrases that state the student "willingly offers a positive comment, then asks a question for clarification or elaboration" and "keeps comments focused on the content of the writing" (p. 12). After reading the outcome and accompanying descriptive phrases, a teacher considers the student's performance and reports progress at one of three levels: *Not Yet, Developing,* and *Achieving.* Parents have supported the use of these forms of reporting; however, parents also indicated that they want a letter grade (Strickland & Strickland, 2000).

Rubrics

A logical extension of the use of checklists is the incorporation of rubrics into reports of student progress. Some authors contend that rubrics with rich descriptors of various levels of achievement illustrated with student work can communicate effectively with parents (Arter & McTighe, 2001; Clarridge & Whitaker, 1994; Guskey & Bailey, 2001; Wiggins, 1994). Shown in Table 10.2 is a section of a progress report used by the Polton Commu-

TABLE 10.2   *Rubrics for Reporting Student Progress in the Language Arts*

	Basic	*Proficient*	*Advanced*
Language Arts Proficiency 3 Reads to construct meaning by interacting with the text, by recognizing the different requirements of a variety of printed materials, and by using appropriate strategies to increase comprehension	Reads varied material, comprehends at literal level; recalls and builds knowledge through related information; begins to use strategies to develop fluency, adjusting rate when reading different material	Reads varied material, comprehends and draws inferences; recalls and builds knowledge through related information; applies strategies to increase fluency, adjusting rate when reading different material	Reads varied material, comprehends literally and interpretively; synthesizes and explores information, drawing inferences; critiques author's intent, analyzes material for meaning and value; applies strategies to increase fluency, adjusting rate when reading different material
Language Arts Proficiency 4 Produces writing that conveys purpose and meaning, uses effective writing strategies, and incorporates the conventions of written language to communicate clearly	Appropriately writes on assigned or self-selected topics; clear main ideas, few details; weak elements in the beginning, middle, end; sentence structure lacks variety and contains error	Appropriately writes on assigned or self-selected topics; clear main ideas, interesting details, clear organization, sequencing, varied sentence structure, edits to reduce errors; appropriate voice and word choice	Appropriately writes on assigned or self-selected topics; connects opinions, details, and examples; effective organization and sequencing; meaningful sentence structure, edits to eliminate most errors; appropriate voice and word choice

As compared to the class in the area of language arts, your child	1	2	3	**Marking Periods**
				Displays strong performance Demonstrates appropriate development Needs practice and support

From Wiggins (1994)

nity Elementary School in Cherry Creek School District (Wiggins, 1994). Each language arts proficiency is accompanied by a scale with labels for the performance levels (i.e., *Basic, Proficient, Advanced*). At each level, the report describes the relevant reading and writing skills and strategies in terms of the quality of student performance.

Originally, the staff at Polton Community School planned to use only the terms *Basic, Proficient,* and *Advanced* to describe the students' performance level for each area of proficiency (Wiggins, 1994). Parents, however, wanted more comparative information to interpret their child's progress. Therefore, the checklist illustrated in Table 10.2 was added. Three times a year the teacher indicates a child's status in the language arts as compared to his or her class. For instance, during the first marking period, a teacher indicates whether a child "Displays strong performance," "Demonstrates appropriate development," or "Needs practice and support" as compared to the other students in the language arts class (p. 31).

Rubrics offer the potential to provide parents with more description about the levels of performance associated with key language arts skills that are the focus of student learning. However, Arter and McTighe (2001) caution that a shift from grades to rubrics is unlikely to happen soon. They note that grades are engrained in the school culture, and a greater understanding and acceptance of rubrics by parents is essential if they are to replace grades. The authors also note that teachers need practice in using rubrics for summarizing and reporting student progress for a grading period.

Narratives

Teacher narratives provide written descriptions of students' capabilities that reflect each student's progress. To provide a framework for writing narratives, some schools specify the areas of student progress to be addressed and general approaches for reviewing student work. The narrative framework designed by teachers in one school, for example, included sections on (a) the growth of the student as a reader, writer, mathematician, and scientist, and (b) the student's contribution to the classroom learning community and growth as a learner (Jennings, 2001; Mills, 2001). The teachers also agreed to write three pluses (positive achievements) and one wish (an area for improvement) for each section (Mills, 1990). In addition, sections on the report include student self-evaluation and parent evaluation.

Similarly, Cunningham and Allington (1999) advocate the use of narrative reports, which they refer to as essays, to report to parents and describe their child as a learner, reader, writer, and citizen. In the essay, the teacher provides information about the child as a learner, details the type of work the student is doing, and attaches samples of student work to illustrate comments in the narrative. The essay informs parents of their child's progress and shares learning goals for the student. Given the demands of writing such reports, Cunningham and Allington propose dispensing with quarterly reports. They recommend, instead, the development of essays for three students each week, thus providing a report to parents approximately every eight weeks. These essays are to be used in conjunction with parent conferences and reviews of student portfolios.

A strength of narrative reports is the dedication of specific sections to address student development as a learner, as a member of a learning community, and as a citizen.

This framework permits a teacher to focus on a student's achievement in the subject-area sections and address achievement-related aspects of performance, such as effort and conduct, in the other sections. In addition, the use of concrete language that is used to instruct students may communicate more effectively to primary students than letter grades. Narratives, however, require even more time to prepare than checklists as well as considerable writing ability (Afflerbach, 1999). In addition, parents initially may express concerns about the lack of a grade (Jennings, 2001).

Portfolios

Chapter 7 discussed portfolios as an assessment system for the classroom. As indicated in that chapter, a portfolio is a purposeful collection of student work that reflects the student's progress. Development of the portfolio involves the teacher and student in the selection of samples of work that provide evidence about the student's capabilities and characteristics. In addition, the portfolio may contain student reflections on the meaning of the work in terms of her learning, the strengths reflected in the work, the challenges still faced by the student, and goals for future growth.

As indicated in Chapter 7, portfolios that go with a child to the next grade may be accompanied by narratives that summarize strengths and areas for improvement. Portfolios also may be combined with checklists to report on student progress. One school district, for example, created the "Can Do Checklist" to include with the portfolio (Schlotterbeck, 1995). Three checklists addressed the language arts areas of speaking, reading, and writing. In reading, skills and strategies were organized into the categories of *Attitude, Book Knowledge,* and *Comprehension.* Teachers checked whether students had demonstrated such capabilities as "holds book with print right way up," "tracks from left to right," and "understands the difference between fiction and nonfiction" (p. 168). Teachers based their decisions for the skills on recorded observations and work samples in the portfolios.

Portfolios also may be used with report cards (Guskey & Bailey, 2001) to provide examples of student work and help parents understand the basis for the grades. In some schools, during parent conferences, teachers use portfolios to illustrate their comments about students' learning (Guskey & Bailey, 2001; Wiener & Cohen, 1997). Similarly, portfolios provide evidence to support teacher judgments when reporting student progress using checklists, rubrics, or narratives.

Portfolios provide concrete examples of student growth; however, without teacher assistance, parents may have difficulty interpreting the material to make judgments about their child's progress. In addition, information about too many aspects of student characteristics and capabilities may overwhelm the parent.

Conferences

Conferences on student progress are focused conversations between the teacher, parents, and the student. In some cases, the teacher leads the conference; in others, the student leads the discussion (Guskey & Bailey, 2001). Whether led by the teacher or student, the conference should address key aspects of the student's understandings in the language arts and his or her attitudes toward the subject area. Some teachers focus the discussion through the use of a checklist to show the student's progress in attaining district and state standards (Strickland & Strickland, 2000). In the language arts areas of listening and speaking, for example, the discussion may focus on whether the student "participates appropriately by contributing and by asking questions" (p. 131). In student-led conferences, work samples from the child's portfolio may frame the conversation in terms of key learning goals (Guskey & Bailey, 2001).

Goal setting also may be part of the conference (Bietau, 1995; Strickland & Strickland, 2000). In one school district, the student, parents, and teacher meet in the fall to set goals for learning. They meet again in December, March, and June to review the student's progress. During the March meeting, the teacher, parents, and student determine if adjustments are to be made in the learning goals.

In another district, goal setting is structured by the parent, student, and teacher together completing a sheet that focuses attention on academic and affective dimensions of student performance (Bietau, 1995). For each academic dimension, the conference addresses the student's strengths and challenges. Based on the perspectives of the group, two student goals are recorded on a goal-setting form. One goal builds on student strengths and the other addresses challenges. The form includes a brief plan for achieving the goal. For example, for the goal that addresses a challenge area, one conference resulted in identifying the goal of "learning to plan and complete a research project" (p. 138). One specific action in the plan stated the student would "research 'Wolf Creek Nuclear Plant'" (p. 131).

Summary

Several methods may be used to report student progress. Although familiar, grades lack specific information about the successes and problems of students. Also, the meaning varies from teacher to teacher because some teachers also incorporate student effort, ability, and/or growth into the computation of grades. Checklists and rubrics, in contrast, can document student achievement of key strategies and skills in the language arts.

Teacher narratives are the most detailed written method of reporting student progress. Specification of the areas to address and approaches for reviewing student progress provide structure for the writing of narratives. They provide teachers the opportunity to separate achievement from other factors, such as student effort. However, narratives are time consuming to prepare. Portfolios also provide extensive information about student progress in that they include examples of student work. They also permit the teacher to document students' interest and study habits. However, in the absence of teacher assistance, accompanying narratives, or checklists, parents may have difficulty interpreting the portfolio material.

Finally, conferences are focused conversations between parents, their child, and the teacher. The student's understandings in the language arts and attitudes toward the subject area provide the focus of the conversation. In addition, the students, parents, and teacher may modify learning goals, establish new goals, and develop a brief plan for achieving the goals.

Review Criteria for Reporting Systems

Various methods for reporting student progress are available; however, they differ in the extent to which they effectively communicate student progress in the language arts. Awareness of the strengths and weaknesses of reporting methods is important because teachers often serve on district committees to develop reporting systems. Seven criteria are important in evaluating the effectiveness of reporting systems. They are focus, clarity, openness, accuracy, reliability, fairness, and information value. This section uses these criteria to review the previously described reporting methods.

Focus

Focus refers to the match between classroom goals and the information provided in the reporting system (see Table 10.3). For example, for the goal of developing skills and strategies in reading, the information in the report should pertain to student achievement of such reading capabilities. In contrast, if the report is to describe students' dispositions toward reading and writing, then the information should address students' interest in and attitudes about language arts.

Focus is diffused when the report blends achievement with other factors, such as attitude and effort, into one summary grade. For example, when progress reports are limited to subject area grades, teachers sometimes consider student effort, ability, and/or conduct in addition to achievement (Cizek et al., 1995/1996; Cross & Frary, 1999). In addition to altering the focus, parents and students are likely to be unaware of the importance allocated to these factors. This problem also can occur with checklists and rubrics if they do not include separate sections for factors other than achievement.

In contrast, teacher narratives, portfolios, and conferences provide opportunities for teachers to communicate a student's progress by separately addressing the student's achievements, attitude, and effort. Given their unstructured nature, however, narratives, portfolios, and conferences require that the teacher carefully frame their delivery in terms of addressing those skills accompanied by actual examples of student work.

Clarity

The extent of understanding of a student's progress report by various audiences is referred to as clarity (Loyd & Loyd, 1997). For example, young students may understand a checklist that includes the skills and strategies they have learned in language arts. Parents, however, may indicate that they prefer a letter grade in addition to the checklist information (Strickland & Strickland, 2000). Both may be needed in such a situation to meet the diverse needs of students and parents.

Checklists and rubrics, because they specify the dimensions of performance in a particular subject area, easily meet the standard of clarity. Next are portfolios, narratives, and conferences. In these forms of reporting, a teacher can provide concrete examples of a student's progress in terms of specific skills, strategies, attitudes, and study habits.

TABLE 10.3   *Criteria for Review of Methods for Reporting Student Progress*

Criteria	Requirements	Example
Focus	Match between classroom goals and the information provided in the reporting system	To separate issues of achievement and behavior, a district committee of teachers, administrators, and parents adds a conduct grade to report cards. The purpose is to discourage the practice of lowering subject area grades due to misbehavior.
Clarity	Students, parents, and others understand the report	A primary-grade checklist sent home to parents indicates specific strategies a student uses to read unfamiliar words.
Openness	Communication of the components of the reporting system to students and parents	A high school teacher describes the weighting of homework, projects, and formal examinations in a written policy that she shares with her students.
Accuracy	Quality assessments are the basis of the report	A teacher uses assessments aligned with her district's language arts standards as the basis for her comments on a narrative report.
Reliability	Similar assessments collected over multiple occasions	During a conference, John shares with his grand-mother his portfolio collection of fictional pieces that he wrote during the grading period.
Fairness	Equal opportunity for each student to earn a grade or achieve a performance level	A district committee rejects the use of grading on the curve because it limits the number of students who can earn an A.
Information value	Evidence for a teacher to examine the effectiveness of instruction	As a teacher prepares to send checklists home to parents, she completes the language arts section of the checklists and notices that many of her students need more learning opportunities to sequence events in a story.

Last in terms of clarity are grades. Their appeal is the summary judgment they represent. However, when these summaries consist of several factors, such as achievement, effort, conduct, and extent of growth, they lack clarity.

Openness

Communication of teacher policies that guide the preparation of progress reports to students and parents constitutes openness (Guskey, 2002; Loyd & Loyd, 1997; O'Connor, 2001; Ory & Ryan, 1993). The importance of openness is that it sends the message that the teacher's decisions are not arbitrary. All reporting methods can meet this criterion if teachers develop evaluation policies and communicate them to students and parents.

Essential components of a policy are (1) the types of assessments that contribute to the progress report, (2) any weighting of assessments, and (3) the method for arriving at a final judgment. For example, a teacher may state that the report is based on projects and tests, but not daily tasks or homework. That is, she may agree with the position that homework and daily tasks are primarily opportunities for students to practice new skills and strategies and should not be included in determining final grades (Cross & Frary, 1999; Frisbie & Waltman, 1992).

The importance of communicating assessment weights is to avoid misunderstandings about the importance of certain tasks. For example, a teacher may weight the grade for students' writing portfolios by a factor of 2. The weighted score is combined with grades for other projects and tests to calculate a nine-week grade. Students who are unaware of this weighting may simply add the grades from the portfolio, tests, and projects and divide by the number of grades. The difference in calculations can result in a B to a student who anticipated earning an A.

Also important is the method for arriving at a final judgment. Teachers often calculate an average or mean score for major assessments, but they may use the median score to determine students' grades (Brookhart, 1999; O'Connor, 2001; Wright, 1994). Particularly important is that the method should be communicated to parents and students. Similarly, the method of selecting comments for narratives or conferences as well as selecting student work samples should be described. For example, guidelines for writing narratives in one school district suggest that teachers include specific examples of student accomplishments, positive phrasing of teacher concerns, and goals and plans for the future (cited in Hogan, 1995, pp. 25, 26–27).

Accuracy

Meeting the criterion of accuracy requires basing the reported information on quality assessments (Loyd & Loyd, 1997; O'Connor, 2001; Ory & Ryan, 1993). That is, accuracy of a reporting system will depend on the extent to which it relies on assessments based on the effective practices described in Chapter 2. Specifically, they are (1) establishing a focus for assessments based on learning goals, (2) aligning assessments with the identified focus, (3) ensuring that instruction provides students the opportunity to learn the identified capabilities and strategies, and (4) ensuring that the selected assessments provide an opportunity for students to demonstrate their learning. To the extent these characteristics of effective assessment practices are addressed, the accuracy criterion can be met by all the reporting methods discussed in this chapter.

An accuracy issue unique to narratives, portfolios, and conferences is the representativeness of the performances used to illustrate student progress. Because only a few samples of student work can be selected, the examples and the comments of the teacher must appropriately represent a student's performance in the language arts. For example, in preparing to report to parents about whether their child "reads a variety of materials," a teacher may consider her observations of the child during independent reading and her review of the student's book log and response journal. To support her conclusions, she may incorporate examples from these sources to share in a conference or to reference in a written narrative. In other words, student samples carry the weight of reflecting the skills and strategies a student has learned and their selection to support narratives, portfolio summaries, and conferences requires careful deliberation.

Reliability

Sufficient evidence about a student's capabilities is the basis for establishing the reliability of the reporting system (Loyd & Loyd, 1997; Ory & Ryan, 1993). The purpose is to be confident that the report reflects patterns of student performances. Reliability in the reporting of student progress requires the inclusion of many instances of student work that are collected over several occasions—a criterion for effective classroom assessment discussed in Chapter 2. The reliability criterion can be met by all the reporting methods discussed in this chapter if a teacher bases progress reports on a broad sample of student performances.

Fairness

The fairness criterion refers to the degree that a reporting method offers equal opportunity for each student to earn a grade or achieve a performance level (Loyd & Loyd, 1997; O'Connor, 2001; Ory & Ryan, 1993). For example, a district may establish a policy that a teacher's grade distributions should approximate 10 percent A's, 20 percent B's, 40 percent C's, 20 percent D's, and 10 percent F's (Frisbie, & Waltman, 1992). This scheme, however, assumes that students' ability to attain important skills and strategies in language arts follow a normal distribution—an assumption not held by all educators (Kohn, 1994; O'Connor, 2001). Consider the impact, for example, in an elective English class in which a majority of the students are avid readers whose insights in class discussions and essays demonstrate advanced understanding of the literary selections. If strictly applied, the policy would limit the number of students in this class who can earn an A or B, even though students may be demonstrating advanced understanding of the material. The predetermination of the number of students does not meet the fairness criterion. Similarly, in the use of rubric, pre-specification of the number of students who can be assigned scores at each performance level (e.g., 15 percent Beginning, 35 percent Developing, 35 percent Proficient, and 15 percent Advanced) is inappropriate. However, grades and rubrics do not require such predetermined rules and, if not restricted to such a scheme, allow reporting that reflects a student's reading and writing achievements.

Information Value

To meet the criterion of information value, a reporting method must provide the teacher with evidence to examine the effectiveness of instruction (Loyd & Loyd, 1997; Ory & Ryan, 1993). After summarizing the information for each student's report, the teacher should be able to use the reports of student progress to examine student accomplishments, partial accomplishments, and capabilities not yet mastered (Loyd & Loyd, 1997, p. 489). In this way, she can make decisions about subsequent instruction.

Checklists and rubrics that record student attainment of specific skills and understandings provide the most information for planning classroom instruction. For example, reports that use checklists may document students' progress in oral presentations by listing such skills and strategies as consideration of audience (e.g., vocabulary and formality), organization of the material (e.g., sequence and summarization), and delivery of the speech (e.g., volume, enunciation, gestures, and pace) (Massachusetts Department of Education, 2001). For example, review of the speaking section of student reports for the grading period may indicate that most students have shown progress in organizing their material into oral presentations; however, many students need additional instructional experiences in the use of gestures to enhance the message.

The narrative, portfolio, or conference has the greatest information value in planning for the individual student. Such reports provide information relevant to each student and will not necessarily address the same skills and strategies for all students. These forms of communication may be used to report a student's unique accomplishments and provide information for setting learning goals for the next reporting period. Information for classroom instruction also may be obtained by reviewing reports across students to determine any general patterns. For instance, after reviewing language arts portfolios with parents, a teacher may notice that students' literary critiques draw exclusively on mainstream authors. Based on this information, the teacher may decide to change the selections for his book talks to reflect more diversity.

Grades provide the least information value for instruction because they do not indicate the effectiveness of instruction in developing specific language arts skills and strategies. The teacher will be able to determine the number of students who have shown overall learning gains, but will not be able to identify specific areas of students' strengths and weaknesses.

Summary

Several types of reporting systems are available, but they are not equally effective in supporting communication between students, parents, and the teacher. In terms of clarity, checklists and rubrics provide feedback about specific capabilities and characteristics. Narratives, conferences, and portfolios allow teachers to share information about specific skills, strategies, and attitudes, but may require the teacher to structure the information carefully to avoid overwhelming students and parents. Grades offer a summary valuation about student progress, and they also may incorporate aspects of student performance (e.g., effort, ability) of which students and parents are unaware.

All reporting systems may meet the criteria of openness, accuracy, reliability, and fairness. Clear communication of the policies and procedures applicable in assessing student progress characterizes systems that meet the openness criterion. Reporting systems based on effective assessments described in earlier chapters meet the accuracy criterion. The reliability criterion is met by those systems in which teachers collect many samples of student work over multiple occasions. Reporting systems that offer each student the opportunity to earn a grade or achieve a performance level (e.g., do not require a teacher to give a certain percentage of A's, B's, C's, D's, and F's) meet the fairness criterion.

Finally, checklists and rubrics provide the most information value in terms of planning class instruction. Narratives, conferences, and portfolios offer information for addressing the goals of individual students. Grades offer little information about specific skills and strategies that students developed or for which additional learning experiences are required.

Summarizing Information

The rich information that teachers collect about students must be summarized in some way to report to various audiences. Information may be summarized qualitatively for reporting with narratives, portfolios, and conferences or quantitatively for letter and numerical grades. Whether based on qualitative or quantitative methods, the process of reviewing and summarizing evidence of student performance should be systematic to report student progress appropriately. The following guidelines provide frameworks for systematically reviewing student performances.

Qualitative Summarizations

Narratives, conferences, and portfolios typically involve the development of a verbal summary (i.e., oral or written) of student performance. In addition, checklists and rubrics that reflect student progress over time require some form of review to reach a conclusion about student performance. To summarize information qualitatively, a teacher verbally processes information from observations, interviews, and student work samples to make decisions about a student's progress. The process parallels that of qualitative research in which interpretations are constructed by reviewing notes and documents and writing successive texts to process the information. These texts describe the context, pose hypotheses, present instances affirming and disconfirming those hypotheses, and, finally, make meaning in order to report to an audience (Denzin & Lincoln, 1994). Many of these elements apply to the qualitative summarization of student progress.

   This section describes a process for qualitatively reviewing evidence of student performance. Guiding the review is (1) a report framework that outlines the areas of learning to be addressed, (2) the development of a student profile within this framework, (3) a review of student evidence for patterns, (4) the formation of initial interpretations of student performance, (5) the examination of student performance for information that supports and challenges the interpretations, and (6) the recording of the conclusions about student progress.

Specifying a Report Framework.   Guiding the review process is a framework that provides a general outline of the areas of learning. The report cards in some districts and schools list specific areas of learning, such as reading, writing, and speaking, for which a teacher writes narratives (Egawa & Azwell, 1995; McAfee & Leong, 1994; Mills, 2001). This outline, or narrative framework, provides a consistent format that helps to organize the report, assures that important information is included, and assists parents in understanding the information (Egawa & Azwell, 1995; McAfee & Leong, 1994). In some instances, additional structure is provided by framing the review and report in terms of students' strengths and needs (McAfee & Leong, 1994).

Developing Student Profiles.   McAfee and Leong (1994) recommend that a teacher compose individual student profiles to help write narratives. The profiles focus on the student learning goals in the report framework, and these goals align with the requirements for the reports of student progress (McAfee & Leong, 1994). If, for example, a report addresses speaking, reading, and writing, then these language arts areas are included in the individual profiles. In completing a profile, the teacher reviews all assessments (e.g., story retellings, reading journals, story maps, and written conversations) and records evidence relevant to the student's learning goal(s). The profile functions as a data display to provide ". . . an organized, compressed assembly of information that permits conclusion drawing" (Huberman & Miles, 1994). The teacher uses this profile to summarize trends that demonstrate growth and to report any breakthroughs in a student's learning (McAfee & Leong, 1994).

Reviewing Evidence for Patterns and Forming Initial Interpretations.   In summarizing information for the learning goals, the teacher looks for patterns of performance to portray a student's typical performance (Anthony, Johnson, Mickelson, & Preece, 1991; McAfee & Leong, 1994). Such patterns may occur across time or across samples of student work. In the area of literacy strategies, for example, a teacher may note on several occasions that a student strategically used predictable word patterns, illustrations, and letter–sound knowledge when reading various selections. Noting patterns of a student's performance over time and literacy experiences provides a basis for reporting a student's capabilities.

Based on these patterns, the teacher generates multiple hypotheses or interpretations about the meaning of student performance (McAfee & Leong, 1994). In other words, a teacher considers all aspects relevant to student learning prior to drawing conclusions about student performance. In this process, the teacher reflects on information of child development, learning goals, past experiences, and examples of student performance.

Reviewing Interpretations.   To avoid premature closure, a teacher considers hypotheses about student performance to be tentative and examines them for convergent and divergent evidence (Anthony et al., 1991). Convergence occurs when evidence supports a hypothesis or interpretation, for example, when ". . . test scores back up work samples and observations" (Huberman & Miles, 1994). Divergence occurs when evidence indicates other factors may be relevant in understanding student performance. Anthony and colleagues (1991) provide an example of a student whose file may lead to an initial hypothesis that her halting oral reading indicates problems with sound/symbol relationships (p. 106). However, additional evidence in the form of writing samples shows broad word choice and correct spelling. This information indicates that other factors, such as performance anxiety, may be contributing to the child's lack of fluency in oral reading.

The student profile allows a teacher to systematically review evidence from previous assessments. The purpose is to detect any convergence of evidence about student performance that demonstrates a trend in development. For example, a sequence of entries in a profile may describe events in which Ricardo initially drew pictures and recited his story. Later entries may describe his use of letters that symbolize key words in his drawings (McAfee & Leong, 1994, p. 123). Such information may be used in qualitatively summarizing the verbal information provided in conferences and writing narratives. It also serves to inform teachers when applying qualitative procedures to summarize information for completing checklists or rubrics.

Students may be involved in the review of the evidence and its interpretation (Lamme & Hysmith, 1991; McAfee & Leong, 1994). Students examine materials and reflect on concepts they have learned or areas in which they have shown improvement over time. Conferences between teachers and students allow them to look for trends in performance. Students may also provide insights to the teacher's initial conclusions about the students' progress.

Recording Conclusions.   A teacher is ready to report her conclusions about student performance after systematically reviewing evidence. The credibility of these interpretations is enhanced by completing student profiles within a framework, generating initial hypotheses, and reviewing for convergence and divergence of evidence. For checklists and rubrics, the teacher records her conclusions by marking the appropriate descriptors of student performance. Narratives and conferences, however, require a verbal summary of the teacher's conclusions. Horm-Wingerd (1992) offers a four-step procedure for developing narrative reports:

1. Open with an overall statement describing a child's progress in broad developmental areas since the last report or conference.
2. Give a specific example of behavior to serve as evidence for your global description of change and to help parents understand exactly what you are describing.
3. State your plans.
4. If appropriate, note what the parents can do at home to facilitate the child's development. (p. 14)

These steps are also relevant to the conduct of parent–teacher conferences.

In conclusion, qualitative summarization of student progress involves the specification of a report framework, development of student profiles within this framework, examination of information for patterns, and formation of initial interpretations of student performance. The teacher then reviews the observations, interviews, and work samples to find instances of convergence for the initial interpretations, as well as instances of divergence that indicate other plausible interpretations should be considered. Finally, the teacher records her conclusions about student performance by placing a check beside demonstrated capabilities on a checklist indicating the appropriate performance level on a rubric, or by verbally summarizing information for a narrative or conference.

Quantitative Summarizations

Letter grades and numerical grades typically are based on a quantitative summarization of information. A hallmark of quantitative summarization is that a teacher assigns numerical values to tasks that students complete during a report period. Two useful quantitative methods to summarize numerical information involve summing or averaging scores.

Summing Scores.   To assign a grade by summing scores, a teacher identifies the major types of evidence of student learning that she will use to assess student progress. For a report period, a high school teacher in the language arts may decide on the following tasks and point values:

Tasks	Points	Total Possible Points
Class Assignments (9)	2	18
Quizzes (4)	5	20
Homework (9)	2	18
Literature Unit Tests (2)	20	40
Writing Portfolio (1)	40	<u>40</u>
Total		136

Key is that the number of points associated with the tasks reflects (a) the importance of the learning assessed in the tasks and (b) the quality of the assessment. In this example, the portfolio and the unit tests receive the highest number of points because these assessments represent important student achievements in the application of the elements of writing and in their understanding of a body of literature.

Note that class assignments and homework receive fewer points. The reduction in points reflects the quality of these assessments. Class assignments and homework occur when a student is still learning and primarily provide opportunities for practice of new reading and writing capabilities. Thus, these assessments help to monitor student learning but may not reflect the student's capabilities at the end of a unit. Also, the quality of homework may reflect student learning, or it may reflect the amount of assistance available in the home. For these reasons, class assignments and homework should contribute less to the final grade because if they heavily influence a student's grade the report may not accurately represent student accomplishments (Frisbie & Waltman, 1992).

Teachers, however, indicate that they use homework in assigning grades, and that homework scores affect final grades from moderately to heavily (Cross & Frary, 1999). To lessen the influence of homework and class assignments on the final grade, a teacher can allocate fewer points to homework and classwork than to assessments that reflect major accomplishments. Notice, in the prior example, the teacher assigned only 18 points to homework out of a possible 136.

After assigning point values to the tasks, the teacher decides on the number of points required to earn each grade. In the current example, he may assign 122 to 136 an A, 109 to 121 a B, 95 to 108 a C, 82 to 94 a D, and below 82 an F. The rationale for this distribution is that an A reflects excellent demonstration of the skills and strategies expressed in the learning goals which is reflected in earning 90 percent or higher of the total points (Gredler, 1999). A B represents performance above average and is reflected in earning 80 to 89 percent of the total points, and so on.

The teacher then communicates the point values and score ranges to students so that they may monitor their progress. At the end of the reporting period, the teacher sums the number of points earned by a student, compares the score to the range specified for each grade, and assigns the appropriate final grade.

Averaging Scores. Teachers also calculate a student's final grade by averaging scores as represented by the mean or median. The mean is calculated by summing a student's scores on tasks for a reporting period and then dividing by the number of tasks. The median is the middle score when a student's scores have been arranged from lowest to highest. Both the mean and median require that all scores be on the same scale, typically a 100-point scale.

Prior to calculating the overall average, a teacher decides whether any scores from minor assessments, such as homework or class assignments, should be grouped before adding them to major tasks, such as compositions, projects, and presentations. Table 10.4 provides an example in which a teacher recorded four assignment scores. If the teacher averages the assignment scores with those for all other tasks, she sums the nine scores and then divides by nine. The final grades will be those labeled Method 1 in Table 10.5. Thus, Dakota's scores are summed as $80 + 84 + 88 + 88 + 92 + 96 + 96 + 92 + 96 = 812$, then $812 \div 9 = 90.2$.

A teacher may decide that class assignments are primarily for practice and he wants to count these minor grades as one score. To do so, he groups the four assignment scores and calculates the mean. Then, to calculate the overall mean, he combines the mean for the assignments with the scores for the three compositions, the project, and the presentation, and divides by six. To continue with the example of Dakota's scores, first the mean for the four assignments is calculated: $80 + 84 + 88 + 88 = 340$, then $340 \div 4 = 85$. Next, the assignment mean is combined with the composition, project, and presentation scores to get an overall mean: $85 + 92 + 96 + 96 + 92 + 96 = 557$, then $557 \div 6 = 92.8$. These final grades are reflected in Method 2 in Table 10.5.

At this point it is important to examine the difference in final grades according to the methods. Note that for Layla the final grade changes from an 82 for Method 1 to an 86 for Method 2. In other words, Layla's final grade went from a C to a B when the method of calculating the mean changed. James' final grade, however, dips slightly from 90 to 89. Because the way grades are calculated will change the final results, it is important to consider which scores should be combined prior to calculation of an overall mean. Combining scores from minor assessments, such as homework, prior to averaging them with scores from key tasks, limits the impact of the minor assessments on the final grade. Also, because the method by which scores are grouped before averaging will result in different

TABLE 10.4 *Grades for Tasks*

Student	*Class Assignments*				*Composition 1*	*Composition 2*	*Composition 3*	*Project*	*Presentation*
Charlie	96	92	96	96	92	92	96	92	96
Dakota	80	84	88	88	92	96	96	92	96
James	88	92	92	96	88	84	84	88	96
Layla	72	68	76	80	88	84	88	92	92

TABLE 10.5   *Final Grades Based on Three Methods for Calculating Averages*

Student	Method 1 *Mean of Individual Tasks*	Method 2 *Mean of Components*	Method 3 *Median of Components*
Charlie	94.2	93.8	94
Dakota	90.2	92.8	94
James	89.8	88.7	88
Layla	82.2	86.3	88

final grades, at the beginning of a report period students should be informed of the teacher's methods for calculating grades.

The mean may not be most representative of student performance because an outlier score, such as a zero, unduly affects the final grade (Canady & Hotchkiss, 1989; Guskey, 2002). Some recommend the use of the median because one poor performance does not pull a final grade down (Wright, 1994). However, a disadvantage is that the effect of a high score also is removed, which is unlikely to be acceptable to students who earned an occasional high score. When the median is used to calculate grades for the scores in Table 10.4, the final grades are those labeled Method 3 in Table 10.5.

Layla's scores provide an example for calculating scores with medians. First, calculations are completed for scores that will be grouped, in this case the class assignments. Because the median is the middle score, the scores for class assignments are arranged from lowest to highest: 68, 72, 76, 80. When the number of scores is odd, the median is the middle score. When the number of scores is even, as it is for Layla's class assignments, the median is the average of the two middle scores: 72 + 76 = 148; 148 ÷ 2 = 74. The median for the grouped scores is then combined with scores from major assignments, and these scores ordered from lowest to highest: 74, 84, 88, 88, 92, 92. In Layla's scores, the central-most scores are 88 and 88; so the median grade is 88 (i.e., 88 + 88 = 176; 176 ÷ 2 = 88). Note that when using the median (Method 3), Layla's final grade increases nearly two points as compared with the calculation of the mean (Method 2). This occurs because the lowest score (i.e., 74 for class assignments) does not significantly impact the median as it does the mean. Again, this example demonstrates the importance of communicating the method of summarizing. Although three students' final grades increase when using the median (i.e., Method 3) rather than the mean (i.e., Method 2), one student's final grade decreases slightly. Without advance knowledge of the method for determining final grades, this student may feel that he was treated unfairly.

Borderline Scores.   Whether a teacher sums or averages scores, instances of students' scores on the borderline between grades will occur. Several authors have raised the issue of reviewing borderline scores before assigning a final grade (Afflerbach & Johnston, 1993; Brookhart, 1999; Frisbie & Waltman, 1992). Loyd and Loyd (1997) state, "it may be that, after scores are combined, there is still a need for the teacher's professional judgment to evaluate what is satisfactory performance and what is outstanding performance" (p. 488). According to Brookhart (1999), the existence of error in assessment of student learning justifies the review of borderline scores. Additional information considered in borderline review should be closely related to learning goals and not be influenced by extraneous factors, such as behavior or effort. Brookhart (1999) indicates that teachers are open to raising a borderline score to a higher grade, but reluctant to lower a borderline score to a lower grade.

In conclusion, quantitative summarization of scores can be achieved through assigning numerical values to tasks and then summing or averaging those scores. In the use of summing, a teacher specifies the number of points associated with each task, assigning more points to major tasks such as unit tests or projects, and fewer points to minor tasks such as homework. The number of points required to earn a grade is then specified. One guide for specifying the points required for each grade is to identify the percentage required for a letter grade, such as a minimum of 90 percent for an A. Then, this percentage is multiplied by the total possible points to identify the number of points required to earn each letter grade.

When all tasks are on the same scale, such as a 100-point scale, averaging scores can be completed through the use of the mean or median. The mean requires that task scores be summed and divided by the number of tasks. An unusually high or low score can significantly affect the mean; so some authors recommend the use of the median. A teacher calculates the median by arranging scores from lowest to highest, then reporting the middle (i.e., median) score as the final grade. A teacher should communicate to students the methods that he will use to summarize scores because final grades differ based on whether grades are grouped before averaging, and whether the mean or median is used to calculate final grades.

Discussion Questions

1. In reporting student progress, what benefit is common in the use of narratives and conferences?

2. List two factors other than achievement that teachers often consider in assigning grades. Explain why these factors may result in miscommunication with parents.

3. What methods of reporting student progress would you use to supplement a parent conference at the end of a grading period? Explain the benefits and limitations in the use of the supplementary methods you selected.

4. After calculating grades for the reporting period, a teacher reviews students' final scores. He changes Therese's borderline grade from B+ to A–. Give one appropriate reason for such a change. Provide an inappropriate reason for such a change.

References

Afflerbach, Peter (1999). Report cards and reading. In S. Barrentine (Ed.), *Reading assessment: Principles and practices for elementary teachers* (pp. 57–65). Newark, DE: International Reading Association.

Afflerbach, P., & Johnston, P. (1993). Writing language arts report cards: Eleven teachers' conflicts of knowing and communicating. *Elementary School Journal, 94*(1), 73–86.

Anthony, R., Johnson, T., Mickelson, N., & Preece, A. (1991). *Evaluating literacy: A perspective for change.* Portsmouth, NH: Heinemann.

Arter, J., & McTighe, J. (2001). *Scoring rubrics in the classroom: Using performance criteria for assessing and improving student performance.* Thousand Oaks, CA: Corwin Press.

Bietau, L. (1995). Student, parent, teacher collaboration. In T. Azwell & E. Schmar (Eds.), *Report card on report cards: Alternatives to consider* (pp. 131–153). Portsmouth, NH: Heinemann.

Brookhart, S. (1994). Teachers' grading: Practice and theory. *Applied Measurement in Education, 7*(4), 279–301.

Brookhart, S. (1999). Teaching about communicating assessment results and grading. *Educational Measurement: Issues and practice, 18*(1), 5–13.

Canady, R., & Hotchkiss, P. (1989). It's a good score! Just a bad grade. *Phi Delta Kappan, 71*(1), 68–71.

Cizek, G., Fitzgerald, S., & Rachor, R. (1995/1996). Teachers' assessment practices: Preparation, isolation, and the kitchen sink. *Educational assessment, 3*(2), 159–179.

Clarridge, P., & Whitaker, E. (1994). Implementing a new elementary progress report. *Educational Leadership, 52*(2), 7–9.

Cross, L., & Frary, R. (1999). Hodgepodge grading: Endorsed by students and teachers alike. *Applied Measurement in Education, 12*(1), 53–72.

Cunningham, P., & Allington, R. (1999). *Classrooms that work: They can all read and write* (2nd ed.). New York: Longman.

Denzin, N., & Lincoln, Y. (1994). Introduction: Entering the field of qualitative research. In N. Denzin & Y. Lincoln (Eds.), *Handbook of qualitative research* (pp. 1–17). Thousand Oaks, CA: Sage.

Egawa, K., & Azwell, T. (1995). Telling the story: Narrative reports. In T. Azwell & E. Schmar (Eds.), *Report card on report cards: Alternatives to consider* (pp. 98–109). Portsmouth, NH: Heinemann.

Frisbie, D., & Waltman, K. (1992). Developing a personal grading plan. *Educational Measurement: Issues and Practices, 11*(3), 35–42.

Guskey, T. (2002). Computerized gradebooks and the myth of objectivity. *Phi Delta Kappan, 83*(10), 775–780.

Guskey, T., & Bailey, J. (2001). *Developing grading and reporting systems for student learning.* Thousand Oaks, CA: Corwin Press.

Hogan, E. (1995). Communicating in a culturally diverse community. In T. Azwell & E. Schmar (Eds.), *Report card on report cards: Alternatives to consider* (pp. 22–34). Portsmouth, NH: Heinemann.

Horm-Wingerd, D. (1992). Reporting children's development: The narrative report. *Dimensions of Early Childhood, 21*(1), 11–16.

Huberman, A. M., & Miles, M. (1994). Data management and analysis methods. In N. Denzin & Y. Lincoln (Eds.), *Handbook of qualitative research* (pp. 428–444). Thousand Oaks, CA: Sage.

Jennings, L. (2001). Inquiry for professional development and continual school renewal. In H. Mills & A. Donnelly (Eds.), *From the ground up: Creating a culture of inquiry* (pp. 33–54). Portsmouth, NH: Heinemann.

Kohn, A. (1994). Grading: The issue is not how but why. *Educational Leadership, 52*(2), 38–41.

Lamme, L., & Hysmith, C. (1991). One school's adventure into portfolio assessment. *Language Arts, 68*, 629–640.

Loyd, B., & Loyd, D. (1997). Kindergarten through grade 12 standards: A philosophy of grading. In G. Phye (Ed.), *Handbook of classroom assessment: Learning, achievement, and adjustment* (pp. 481–489). San Diego, CA: Academic Press.

Massachusetts Department of Education (2001). Massachusetts English language arts curriculum framework. MA: Author.

McAfee, O., & Leong, D. (1994). *Assessing and guiding young children's development and learning.* Boston: Allyn and Bacon.

Mills, H. (1990). Teachers and children: Partners in learning. In H. Mills & J. Clyde (Eds.), *Portraits of whole language classrooms* (pp. 43–63). Portsmouth, NH: Heinemann.

Mills, H. (2001). Critical incidents throughout the beginning of our journey. In H. Mills & A. Donnelly (Eds.), *From the ground up: Creating a culture of inquiry* (pp. 33–54). Portsmouth, NH: Heinemann.

O'Connor, K. (2001). The principal's role in report card grading. *National Association of Secondary School Principals Bulletin, 85*(621), 37–46.

Ory, J., & Ryan, K. (1993). *Tips for improving testing and grading.* Newbury Park, CA: Sage.

Schlotterbeck, K. (1995). Drawing a portrait of emergent learners. In T. Azwell & E. Schmar (Eds.), *Report card on report cards: Alternatives to consider* (pp. 165–174). Portsmouth, NH: Heinemann.

Sperling, D. (1994). Assessing and reporting: A natural pair. *Educational Leadership, 52*(2), 10–13.

Strickland, K., & Strickland, J. (2000). *Making assessment elementary.* Portsmouth, NH: Heinemann.

Thorndike, R. M., Cunningham, G. K., Thorndike, R. L., & Hagen, E. P. (1991). *Measurement and evaluation in psychology and education* (5th ed.). New York: Macmillan Publishing.

Tomlinson, C. (2001). Grading for success. *Educational Leadership, 58*(6), 12–15.

Wiener, R., & Cohen, J. (1997). *Literacy portfolios: Using assessment to guide instruction.* Upper Saddle River, NJ: Merrill.

Wiggins, G. (1994). Toward better report cards. *Educational Leadership, 52*(2), 38–41.

Wright, R. (1994, May). Success for all: The median is the key. *Phi Delta Kappan, 75*(9), 723–725.

11

Major Types of Published Assessments

As is the case with all complex human phenomena, there is no single answer to the issue of literacy assessment. The challenge for modern-day educators is to take the best of what current research and theory have to offer and integrate it with the best of what has been successful and useful in the past.

—Marzano, 1994, p. 45

A second-grade teacher is concerned about the progress of Patrick, a new student who is struggling with reading. To explore the possibility that Patrick's attitude towards reading is impeding his progress, the teacher administers a published instrument, the *Elementary Reading Attitude Survey* (McKenna & Kear, 1999). During the assessment, Patrick listens as his teacher reads statements such as, "How do you feel when you read a book in school during free time?" and "How do you feel about learning from a book?" (pp. 205–208). He responds to each by indicating the degree to which the statement makes him feel "very happy," "a little happy," "a little upset," or "very upset" (p. 204). Results from the *Elementary Reading Attitude Survey* indicate that Patrick's attitude about reading is relatively positive. The teacher now begins to explore other possibilities through classroom assessments, such as reading interviews, miscue analyses, and observations.

Among the published literacy instruments that may be useful for different purposes are assessments that accompany classroom texts, those found in articles, and standardized assessments (interest inventories, attitude surveys, and achievement tests). This chapter first discusses the major forms of published assessments, including two student profiles on two different standardized tests. Then the chapter describes the criteria for reviewing published instruments. Finally, sources of information for published assessments are discussed, including sample reviews of three standardized assessments.

Types of Published Assessments

Published instruments assess dimensions of literacy that include phonemic awareness, phonics knowledge, awareness of strategic reading processes (metacognition), understanding of text, and attitudes toward and interest in the language arts. This section first discusses text-based assessments and supplementary assessments, including the requirements for multiple-choice items. Then standardized tests are discussed, including the two types of scoring, criterion-referenced and norm-referenced. Two student profiles also are described.

Text-Based and Supplementary Assessments

Text-based assessments, unlike other commercially available assessments, are designed by publishers to reflect their basal reading programs or literature anthologies. The various formats in these materials include open-ended questions, observational checklists, student self-reports, holistic comprehension measures, and traditional tests with multiple-choice items (Calfee & Chambliss, 1999; Greer, 1992). For example, the anthologies in the *Elements of Literature* series (Holt, Rinehart, & Winston, 2000) include the following resources: *Formal Assessment, Portfolio Management Systems with Rubrics for Assignments, Standardized Test Preparation,* and *Test Generator.*

An important consideration in text-based tests is the extent to which they reflect best assessment practices (Greer, 1992). Nitko (2001) warns that experienced item writers often have not developed the text-based assessments. Moreover, text-based assessments often measure low-level cognitive skills and have incorrectly keyed answers (p. 373).

However, a review by Greer (1992) of three basal programs reported some positive findings about text-based assessments. First, the assessments used authentic texts written by children's authors that addressed various genres and matched the topics addressed in the particular unit. Second, in terms of thinking skills, the tasks and questions extended beyond the literal level and required inferential reasoning. Third, the materials provided teachers with descriptions of procedures to support the implementation of portfolio assessment.

Unlike text-based assessments, supplementary assessments are independent of particular texts, and address both the cognitive and affective aspects of reading and writing. Two examples of supplementary assessments that focus on student understanding of text are the commercially available Accelerated Reader® and the free website Book Adventure®. Both assessment systems provide progress reports to the teacher on individual students and the class, based on quizzes administered by the system. However, they function in somewhat different ways. The goal of Accelerated Reader (AR) is to increase literature-based reading (Paul, VanderZee, Rue, & Swanson, 1996). Students read trade books identified for their reading level. They then complete a multiple-choice test of five, ten, or twenty items, depending on the length or difficulty of the book (Topping & Sanders, 2000). Items, however, primarily assess literal comprehension. Reports for the teacher include the number and difficulty of completed readings and the average percent correct on the tests.

A suggested benefit from AR is the improvement of student achievement associated with the number of books read, the average book level, and the percent correct on AR tests

(Topping & Sanders, 2000). However, encouraging students to attempt books that are beyond their reading level resulted in few achievement gains (p. 329). A disadvantage includes the tendency in some schools for the reading program to narrow into the AR program (Biggers, 2001). For example, in some schools, the media center is divided into AR and regular circulation sections and students are denied access to materials that are not at their levels.

In contrast, the free website, Book Adventure (www.bookadventure.org) is sponsored by the Sylvan Learning Foundation and various business advertisements. The website (1) generates book lists for students based on their interests and preferred reading level, (2) offers quizzes for more than 5,000 titles from kindergarten to eighth grade, and (3) provides the teacher with score information for individual students and the class in the Teacher's Lounge section.

The basis for the booklist generated for each student is the student's interests (e.g., animals, drama, ethnic studies, legends or fables, science fiction) and preferred reading level (e.g., books at my grade level, easier books) entered by the student on the Bookfinder page. Clicking on an icon also generates brief annotations for many of the titles. After reading each selection, the student completes the related ten-item test from the Quiz-O-Matic page of the website. On successful completion of each test, students earn points that can be redeemed for prizes from businesses associated with the website. A review of the test items associated with two literary selections on the website indicated that the items focus primarily on literal comprehension.

Guidelines for Reviewing Multiple-Choice Items

Accelerated Reader and Book Adventure, as well as other published instruments, use multiple-choice items to assess student learning. In addition, the multiple-choice format is used by a majority of states in their testing programs (Olson, Bond, & Andrews, 1999). The widespread use of this format requires educators to be familiar with the characteristics of effective multiple-choice questions.

Some educators have questioned the utility of multiple-choice questions, given the acceptance of performance and portfolio assessments. However, Myers and Pearson (1996) noted that several students who scored only 0 or 1 on performance tasks in the California Learning Assessment System demonstrated some comprehension and reasoning ability on multiple-choice items on reading. Myers and Pearson (1996) concluded that such items may provide information about students who may perform only at minimal levels on other assessments. Therefore, reviewing multiple-choice items to ensure that they are effective is important.

Six major criteria are essential for effective items. First, the items in an assessment should represent a range of cognitive skills. One view of the multiple-choice format is that it can measure only the recall of information. However, others note that well-constructed items can measure students' abilities to analyze situations, synthesize information, make comparisons, draw inferences, and evaluate ideas (Worthen & Spandel, 1991). The first item in Table 11.1, for example, requires analysis.

A second, and related criterion, is that items should gauge student understanding of major concepts, not trivial details. For example, in the chapter "The Happy Medium" of

TABLE 11.1 *Criteria for Reviewing Multiple-Choice Items*

Criteria	Item	Explanation

1. Items should sample from a range of cognitive skills such as recall, comprehension, analysis, and application.	**Use the following poem to answer the item.**
	
	Silent city roads.
	Night. Heavy with snow, pines lean
	Toward sole travelers.
	
	The above poem is a(n) _____.
	  a. acrostic
	  b. cinquain
	  c. couplet
	  d. haiku*
		The item requires a student to analyze a poem to determine that its topic and structure follow the conventions associated with haiku.

2. Items should address important topics, skills, and strategies, not minor points.	In *A Wrinkle in Time,* the color of the homes in Camazotz was _____.
	  a. blue
	  b. gray*
	  c. white
	  d. yellow
		The rich description of a neighborhood to illustrate conformity has been trivialized in this item.

3. The stem of the item should ask a question or establish a problem.	In describing Treasure, Francie refers to "his fat orange caterpillar tail." This phrase is an example of a(n) _____.
	  a. analogy
	  b. idiom
	  c. metaphor*
	  d. simile
		The stem of the item presents a phrase and asks students to classify it according to the appropriate form of figurative speech.

4. An item should contain one correct answer and alternatives should be plausible distractors.	See the choices in the above item.	The choices are all plausible answers because they are terms associated with figurative language.

5. Items should not provide inadvertent clues to answers.	A haiku is a three-line poem that _____.
	  a. tells a humorous story
	  b. rhymes on the first and last line
	  c. always has a 5-7-5 syllable pattern
	  d. typically describes a scene in nature*
		The use of the term "always" cues students to consider other choices because absolute statements are typically not the correct answer. Also, if in the same test, item 5 provides a clue in answering item 1.

6. Items should not be tricky.	The syllable pattern for a cinquain is _____.
	  a. 5-7-5
	  b. 24-6-8-2
	  c. 2-4-6-8-2*
	  d. 8-8-5-5-8
		Choice b is a tricky distractor because the use of the 24 may confuse a student who knows the correct pattern is 2-4-6-8-2.

the novel *A Wrinkle in Time,* L'Engle (1962) portrays a society in which everyone has the same type of house and yard and acts the same as their peers. In this society, everything happens in rhythm. As some children bounce their balls, the skipping ropes of others hit the sidewalks—in *perfect* rhythm. In this town, mothers simultaneously appear at the doors of their identical houses to call their children in from play. The author uses this scene to convey a powerful message about conformity. If, as indicated in Table 11.1, test items focus on minor details, then the chapter's message is trivialized. Instead, items should focus on major ideas, in this case the author's use of the physical setting to reflect the values held by a particular society.

Review of items in text-based and supplementary assessments for these two criteria is particularly important because these systems often focus on only literal comprehension. Adoption of these systems may require that classroom assessments be used to achieve a more comprehensive assessment of student learning.

The third criterion is that the stem of the multiple-choice item should not be simply an open-ended sentence. Instead, as illustrated in example 3 in Table 11.1, the item should ask a question or establish a problem.

Item 3 also illustrates the fourth criterion, which is, each item should have one correct answer and *plausible* alternatives. Sometimes referred to as distractors, plausible alternatives are choices that are similar. In item 3, knowledgeable students will recognize the direct comparison of a cat's tail to a caterpillar and select "metaphor." Item 3 also is one that can identify students who may be having difficulty with the types of figurative speech. Confusing "metaphor" and "simile," for example, is a common mistake, and item 3 addresses this difficulty.

Fifth, items should not include inadvertent clues to the correct answer. Item 5 in Table 11.1, illustrates one type of inadvertent clue: the use of absolute terms such as "none," "never," "all," or "always." These words cue students to look more closely at the other alternatives because absolute statements rarely are the correct answer.

Another type of inadvertent clue is the use of grammatical structure that signals a particular answer as correct. An example is the use of "a" or "an" in the stem that indicates whether the correct answer is the one that begins with a vowel or a consonant. Instead, the stem should use "a(n)." For younger students, to avoid confusion, the appropriate article should be placed with each alternative (e.g., an idiom, a metaphor). Another grammatical clue is the use of "is" or "are" instead of "is/are" in the stem.

Further, if items 5 and 1 from Table 11.1 are in the same test, item 5 will cue students to the answer to the prior item. The information in item 5 (a haiku is a three-line poem) can be used to correctly identify the answer in item 1 as "c." The problem is corrected by deleting the phrase "three-line" from the stem in item 5.

Finally, items should not be tricky. Instead, an item should assess understanding of the concepts presented in a unit. In item 6 of Table 11.1, a student who knows the pattern is 2-4-6-8-2 may miss the item because of quickly noting the pattern in option "b" and selecting that response. However, option "b" is tricky because the use of 24 in place of the 2-4 creates confusion.

In summary, assessment materials that accompany texts, computer-based tests, and other published assessments often include multiple-choice items. A major purpose of assessment is to provide information to the teacher about students' understanding of major concepts and ideas. Flawed multiple-choice items, however, can lead to inappropriate inferences about students' thinking. These items should be reviewed on the criteria essential for effective items.

Standardized Achievement Tests

The term *standardized* often is used to refer to tests that are commercially available or are norm-referenced assessments. Any assessment, however, that includes a standard set of directions, a specified scoring system, and a prescribed method of administration is standardized. Included are attitudinal surveys, individually administered tests, aptitude and achievement tests, and statewide assessment systems. In the affective area, assessments address students' motivation to read and write, their self-perceptions about themselves as readers and writers, or their attitudes toward these activities. For example, the *Elementary Reading Attitude Survey* (ERAS) used by Patrick's teacher consists of twenty statements that address recreational reading (e.g., How do you feel about reading for fun at home?) and academic reading (e.g., How do you feel about the stories you read in reading class?).

When answering the questions, students select one of four poses of the Garfield character that conveys the feelings "very upset," "a little upset," "a little happy," and "very happy" (McKenna & Kear, 1999, p. 204). Students' responses (range = 1 to 4) are summed for a total score between 20 and 80. A high score indicates that a student has a positive attitude toward reading, whereas a low score indicates a negative attitude. A teacher can use the results from the ERAS, for example, to identify positive aspects of a student's attitudes and to form initial hypotheses about problem areas.

Standardized assessments provide various types of information to parents, teachers, schools, districts, and states about student aptitudes, attitudes, and achievements. For example, the English language arts component of the Palmetto Achievement Challenge Test (PACT) in South Carolina reports the performance level of the student—Below Basic, Basic, Proficient, or Advanced—on reading and writing. Also, the percentage of students in the school, district, and state at each of the four performance levels is reported. In addition, the assessment provides extended writing scores for the student in four areas: content and development, organization, voice, and conventions. That is, student essays are scored on a scale of 0 to 4 for the dimensions of content and development, organization, and conventions, and a scale of 0 to 3 for the dimension of voice.

In the 1980s, educators criticized the standardized assessments used by districts and states for being "inauthentic" and uninformative for instruction. Currently, however, both statewide and several commercially available assessments of achievement have developed information that is useful for instruction. An example is the extended writing scores on student essays in the PACT assessment.

Understanding the methods of reporting used in standardized assessments is important for two reasons. One is the information provided about student strengths and weaknesses in language arts. The other is that students and parents often are unfamiliar with the reporting methods (Bisesi, Farr, Greene, & Haydel, 2000). Faced with unfamiliar language, parents view their child's teacher as a resource in understanding this information. Parents are likely to ask, "What do these scores mean?" If the information in the report is inconsistent with other reports about student progress, parents may ask, "Why does my child's performance on the standardized test scores not match the information you provide about our child's performance?" Also, concerned parents may ask, "What can we do to help our child do better next time?" To begin to answer these questions, teachers should be familiar with the language that standardized tests use to describe student performance.

The two major approaches to summarizing student performance are criterion-referenced and norm-referenced interpretations. As the designations indicate, these approaches differ in the frame of reference used to interpret student performance.

Criterion-Referenced Interpretations. Currently, forty-two states report criterion-referenced scores in their assessments of student progress in reading (Council of Chief State School Officers, 2002). The basis for summarizing student performance in a criterion-referenced interpretation is a preset standard of acceptable performance (Stiggins, 2001) in a clearly defined domain of tasks (Linn & Gronlund, 2000, p. 24). An example is "Richard answered correctly 12 of the 14 items related to main ideas and supporting details. His score of 86% indicates mastery of this domain."

The two major types of criterion-referenced scores are pass/fail designations and quality ratings. As suggested by the terms, met standard or pass/fail designations indicate whether the student has demonstrated the attainment of identified skills. Quality ratings, however, are developed in either of two ways. One is to directly apply a holistic rubric to evaluate essays, portfolios, or other student products. An example is the NAEP Writing Assessment Rubric for eighth grade (see Figure 6.5). A student who performs at the highest level, Excellent Response, for example, "tells a clear story that is well developed and shaped with well-chosen details across the response. [Response] is well organized with strong transitions; sustains variety in sentence structure and exhibits good word choice . . ." (Greenwald, Persky, Campbell, & Mazzeo, 1999, p. 138).

Some assessments, however, do not identify a particular standard of performance for student scores. For example, the Indiana Statewide Testing Progress (ISTEP) reports only percentage of items correct for identified English language arts skills (Bisesi et al., 2000). Student reports include "Points Obtained," "Points Possible," and "Percent of Points Possible" for particular skills. For example, for the domain of "Make Inferences," a total of 11 points (points obtained) out of 14 possible points is a score of 79 percent (Percent of Points Possible).

Figure 11.1 illustrates a simulated criterion-referenced report for third-grader Frances Dezurik. As indicated on the chart, Frances scored 296 on the ELA test. The narrative below the chart explains that the score of 296 is in the Basic category. The narrative also indicates that Frances performed at the Basic level for the reading subtest and Below Basic for the writing subtest. In the Extended Writing section, Frances' scores of 2.0 to 2.5 indicate that she addresses some of the skills associated with each dimension, but she needs to develop additional writing skills. Finally, the chart at the bottom of the report provides the percentage of third-grade students in each performance level. For example, 44 percent of students in Frances' school, Moore Elementary, performed at the Basic level for the ELA assessment. Approximately 39 percent of students in the Florence district and 41 percent of third-graders in the state performed at the Basic level.

Norm-Referenced Interpretations. Currently, thirty-three states include norm-referenced reading scores in reports of student progress (Council of Chief State School Officers, 2002). Unlike criterion-referenced interpretations, norm-referenced scores report

Palmetto Achievement Challenge Tests

PACT

INDIVIDUAL STUDENT REPORT FOR
DEZURIK, FRANCES A.

GRADE 3

Test Date: SPRING 2001

Student's Birth Date: 09/01/91   District: 00 MIDDLEVILLE
Student's ID Number 000064817   School: 00000 MIDDLEVILLE ELEMENTARY   HOME COPY

ENGLISH LANGUAGE ARTS SUMMARY FOR DEZURIK, FRANCES A.
Test Administrator: VEIT   MJ

Total Scale Score:	**296**
Met Standard?	**YES**
Modifications:	

Performance Level:	**BASIC**
State Standard:	**296**
State Score Range:	**253-352**

Below Basic	Basic	Prof.	Advanced
253	296	310	331	352

FRANCES met the state standard in English language arts (ELA) for grade 3.

FRANCES' scale score of 296 falls in the score category of BASIC for the grade 3 ELA test.

FRANCES scored BASIC on the reading portion of the grade 3 ELA test and BELOW BASIC on the writing portion of the grade 3 ELA test.

FRANCES' extended writing scores are shown below. Information about these scores is provided on the back of this report. For more information about the test, contact FRANCES' school.

Extended Writing

Content and Development	2.0
Organization	2.5
Voice	2.0
Conventions	2.0

Grade 3 ELA PACT Summary Results				
	Below Basic	Basic	Proficient	Advanced
Moore Elementary	20.5%	44.0%	30.0%	5.5%
Florence 1	27.0%	38.5%	27.0%	7.5%
South Carolina	32.0%	41.0%	23.4%	3.6%

FIGURE 11.1   A Simulated Student Report for the Palmetto Achievement Challenge Tests

a student's performance in comparison to other students who have completed the test. An example is the statement that Ahmet's percentile rank in reading is 95. This means that Ahmet scored the same or higher than 95 percent of the students in the national comparison group.

To develop the information for comparing student performance, the test publisher administers the test to a representative group of examinees. These students are selected to reflect the characteristics of students across the nation, and they are referred to as the norm or comparison group. In subsequent years, the performance of this large group of students is the basis of comparison for students within a district or a state who take the test. Three major types of norm-referenced scores are percentile ranks, normal curve equivalents, and stanines. They differ somewhat in meaning and have different advantages and disadvantages.

Percentile Ranks.   As indicated in the prior example about Ahmet, percentile ranks indicate the percentage of students who scored at or below a particular score on a test (see Table 11.2). Suppose, for example, that half (50%) of the norm group scored at or below 110 on a language arts assessment. On that assessment, 110 is equivalent to the fiftieth percentile. On another test, 50 percent of the students may score at or below a score of 60. On that assessment, a score of 60 is the fiftieth percentile.

On any assessment, percentile ranks below 50, such as 6, 25, or 32 indicate that a student's performance on the test was below that of many of the students in the norm group. These ranks indicate, respectively, that the students scored at or higher than only 6, 25, and 32 percent of the comparison group students. In contrast, percentile ranks of 55,

TABLE 11.2   *Types of Norm-Referenced Scores Reported in Published Tests*

Name	Definition	Examples
Percentile rank	The percentage of students in a norm group who scored at or below a particular raw score	Thirty-nine percent of the norm group for a test earned at or below a raw score of 30. Therefore, Tam's raw score of 30 places her at the 39th percentile.
Normal curve equivalent	A standard score on a scale from 1 to 99 with 50 being the mean	Teachers implemented a new literacy program and wanted to compare reading achievement scores for the previous year and current year. They used normal curve equivalents to calculate class averages for the two years.
Stanine	A standard score on a scale of 1 to 9 with 5 being average	The stanine of 8 on the language arts section of the norm-referenced test indicated Chloe scored above average.

70, or 84 indicate, respectively, that the students scored the same as or higher than 55, 70, or 84 percent of the comparison group (see Table 11.2).

Percentile ranks range from 1 to 99 and are easy to interpret. However, they have two major disadvantages. One is that they are sometimes misinterpreted to mean the percentage of items answered correctly. Instead, they refer to the percentages of students who scored at or below a particular raw score. Second, percentile ranks are not equal intervals. Those around the midpoint (45 to 55) are closer together than those at the upper and lower extremes (1 to 15 and 85 to 99). The reason is that more students are clustered around the midpoint, the fiftieth percentile. Therefore, percentile scores cannot be averaged.

Normal Curve Equivalents (NCEs).   Unlike percentile ranks, normal curve equivalents do represent equal intervals. Specifically, they are mathematical transformations of percentile ranks that overcome the disadvantage of percentiles. Students whose NCE scores are above 50 have scored above average as compared to students in the comparison group. Scores below 50, such as 19, 36, or 45, are below average. Of importance is that the conversion of scores from percentile ranks to normal curve equivalents does not change a student's relative position in relation to others who took the test. For example, if Debra's percentile rank is higher than Bill's, her NCE score also will be higher than his.

Stanines.   The scores referred to as *stanines* (a contraction of the phrase "standard nines") range from 1 to 9. A benefit is that they are easily interpreted. Specifically, 1 to 3 is below average, 4 to 6 is average, and 7 to 9 is above average. However, stanines provide less precise information about student performance. For example, a student with a score of 5 may have a percentile rank in the range from 40 to 59 (see Table 11.3). If the stanine were the only reported score, a teacher would not know if the student performed at the forty-second percentile rank (below many in the norm group) or at the fifty-eighth percentile (above many in the norm group).

Figure 11.2 illustrates a student report for the *Stanford Diagnostic Reading Test, 4th Edition* (SDRT4). This simulated report is for Debra Belknap, a fourth-grade student. The

TABLE 11.3   *Comparison of Stanines, Percentile Ranks, and Normal Curve Equivalents (NCEs)*

Stanine	Percentile Range	NCE Range
9	96 or higher	86.9 to 99
8	89 to 95	75.8 to 84.6
7	77 to 88	65.6 to 74.7
6	60 to 76	55.3 to 64.9
5	40 to 59	44.7 to 54.8
4	23 to 39	34.4 to 44.1
3	11 to 22	24.2 to 33.7
2	4 to 10	13.1 to 23.0
1	below 4	1.0 to 10.4

SDRT

Stanford Diagnostic Reading Test, 4th Edition

TEACHER:	LUCIO	GRADE:	04
SCHOOL:	NEWTOWN ELEM	1995 NORMS:	SPRING
DISTRICT:	NEWTOWN	LEVEL:	PURPLE
TEST DATE:	04/95	FORM:	J

INDIVIDUAL DIAGNOSTIC REPORT
for
DEBRA G BELKNAP

Subtest and Total Scores
The scores below show the student's performance compared to that of students who took SDRT at the same time of year.

Subtests and Total	No. of Items	Raw Score	Scaled Score	Grade Equivalent	National NCE	Local PR	Local S	National PR	National S
Vocabulary	30	14	571	2.6	15.4	15	3	5	2
Comprehension	54	22	583	2.2	21.8	11	3	9	2
Scanning	30	20	649	5.3	53.2	75	6	56	5
SDRT Total	**114**	**56**	**598**	**2.6**	**25.3**	**23**	**4**	**12**	**3**

NATIONAL PERCENTILE BANDS: 1   10   30   50   70   90

Skills Analysis
This analysis shows the number of questions the student answered correctly out of the number possible for each skill. A shaded oval indicates that the score is at or above the Progress Indicator cutoff score.

14/30 VOCABULARY

9/19 Synonyms
3/5 Classification

2/3 Word Parts
0/3 Content Area Words

22/54 COMPREHENSION

6/18 Recreational Reading
7/18 Textual Reading
9/18 Functional Reading

11/18 Initial Understanding
8/25 Interpretation
1/6 Critical Analysis
2/5 Process Strategies

Reading Strategies Survey
Date ___
Level ___
___ % Correct

Reading Questionnaire
Date ___
Level ___
___ % Correct

Story Retelling

Date	Level	Oral	Written
Introduction	0 1 2 3		Sequence 0 1 2 3
Setting	0 1 2 3		Literal Information 0 1 2 3
Character(s)	0 1 2 3		Inferences 0 1 2 3
Problem	0 1 2 3		Critical Analysis 0 1 2 3
Plot/Events	0 1 2 3		Summarize/Generalizations 0 1 2 3
Resolution	0 1 2 3		Prior Knowledge 0 1 2 3
Theme	0 1 2 3		Creativity/Expressiveness/Aud. 0 1 2 3

Performance Assessment
Instrument ___
Date ___
Level ___
Performance Level ___

FIGURE 11.2 A Simulated Student Report for the Stanford Diagnostic Reading Test, Fourth Edition

report includes both norm-referenced and criterion-referenced information. A review of the student report for the SDRT4 shows that for the Scanning subtest Debra answered 20 of the 30 items correctly. The report provides the corresponding national percentile rank of 56 in the column labeled "National PR." With a percentile rank of 56, Debra scored in the average range for the subtest of Scanning. The score is interpreted as follows, "For the Scanning subtest, Debra scored as well or better than 56 percent of the 4th grade students in the norm group." Debra did not perform as well on the Comprehension subtest where she scored as well as or better than 9 percent of the students in the norm group.

These scores sound more exact than they actually are; so care must be taken to not over-interpret them. All assessments contain some unreliability, so students' scores would be likely to vary somewhat if they were to complete the test on another occasion or complete another form of the test. To reflect the possible variation in performance, student reports often contain score bands that represent the range of scores that reflect a student's true performance. The column labeled "National Percentile Bands" provides this form of information. Thus, interpretation of the national percentile band for the Scanning subtest indicates that an estimate of Debra's true performance on the Scanning subtest is somewhere between the forty-fifth and sixty-fifth percentile rank.

In the SDRT4 student report, Debra has a NCE score of 25.3 for SDRT Total. Because the mean of the NCE scale is 50, Debra's total score may be interpreted as below average in comparison to other fourth-grade students. Debra's stanine score of 3 for the SDRT Total (shown in the column labeled "National S") also reflects that Debra's performance was below average.

The scores in the section labeled Skills Analysis provide some criterion-referenced interpretations of Debra's performance. For each language arts skill, the report indicates the number of correctly answered items of the total number in that cluster. For example, the report indicates that Debra answered correctly 11 of the 18 items in the skill cluster of Initial Understanding. Also, the oval is shaded, indicating that Debra's score exceeded a cutoff score for these skills. In contrast, the unshaded oval for the Interpretation skill cluster shows that Debra answered only 8 of the 25 items correctly, and her score did not exceed the cutoff score for this cluster. Because of the small number of items in a skills cluster, Linn and Gronlund (2000) recommend a teacher use skills analyses as "clues for further study" (p. 497). In addition, in the critiques at the end of this chapter, a reviewer suggests that caution in the interpretation of the cluster scores is warranted.

Summary

Standardized achievement tests require students to complete the same or similar sets of test items under similar conditions. Components of the assessment that may be standardized include student directions, the time allocation for the test, and conditions and dates for administration. Students' scores are reported in either a criterion-referenced or norm-referenced framework. Criterion-referenced scores describe a student's performance on the test in terms of a preset standard of acceptable performance in a clearly defined domain, such as quality ratings and pass/fail designations. Norm-referenced scores describe a student's performance in comparison to a nationally representative group of students referred to as a norm group. Interpretation of these scores focuses on whether a student's performance is below average, average, or above average in relation to the norm group. Examples of norm-referenced scores are percentiles, normal curve equivalents, and stanines.

Reviewing Published Assessments

Teacher involvement in the development and review of standardized assessments in school districts and states is increasingly commonplace. Included are the development of new tasks, review of item quality, the scoring of constructed-response tasks, and the selection of standardized assessments for use in testing programs (Johnson, Willeke, & Steiner, 1998; Kapinus, Collier, & Kruglanski, 1994; Myers & Pearson, 1996; Valencia, Hiebert, & Afflerbach, 1994). Teacher involvement is important because it increases the likelihood that assessments will effectively address student understanding, interests, and attitudes.

In Maryland, for example, language arts supervisors and teachers in reading, special education, and vocational education from twenty-four school districts developed English language arts items for a state assessment (Kapinus et al., 1994). They first reviewed examples of different types of tasks and the characteristics of performance assessments. Then, using authentic texts, including stories, poems, articles, directions, and trade books, they developed assessment tasks. Next, another committee of teachers and language arts supervisors reviewed the tasks for (1) possible bias, (2) the likelihood of reliable scoring, (3) the extent of content coverage, and (4) required thinking activities. Tasks identified as problematic were revised by the development team.

Teachers who want to assess student attitudes, reading strategies, and understanding, and who face time constraints in developing an assessment, may supplement their classroom assessments with commercially published tests (Cizek, Fitzgerald, & Rachor, 1995/1996). However, the quality of published assessments varies. Therefore, "Teachers and administrators must carefully review and select assessment tools to assure that they reflect important instructional goals and that they are assessed in reasonable and authentic ways" (Greer, 1992, p. 652).

Validity and reliability, two important issues in classroom assessments discussed in Chapter 2, also apply to the review and selection of published instruments. In addition to these issues, this section also discusses the nature of the norming group, an important consideration in the selection of norm-referenced tests.

Reliability

In relation to published assessments, reliability addresses the consistency of students' scores (1) on different items within a single assessment, (2) on different test forms that assess the same content, (3) on the same assessment across different occasions, or (4) assigned by different raters. Manuals that accompany commercially available instruments use any of several terms to indicate reliability. They are Kuder-Richardson 20 (KR-20), Kuder-Richardson 21 (KR-21), Cronbach's alpha, Pearson's correlation, and Spearman's rank-order correlation. Each term refers to a number, referred to as a *reliability coefficient,* that ranges from 0 to 1.0. As the coefficient approaches 1.0, student scores are more reliable. Of importance is that we are looking for a reliability coefficient of approximately .90 or higher when reviewing published instruments for assessing individual student performance. This numerical value indicates that the assessment yields consistent scores, and therefore teacher decisions about student performances will be consistent.

Validity

The question in reviewing validity is, Will information from an assessment support teachers in making accurate decisions about student capabilities, interests, and attitudes? Validity requires examining the evidence supporting the interpretations and uses of an assessment. Evidence relevant in a review of the validity of a literacy assessment includes (1) the extent that the instrument reflects current conceptualizations of literacy, (2) the similarity of students' scores on the instrument with scores on other literacy assessments, and (3) the consequences of using an assessment.

Current Conceptualizations of Literacy.
An instrument should reflect current conceptualizations about students' capabilities, motivation, or attitudes. When reviewing language arts assessments, a teacher asks, "Do the test developers provide a framework for the development of the instrument that is based on the current thinking of researchers and practitioners in the literacy field?"

As indicated in Chapter 1, current conceptualization of literacy extends reading and writing capabilities to include those of speaking, listening (Bembridge, 1994), communicating through technology, viewing (Cooper, 2000), and representing (Myers & Spalding, 1997). In addition, central to the current literacy framework is the learner's construction of meaning. Thus, the validity of a literacy assessment is supported to the extent that the instrument addresses this current framework. State or district testing programs that focus solely on reading and writing address only two of the seven literacy capabilities. Similarly, assessments that solely rely on multiple-choice items measure student capability to construct meaning in a limited way.

To assist educators in determining whether an assessment reflects current conceptualizations, published literacy instruments should include a table of specifications that outlines the language arts standards assessed by the tasks and items. For example, the table may list such skills as "identify the main idea," "use key events to summarize a story," and "explain the conflict and resolution in a story." The number of each item in the instrument is then listed by the content standard that is the focus of the item. Committee members who are reviewing an instrument for possible use in their district or state testing program can examine the specifications table to determine whether the items in the instrument align with the content standards of their district or state.

Similarity of Scores.
Test manuals and published reviews of instruments also discuss validity in terms of the similarity of student scores on an instrument and their scores on other measures of the same capabilities or characteristics. For example, if two instruments assess student reading capabilities, such as the *Stanford Diagnostic Reading Test, Fourth Edition* and the *STAR Reading®* (Advantage Learning Systems, 1997), then students' scores should be similar on the two tests. Students who experience difficulty in reading are

likely to score low on both assessments, and students who are proficient readers are likely to score high on both instruments. If the information about student reading capability is the same on two different tests, then use of test scores is likely to result in accurate decisions about instruction based on students' strengths and weaknesses.

The similarity of scores across two different tests is reported in the form of a numerical index, often referred to as a validity coefficient. The range of values in the analysis of score similarity across tests is from 0 to 1.0. Although a reliability of .9 and higher is often reported for achievement tests, McDaniel (1994) indicates that validity coefficients are not typically high. McDaniel provides a general guideline that instruments with validity coefficients of .40 or higher may provide useful information for making decisions about students. Of importance is the understanding that as validity coefficients approach 1.0, then the scores from the two different assessments reflect similar information about a student.

Consequences of Use. Also relevant in the collection of validity evidence are the consequences associated with the use and interpretation of the results of the assessment (Messick, 1988, 1993). The statewide assessment implemented in Connecticut provides an example of consequential validity (Chudowsky & Behuniak, 1998). In this assessment system, high school students receive a designation of *certification of mastery* on their high school transcript for each subject area in which they meet the state standard for a pass score on a criterion-referenced assessment. The assessment, the *Connecticut Academic Performance Test* (CAPT), consists of multiple-choice and constructed-response items in language arts, mathematics, science, and an interdisciplinary task in reading and writing. When asked about the consequences associated with the CAPT, teachers reported such positive changes as instruction including more writing in all content areas and students being required to use more support and evidence in their writing. Negative consequences included the disruption of the school schedule during test administration and the narrowing of the curriculum to the content-area skills and strategies emphasized on the CAPT. Thus, in the review of an assessment for adoption, the members of the committee should consider the consequences of implementing the assessment or an alternative to ascertain if the benefits of the assessment exceed the detriments.

Composition of the Comparison Group

In the case of assessments with norm-referenced scores, reviewing the composition of the comparison group for relevance and representativeness is also important. Relevance requires that the norm group provides a meaningful basis for comparison. An example of relevance is provided by the *Diagnostic Inventory for Screening Children* (Amdur, Mainland, & Parker, 1988). The inventory can be used to monitor the development of preschool children in such areas as language and motor skills. However, the norms for the test are based on children from three counties in Ontario who were categorized as English, French, and other (Watson & Henington, 1998). Early childhood educators considering the use of this instrument would ask if comparisons to this group of Canadian children from different cultural backgrounds are relevant in assessing the preschool children in their district. Watson and Henington, in their review of the instrument, questioned the utility of information for diverse groups of U. S. preschoolers. Relevance is supported when the students in a school or district are similar to those in the norm group. Under such circumstances the norm group will provide a meaningful comparison.

Also important is the representativeness of the norm group. A norm group is a sample of a larger population. For example, a sample of fourth-grade students from across the nation provides the basis for the norm-referenced scores in the fourth-grade report for the SDRT4. For the sample to be representative of fourth-graders, students selected for the norm group must reflect the characteristics typical of this grade level across the nation. Characteristics to consider in reviewing the representativeness of norm groups are the ages, grade level(s), socioeconomic status, ethnicity, and region (e.g., Midwest, Northeast, Southwest). To continue the example, if a district plans to compare the achievement of its fourth-grade students with that of a national sample, then the norm group should be composed of fourth-grade students across these various subgroups. In addition, the proportion of students in each of these categories should reflect the population distribution reported by the United States Census Bureau. As part of its technical documentation, a test publisher should provide a description of the characteristics of students in the comparison group.

Summary

Reviews of published assessments typically attend to the criteria of reliability, validity, and, in the case of instruments with norm-referenced scores, the composition of the norming group. Reliability addresses the consistency of student scores and is reported in the form of a reliability coefficient that ranges from 0 to 1.0. Reliable scores are indicated by coefficients in the .90 range and higher. When scores are unreliable, perhaps high on one occasion and low on another, the decisions a teacher makes about a student's literacy capabilities may be in error. Validity examines the likelihood that the assessment results will support accurate decisions about student capabilities and characteristics in the language arts. Validity is supported when a published instrument is developed based on current conceptualizations of literacy and when student scores on the instrument are similar to his or her scores on other measures of the same capabilities or characteristics. Further, for norm-referenced instruments, teachers and other members of the review committee should examine the composition of the norm group to determine its relevance and representativeness. Application of these criteria assists in the selection of published literacy instruments that are effective in assessing student understandings, interests, and attitudes.

Illustrative Critiques of Published Assessments

This section illustrates the application of the key criteria in the critique of published assessments. First, the section describes several resources that provide information about published assessments. Next, information from these sources is used to critically review published instruments that assess phonemic awareness, reading comprehension, and attitudes toward writing. The reviews are for illustration only and should not be viewed as endorsements.

Sources of Review Information

As indicated in Table 11.4, four major sources provide information about published assessments. Two resources, the *Reading Teacher* and *A Practical Guide to Reading Assessment* (Kame'enui, Simmons, & Cornachione, 2000) specifically address assessments in language arts. For example, assessments discussed in articles in recent years in the *Reading Teacher* include a comparison of different informal reading inventories (Pikulski, 1990) and an assessment of phonemic awareness (Yopp, 1995).

Assessments described in *A Practical Guide to Reading Assessment* address a variety of capabilities. Included are concepts about print, phonemic awareness, alphabetic understanding, spelling, vocabulary, reading achievement, and reading comprehension. In addition to descriptive information, the text discusses interpretation of results and instructional implications of each assessment. The text may be obtained from the International Reading Association.

Another resource, the *Mental Measurement Yearbook* (MMY), addresses published standardized assessments that range from a variety of curriculum assessments to attitudes and metacognition. Each yearbook provides reviews of the standardized tests published since the last issue. In addition to descriptive information, two reviewers critique each instrument.

Finally, the test manuals that accompany published standardized assessments provide information about administration and interpretation, the norming group, and validity

TABLE 11.4   *Sources of Information about Published Assessments*

Source	*Description*	*Examples*
Reading Teacher	Journal published by the International Reading Association; periodically includes articles about assessments in language arts	*Writing Attitude Survey* (WAS) in Kear, Coffman, McKenna, and Ambrosio (2000)
A Practical Guide to Reading Assessment	Text discusses reading assessments, including publisher, purpose, format, administration, interpretation of results, and instructional implications	*An Observation Survey of Early Literacy Achievement* (Clay, 1993, 2002 [2nd edition])
Mental Measurement Yearbook	Text includes reviews of standardized tests in a variety of areas; provides descriptive information and critiques by two reviewers for each instrument	*STAR Reading* (Advantage Learning Systems, 1997), a norm-referenced, computer-based test, reviewed by Volpe-Johnstone (2001) and Ward (2001)
Test manuals accompanying published standardized instruments	Manuals include administration requirements, validity and reliability indices, norming group information, and interpretations of test results	Manuals for the SDRT4 (Karlsen & Gardner, 1996a, 1996b)

and reliability indices. Absent from the manuals, however, is any critique of potential weaknesses in the instrument.

Several of these resources were used in summarizing information about the three language arts assessments in the following section. The critiques that follow serve to model the process of identifying key information used to review the adequacy of a published instrument for assessing student progress. Each critique begins with a general description of the assessment, followed by the application of the effectiveness criteria: reliability, validity, and, if applicable, norm group. Each review ends with a general conclusion about the effectiveness of the instrument in the assessment of students.

Phonemic Awareness

Description.   The *Yopp-Singer Test of Phonemic Segmentation* measures a student's ability to separately articulate the sounds of a spoken word in the correct order (Yopp, 1995, p. 21). The instrument, listed as a measure of phonemic awareness in *A Practical Guide to Reading Assessments*, consists of a list of twenty-five words of which three are practice items and twenty-two are test items. The test is administered individually and requires 5 to 10 minutes per child. The student's score is the number of items correctly segmented into all phonemes. Partial credit is not awarded for an item; so ". . . if a child says '/c/-/at/' instead of '/c/-/a/-/t/,' the response . . . is considered incorrect for purposes of scoring" (p. 21). To receive credit, a student must articulate each phoneme separately. High scores indicate phonemic awareness. Students who are not able to segment items are likely to experience difficulty with reading and spelling.

The *Yopp-Singer Test of Phonemic Segmentation* allows early identification of students who may experience difficulty reading and spelling. For students who score low on the test, instruction can be planned to develop phonemic awareness. For example, as part of a larger literacy program, a teacher may use rhyme, assonance, and alliteration in read-aloud books to develop students' phonemic awareness (Yopp, 1995, p. 27).

Application of Criteria.   The reliability of the test is a respectable .95 (Yopp, 1995). The author investigated validity by comparing the similarity of students' scores from kindergarten with their scores in grades 1 through 6 on the reading and spelling subtests of the *Comprehensive Test of Basic Skills,* a multiple-choice, norm-referenced test. Validity coefficients ranged from .38 to .78 with the typical coefficient in the .60s. These validity coefficients indicate that a student's performance on the *Yopp-Singer Test* is somewhat predictive of his or her performance on reading and spelling tests in later grades.

Conclusion.   The *Yopp-Singer Test of Phonemic Segmentation* provides support for claims of reliability and validity. It may serve as one resource for gauging student development of phonemic awareness.

Identifying Strengths and Weaknesses in the Reading Process

Description.   The *Stanford Diagnostic Reading Test, Fourth Edition* (Karlsen & Gardner, 1996b), a test of reading comprehension, was listed in *A Practical Guide to Reading*

Assessments and reviewed in *The Thirteenth Mental Measurement Yearbook* (Impara & Plake, 1998). Both sources indicate that the purpose of the assessment includes diagnosing a students' strengths and weaknesses in reading (Engelhard, 1998; Kame'enui et al., 2000). The test may be administered to students at the end of first grade to the first year of college. The subtests of the assessment are Phonetic Analysis (grades 1.5–4.5), Vocabulary (1.5–13), Comprehension (1.5–13), and Scanning (grades 4.5–13) (Swerdlik & Bucy, 1998). Beginning in second grade, comprehension assessment includes various types of text: recreational, textual, and functional.

The test has two parallel forms, J and K, which use different reading passages and multiple-choice items, but assess the same reading skills. In addition, the two forms have the same number of items, and the items are of approximately the same level of difficulty. The test is administered to students as a group and requires approximately 1 1/2 hours to complete.

The SDRT4 provides criterion-referenced and norm-referenced scores. The purpose of the criterion-referenced scores, Progress Indicator Cut (PIC) scores, is to indicate whether students will make satisfactory progress in a regular developmental reading program. The PIC scores are shown in the section labeled Skills Analysis of the SDRT4 report (see Figure 11.2).

The types of norm-referenced scores in the SDRT4 include percentile ranks, stanines, and normal curve equivalents. As stated in the *Practical Guide,* the scores in the SDRT4 "allow comparison to a normed group" (Kame'enui et al., 2000, p. 40). The norm groups included approximately 33,000 examinees in the fall of 1994 and 20,000 in the spring of 1995. In forming the groups to reflect national norms, publishers attended to geographical region, socioeconomic status, urbanicity, ethnicity, handicapping condition, and nonpublic schools.

Application of Criteria.   To determine if comparisons with a norm group are appropriate requires that a review committee examines the composition of the comparison group. The MMY reviews indicate the norm groups generally concur with national school enrollment statistics (Engelhard, 1998; Swerdlik & Bucy, 1998). However, they also indicate the spring sample appears to have some over-representation of rural students and under-representation of urban students. Also, the fall sample over-represents students in private schools, and the fall and spring sample has some under-representation of Hispanic students.

Scores are reported for the total test, subtests, and skill clusters. Therefore, reliability for each type of score should be considered. One method for estimating reliability is to compare student performance across parallel forms of a test. Using this approach, the reliability for total scores ranged from a respectable .86 to .88. Thus, a teacher's decision about a student's performance is likely to be the same whether the student completes Form J or Form K. Reliability for the four subtests of Phonetic Analysis, Vocabulary, Comprehension, and Scanning ranged from .62 to .82, indicating that caution is needed in interpreting subtest scores.

Another way of estimating reliability is to examine the consistency of students' scores on different items within the same form. Using this method, KR-20 estimates of reliability ranged from .95 to .98 for the total scores and .70 to .94 for the four subtests

(Engelhard, 1998). Swerdlik and Bucy (1998) indicated that these reliability coefficients exceeded .85 for all subtests except Vocabulary in grade 2. They also indicated that such reliability levels suggest that the total score and subtest scores ". . . are of sufficient reliability to pinpoint specific domains of reading strengths and weaknesses" (p. 942).

Reliability estimates for the skill clusters associated with the PIC scores were low, for example, a KR-21 of .59 for a skill cluster related to "long vowels." Low reliability estimates for the clusters indicate ". . . they are too unreliable to assess strengths or weaknesses" (Swerdlik & Bucy, 1998, p. 943).

The validity of the SDRT4 is supported by the inclusion of a detailed description in the teacher's manual of the language arts objectives and items that comprise the test (Karlsen & Gardner, 1996b). In addition, the inclusion of reading passages with recreational, textual, and functional narrative addresses the need to assess student reading across various forms of text because student comprehension differs according to the type of narrative (Lipson, 1994). Finally, students' scores on the SDRT4 correlate with their scores on the previous version of the assessment with validity coefficients ranging from .80 to .90 for total scores (Karlsen & Gardner, 1996a). These high correlations indicate that interpretations of student performance based on the SDRT4 would be similar to conclusions about student performance based on the SDRT3. Finally, Engelhard (1998) discourages use of PIC scores due to the lack of validity information to support the claim that the scores predict success of students in reading programs.

Conclusion.   The SDRT4 demonstrates desirable levels of reliability and validity and uses a representative norm group for comparison purposes. Teachers may find the total scores and subtest scores useful in providing general information about student reading capabilities, but cluster scores should not be relied on for diagnosing individual student needs.

Attitudes Toward Writing

Description.   The purpose of the *Writing Attitude Survey* (WAS) (Kear, Coffman, McKenna, & Ambrosio, 2000) is to allow comparison of students' attitudes about writing with grade and age peers in a norm group. Kear et al. (2000) suggest that teachers use scores to plan interventions for students whose low scores indicate poor attitudes, and then use the WAS to investigate whether the interventions changed students' attitudes.

The 28-item instrument includes norm-referenced scores based on 974 students in grades 1 through 12. The size of the norm groups ranged from a low of 55 students in the fifth grade to a high of 159 students in the sixth grade. The students represent 19 school districts in the east, central, and west regions of the United States. Administered to the norm groups in the spring of 1997, the sample contains 509 males and 465 females. The proportions of African American and Hispanic students are within 4 percent of national proportions by grade.

The instrument may be administered to individuals or groups. Students respond to items that reflect their attitudes about writing in various situations. For example, one item asks, "How would you feel writing a letter to the author of a book you read?" (Kear et al., 2000, p. 16) and another asks, "How would you feel about writing a story instead of watching TV?" (p. 18). Students record their responses using a 4-point scale that shows the Garfield character in poses that convey the feelings "very happy," "somewhat happy," "somewhat upset," "very upset" (Kear et al., 2000, p. 23). Raw scores range from 28 to 112.

Application of Criteria. Reliability for the total score ranges from .85 to .93 across the grade levels. Validity claims depend on the development of the instrument based on a review of previously published writing scales. No validity information examines the similarity of students' WAS scores and their scores on other scales.

Conclusion. Acceptable levels of reliability and some basis in the literature make this an assessment that teachers may use, but decisions about student attitudes must be tentative due to scant validity information.

Summary

Resources available to teachers for the review of published instruments include the professional journal the *Reading Teacher;* the publication, *A Practical Guide to Reading Assessments;* and the reference tool, the *Mental Measurement Yearbook.* These resources provide such information as to the purpose of the assessment, a description of the instrument, the test author, and the publisher. The *Mental Measurement Yearbook* also provides critical reviews that evaluate the instrument by considering its reliability and validity, and, in the case of norm-referenced instruments, the composition of the norm group. Information from these sources generally supports the use of the *Yopp-Singer Test of Phonemic Segmentation,* the *Stanford Diagnostic Reading Test, Fourth Edition,* and the *Writing Attitude Survey.* As modeled by these critiques, teacher awareness of effective published instruments can contribute a discerning voice in the selection of instruments to assess student understanding and dispositions in the English language arts.

Discussion Questions

1. Review the student report in Figure 11.1. Based on the report, in which area, reading or writing, does the student need more learning opportunities? Provide a reason for your answer.

2. In the student's report for the SDRT4 (Figure 11.2) locate the national stanine for the Vocabulary subtest. Was the student's performance on the Vocabulary subtest below average, average, or above average? Provide a reason for your answer.

3. Provide an explanation that could be given to a parent who asks about the national percentile band associated with her child's score. Use the SDRT4 Total score in Figure 11.2 to provide an example. State the band of scores associated with Debra's score and the meaning of this score band.

4. Which item-writing guideline does the following item violate?

In *A Wrinkle in Time*, what was the color of Calvin's hair?

a. Black
b. Blond
c. Brown
d. Red

Use the following information about the *STAR Reading* achievement test to answer questions 5 and 6:

> *STAR Reading* is a norm-referenced, computer-adaptive reading test (Advantage Learning Systems, 1997). One use of the achievement test is to determine students' reading levels for Accelerated Reader. *STAR Reading* determines a student's reading level through the use of a modified cloze procedure in which examinees select the best word to complete a sentence or passage (Ward, 2001). The assessment is individually administered and takes about 10 minutes to complete. In a review of *STAR Reading*, Volpe-Johnstone (2000) reported that reliability estimates for the total score ranged from .85 to .95 across grade levels.

5. Are the reliability levels reported for *STAR Reading* reasonable for using the instrument to make decisions about student reading levels? Why or why not?

6. What additional information about *STAR Reading* would you want to know in considering its adoption for use in your school?

References

Advantage Learning Systems, (1997). *STAR Reading*. Wisconsin Rapids, WI: Author.

Amdur, J., Mainland, M., & Parker, K. (1988). *Diagnostic Inventory for Screening Children*. San Antonio, TX: The Psychological Corporation.

Barrentine, S. (1999). Formal assessment instruments. In S. Barrentine (Ed.), *Reading assessment: Principles and practices for elementary teachers* (p. 165). Newark, DE: International Reading Association.

Bembridge, T. (1994). A Multilayered Assessment Package. In S. W. Valencia, E. H. Hiebert, & P. Afflerbach (Eds.), *Authentic reading assessment* (pp. 167–184). Newark, DE: International Reading Association.

Biggers, D. (2001). The argument against Accelerated Reader. *Journal of Adolescent and Adult Literacy, 45*(1), 72–75.

Bisesi, T., Farr, R., Greene, B., & Haydel, E. (2000). Reporting to parents and the community. In E. Trumbull & B. Farr (Eds.), *Grading and reporting student progress in an age of standards* (pp.157–184). Norwood, MA: Christopher-Gordon Publishers.

Calfee, R., & Chambliss, (1999). Cognitive perspectives on primers and textbooks. In D. Wagner, R. Venezky, & B. Street (Eds.), *Literacy: An international handbook* (pp. 179–185). Boulder, CO: Westview Press.

Chudowsky, N., & Behuniak, P. (1998). Using focus groups to examine the consequential aspect of validity. *Educational Measurement: Issues and Practices, 17*(4), 28–38.

Cizek, G., Fitzgerald, S., & Rachor, R. (1995/1996). Teachers' assessment practices: Preparation, isolation, and the kitchen sink. *Educational assessment, 3*(2), 159–179.

Clay, M. (2002). *An observation survey of early literacy achievement* (2nd ed.). Portsmouth, NH: Heinemann.

Cooper, J. D. (2000). *Literacy: Helping children construct meaning.* Boston: Houghton Mifflin.

Council of Chief State School Officers (2002). *Annual survey of state student assessment programs, 2000–2001.* Washington, DC: Author.

Engelhard, G. (1998). [Review of *Stanford Diagnostic Reading Test,* Fourth Edition]. *The Thirteenth Mental Measurements Yearbook* (pp. 939–941). Lincoln, NE: Buros Institute of Mental Measurements.

English, K. (1999). *Francie.* New York: Farrar, Straus, and Giroux.

Greenwald, E., Persky, H., Campbell, J., & Mazzeo, J. (1999). *The NAEP 1998 Writing Report Card for the Nation and the States* (NCES 1999-462). Washington, DC: U.S. Government Printing Office.

Greer, E. (1992). Basal assessment systems: "It's not the shoes." *Reading Teacher, 45*(8), 650–652.

Holt, Rinehart, & Winston (2000). *Elements of Literature.* Austin, TX: Author.

Impara, J. & Plake, B. (Eds.). (1998). *The Thirteenth Mental Measurements Yearbook.* Lincoln, NE: Buros Institute of Mental Measurements.

Johnson, R., Willeke, M., & Steiner, D. (1998). Stakeholder collaboration in the design and implementation of a family literacy portfolio assessment. *American Journal of Evaluation, 19*(3), 33–353.

Kame'enui, E., Simmons, D., & Cornachione, C. (2000). *A practical guide to reading assessments.* Newark, DE: International Reading Association.

Kapinus, B., Collier, G., & Kruglanski, H. (1994). The Maryland School Performance Assessment Program: A new view of assessment. In S. W. Valencia, E. H. Hiebert, & P. Afflerbach (Eds.), *Authentic reading assessment* (pp. 255–276). Newark, DE: International Reading Association.

Karlsen, B., & Gardner, E. (1996a). *Stanford Diagnostic Reading Test, Fourth Edition: 1995 multilevel norms book and technical information.* San Antonio, TX: Harcourt Brace Educational Measurement.

Karlsen, B., & Gardner, E. (1996b). *Stanford Diagnostic Reading Test, Fourth Edition: Teacher's manual for interpreting.* San Antonio, TX: Harcourt Brace Educational Measurement.

Kear, D., Coffman, G., McKenna, M., & Ambrosio, A. (2000). Measuring attitude toward writing: A new tool for teachers. *Reading Teacher, 54*(1), 10–23.

L'Engle, M. (1962). *A wrinkle in time.* New York: Farrar, Straus, and Giroux.

Lipson, M. (1994). [Commentary on the chapter A Multilayered Assessment Package]. In S. Valencia, E. Hiebert, & P. Afflerbach (Eds.), *Authentic reading assessment: Practices and possibilities* (pp. 185–192). Newark, DE: International Reading Association.

Linn, R., & Gronlund, N. (2000). *Measurement and assessment in teaching* (8th ed.). Upper Saddle River, NJ: Prentice-Hall.

Marzano, J. (1994). [Commentary on the chapter Literacy portfolios: Windows on potential]. In S. Valencia, E. Hiebert, & P. Afflerbach (Eds.), *Authentic reading assessment: Practices and possibilities* (pp. 41–45). Newark, Delaware: International Reading Association.

McDaniel, E. (1994). *Understanding educational measurement* (2nd ed.). Madison, Wisconsin: WCB Brown & Benchmark Publishers.

McKenna, M., & Kear, D. (1999). Measuring attitude toward reading: A new tool for teachers. In S. Barrentine (Ed.), *Reading assessment: Principles and practices for elementary teachers* (pp. 199–214). Newark, DE: International Reading Association.

Messick, S. (1988). The once and future issues of validity: Assessing the meaning and consequences of measurement. In H. Wainer & H. Braun (Eds.), *Test validity,* (pp. 33–45). Hillsdale, NJ: Lawrence Erlbaum Associates.

Messick S. (1993). Validity. In R. Linn (Ed.), *Educational measurement,* (3rd ed., pp. 13–103). Washington: American Council on Education.

Myers, M., & Pearson, P. (1996). Performance assessment and the literacy unit of the New Standards Project. *Assessing Writing, 3*(1), 5–29.

Myers, M., & Spalding, E. (1997). *Standards exemplar series: Assessing student performance grades K–5.* Urbana, IL: National Council of Teachers of English.

Nitko, A. (2001). *Educational assessment of students* (3rd ed.). Upper Saddle River, NJ: Merrill Prentice Hall.

Olson, J., Bond, L., & Andrews, C. (1999). *Annual survey of state student assessment programs: A summary report.* Washington, DC: Council of Chief State School Officers.

Paul, T., VanderZee, D., Rue, T., & Swanson, S. (1996, October). *The impact of the Accelerated Reader on overall academic achievement and school attendance.* Paper presented at the National Reading Research Center Conference, Atlanta, GA.

Pikulski, J. (1990). Informal reading inventories. *Reading Teacher, 43,* 514–516.

Stiggins, R. (2001). *Student-involved classroom assessment* (3rd ed.). Upper Saddle River, NJ: Merrill Prentice Hall.

Swerdlik, M., & Bucy, J. (1998). [Review of *Stanford Diagnostic Reading Test, Fourth Edition*]. *The Thirteenth Mental Measurements Yearbook* (pp. 941–943). Lincoln, NE: Buros Institute of Mental Measurements.

Topping, K., & Sanders, W. (2000). Teaching effectiveness and computer assessment of reading: Relating value added and learning information system data. *School Effectiveness and School Improvement, 11*(3), 305–337.

Valencia, S., Hiebert, E., & Afflerbach, P. (1994). Realizing the possibilities of authentic assessment. In S. W. Valencia, E. H. Hiebert, & P. Afflerbach (Eds.), *Authentic reading assessment* (pp. 286–300). Newark, DE: International Reading Association.

Volpe-Johnstone, T. (2001). [Review of *STAR Reading*]. *The Fourteenth Mental Measurements Yearbook* (pp. 1175–1177). Lincoln, NE: Buros Institute of Mental Measurements.

Ward, S. (2001). [Review of *STAR Reading*]. *The Fourteenth Mental Measurements Yearbook* (pp. 1177–1179). Lincoln, NE: Buros Institute of Mental Measurements.

Watson, T. S., & Henington, C. (1998). [Review of *Diagnostic Inventory for Screening Children*]. *The Thirteenth Mental Measurements Yearbook* (pp. 366–368). Lincoln, NE: Buros Institute of Mental Measurements.

Worthen, B., & Spandel, V. (1991). Putting the standardized test debate in perspective. *Educational Leadership, 48*(5), 65–69.

Yopp, H. (1995). A test for assessing phonemic awareness in young children. *Reading Teacher, 49*, 20–29.

Author Index

Subject Index